THE BIG BRAIN TEASERS BOOK FOR KIDS

Woo! Jr. Kids Activities Founder: Wendy Piersall

Book Layout and Cover Design by: Lilia Garvin
Production Designer: Ethan Piersall

Published by DragonFruit, an imprint of Mango Publishing, a division of Mango Publishing Group, Inc.

For permission requests, please contact the publisher at:

Mango Publishing Group
2850 Douglas Road, 4th Floor
Coral Gables, FL
33134 USA
info@mango.bz

For special orders, quantity sales, course adoptions and corporate sales, please email the publisher at sales@mango.bz. For trade and wholesale sales, please contact Ingram Publisher Services at customer. service@ingramcontent.com or +1.800.509.4887.

The Big Brain Teasers Book for Kids: Logic Puzzles, Hidden Pictures, Math Games, and More Brain Teasers for Kids

ISBN: (p) 978-1-64250-640-2 (e) 978-1-64250-641-9
BISAC: JNF021070, JUVENILE NONFICTION / Games & Activities / Word Games

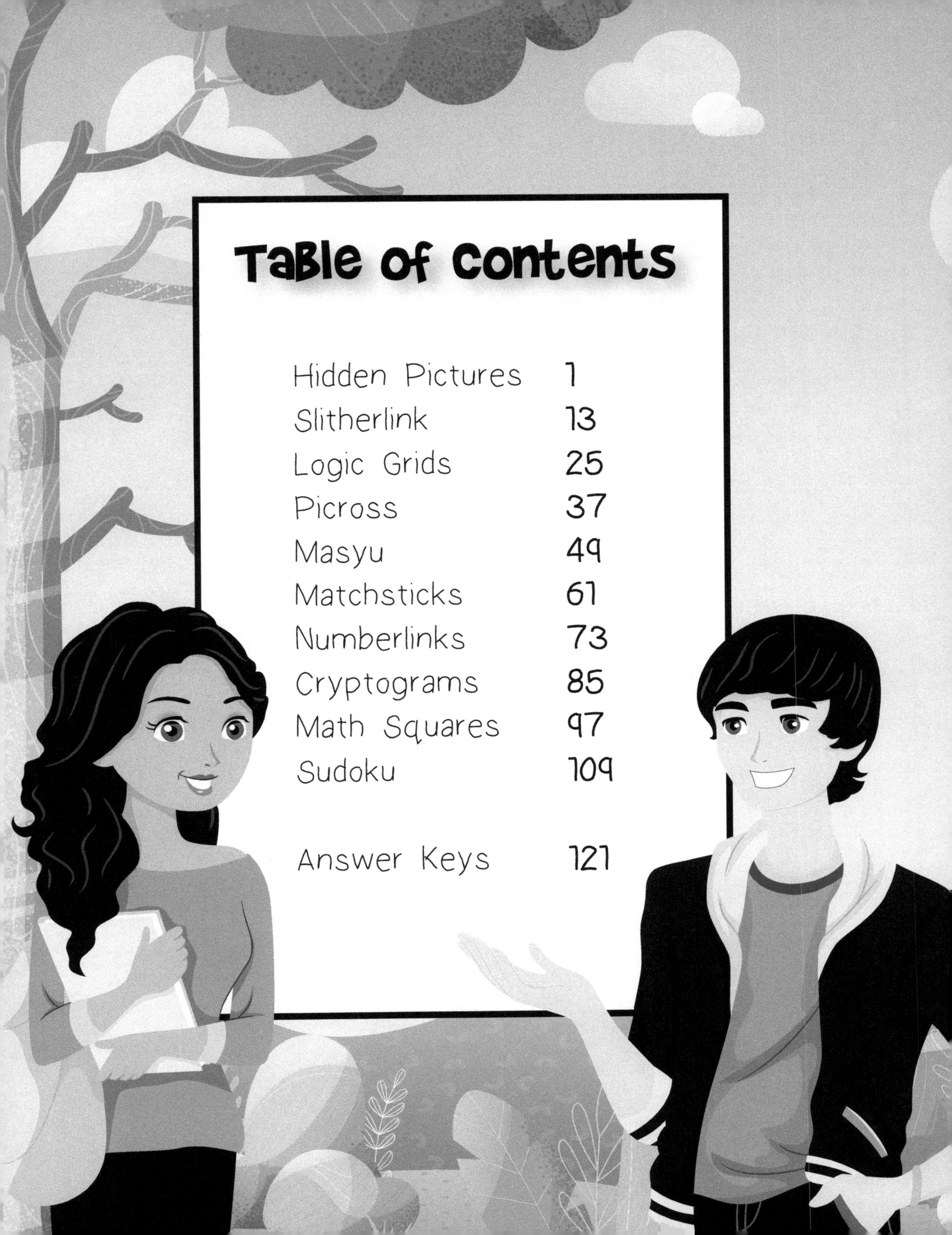

Table of Contents

Hidden Pictures

How to: Hidden Pictures

Puzzle 1

Puzzle 2

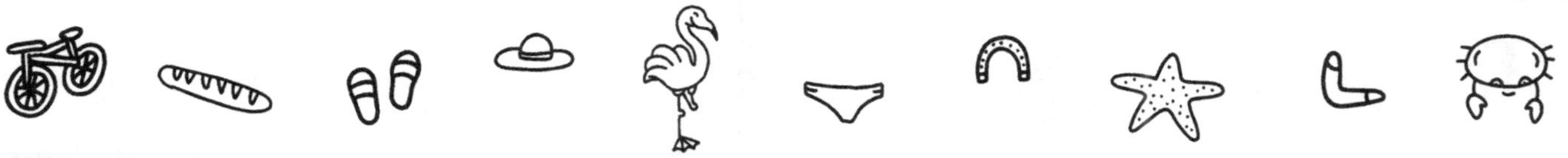

Puzzle 3

Puzzle 4

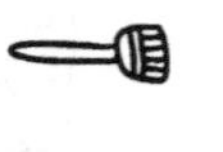       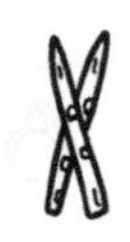 

Puzzle 5

Hidden Pictures

Puzzle 6

Puzzle 7

Puzzle 8

Puzzle 9

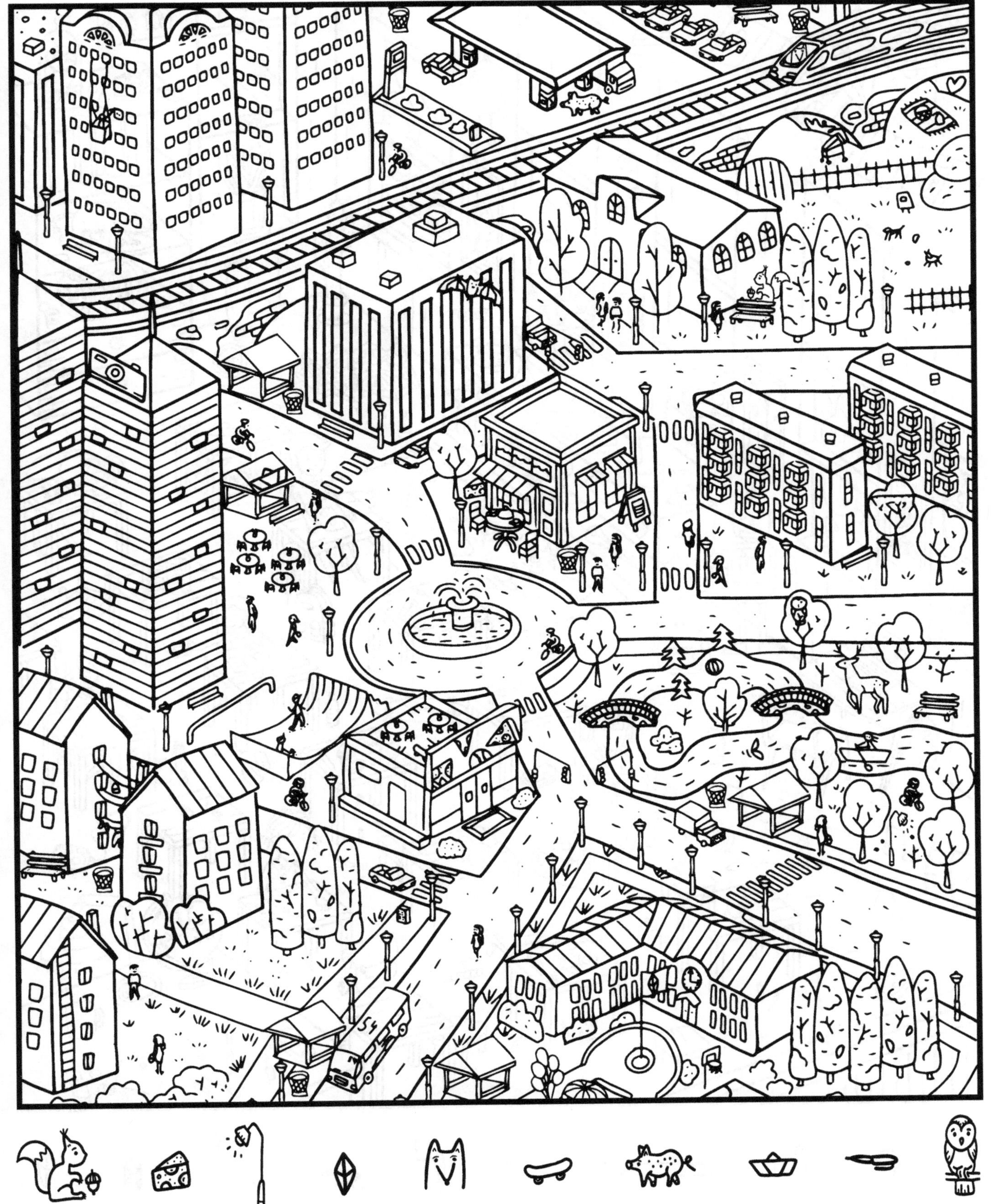

PUZZLE 10

Slitherlink

How to: Slitherlink

Draw a complete loop past each number, traveling only vertically or horizontally between dots. Each number cannot have more lines next to them than its number. So for example, a 3 should have exactly 3 lines around it—not 2, and not 4.

See if you can finish this example!

Puzzle 1

0	0		1	
	2			
	1			2
1		3	2	2
2	2	2	2	

Puzzle 2

	3	3		
	1		0	3
	0	0		
	2			3
	1	2		

Puzzle 3

1	1	2		
				3
1		2		
	2	0		
	2	2	3	3

Puzzle 4

	2			
		3	1	
3				2
	1	0	1	2
1		3	2	

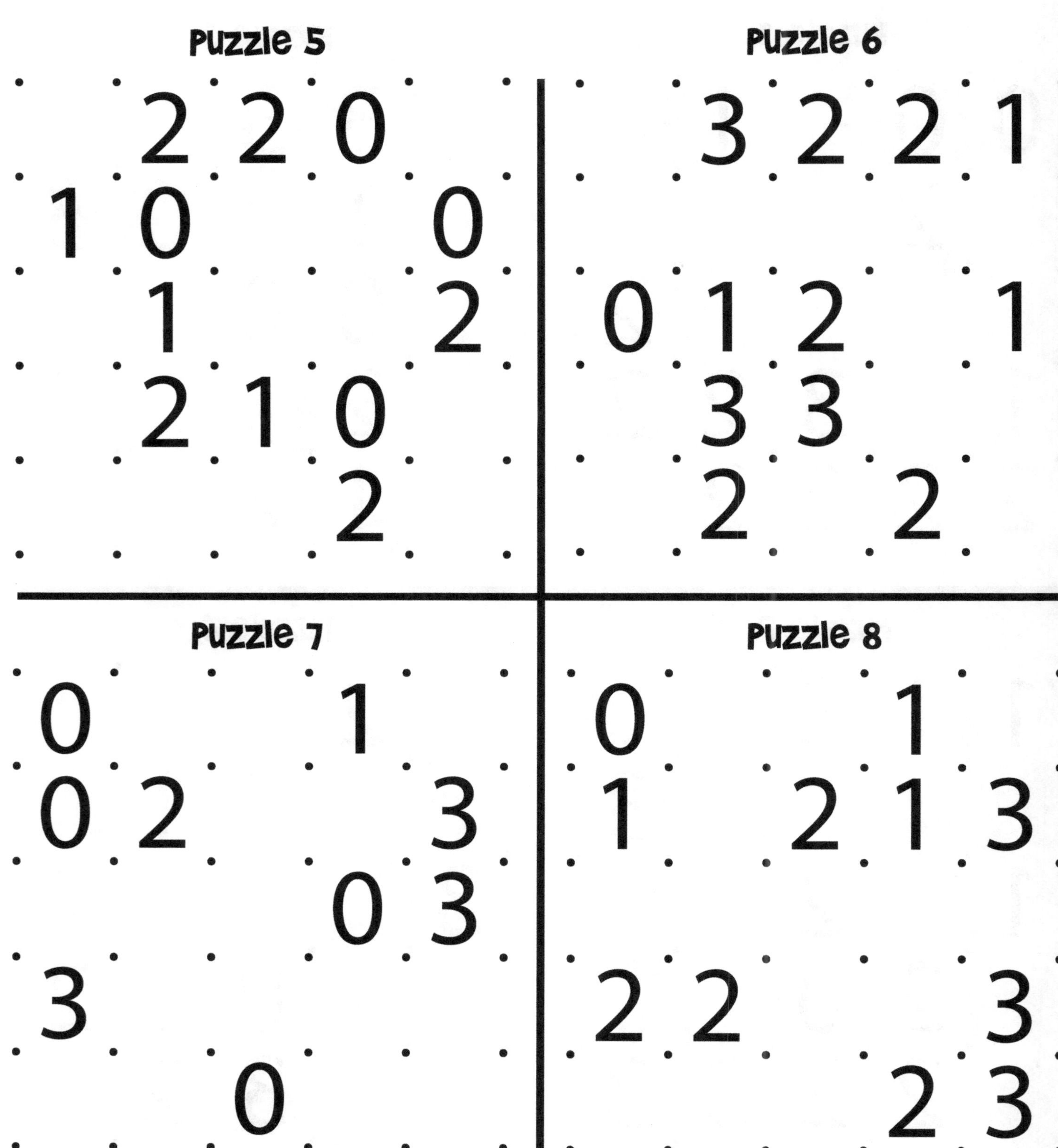

Puzzle 5
Puzzle 6
Puzzle 7
Puzzle 8

Slitherlink

Puzzle 9

0		2		1
		2		
3	1	0	0	2
2			1	2
		2	2	

Puzzle 10

		2	2	
2	1	1		
1	0	1		2
		3		0
2	2	3		

Puzzle 11

2	1	3		3
	1			3
		2	1	3
1		2	3	

Puzzle 12

0	1	2	2	
0				
		1	2	1
1	2	1	2	
0		1	1	

Puzzle 13

		3		
	2	0	1	3
2	0			
				1
3	2	2		

Puzzle 14

3	3		3	
1				
		0		3
		0	2	
3	1			

Puzzle 15

				3
1	3		3	
		0		1
2	1		3	3
1		1		

Puzzle 16

	3	2	2	
	2		1	
2	0			
	0			1
	1		2	0

Slitherlink

Puzzle 17

1	3			3	
					0
	1		2	2	
3		1		2	
2		0	0	0	
	3			2	

Puzzle 18

	3				3
	1	2	2		
3			3	2	2
	3				3
3			0		
2		3	2	2	

Puzzle 19

			1		3
3	3				2
				1	1
	2			1	2
2	1	1			2
2	2	2	3	3	1

Puzzle 20

1	1				2
				1	1
	3		1		
		0		3	
1	2				
2				3	3

Slitherlink

Puzzle 21

1		1	3		1
2	2				
2				0	3
			1		2
1	2				
	3	2	1		3

Puzzle 22

2	2		2		0
	1	1	2		
		2		3	3
3		3		2	
					1
1		1	2		

Puzzle 23

	1		2	2	
3		1		1	2
3			2	1	
		1		2	
1				1	2
	0	1			

Puzzle 24

2	3			3	
3	1		1		
			1	3	
	2		1		2
					3
	0	1	2	1	

Puzzle 25

1			2		
3			1		3
		2		3	
2					
2	1	1		2	2
	2	1		3	1

Puzzle 26

	2	3		2	1
			1		1
1	2	1			
			1	1	
3		0		1	2
2			2	2	

Puzzle 27

	2	2	1	1	1
	1				
	2				1
3	0				
			1	1	3
		3		0	

Puzzle 28

	2	3	2	2	
2		1	3	2	
2	1	1	1		
2	2				1
		2	1	1	3
	3		2		

Slitherlink

Puzzle 29

2					1	3
3		1	2			
	2			2		1
3				3		3
				1		
2	2	2	1	3		
					2	1

Puzzle 30

0	2			3		1
1				1	2	
2		1	1	3		2
					1	
3		2		3	2	
	1			2	1	2
2	2		3		2	

Puzzle 31

				3		1
2	1	2				
	1			2		
1				3	3	
3		2				
		0	0	1	2	1
	2	2		1		

Puzzle 32

	3		1			3
1			1		2	3
0	2					
				3	1	
	1	0	2			
	2				1	1
			0			1

Puzzle 33

	3					1	0
	1		1			2	2
1				2			
1	1	2	1	2			
			1				2
	1	0		2	3		
1		2	3				1
		3	2	2	2		

Puzzle 34

1		0			2	1	
		0				1	2
		3	2			2	2
1	1		1				1
		1	1			2	2
	2		2	3			
1	2	1				1	
	2			2	3		1

Puzzle 35

	2			1		2	1
		3			0		1
3	0	1				1	
2				2		1	
2					1	3	1
		1	1		2		
3				2		2	
1			2			2	

Puzzle 36

		3	3		2		
1		2		2	1		0
						2	0
			0				2
3			2				
	0	0			1		3
2		1		1	0	1	
2				1		2	

Puzzle 37

	2		3	3	2	3	
	0					1	3
2	1		1		1		
	2	1			3	2	2
	1						
3		1	1				
	1	1	3		1	2	
	2	2		3		1	1

Puzzle 38

2	3		3			0	
				2	2	3	
	1		2				2
0						1	1
2	2	2		3	3		
3							
		1	1		2	3	
		1	2				3

Puzzle 39

1			0	2	2		1
1	1			2			
			2			0	
						0	
2		3				0	2
		0	2	1			
1							
2	2		2	1			0

Puzzle 40

0		2	1	3	1	2	
	1		2			3	
1							
	1			0	2		
	2		1				
							1
	2	0		0		1	
3		3		2			0

Logic Grids

How to: Logic Grid Puzzles

Four friends each have different favorite colors. What color is each friend's favorite?

1. Brian nor Greg like red.
2. Greg does not like blue.
3. Don's favorite color is yellow.

	Red	Yellow	Green	Blue
Brian	X			
				X

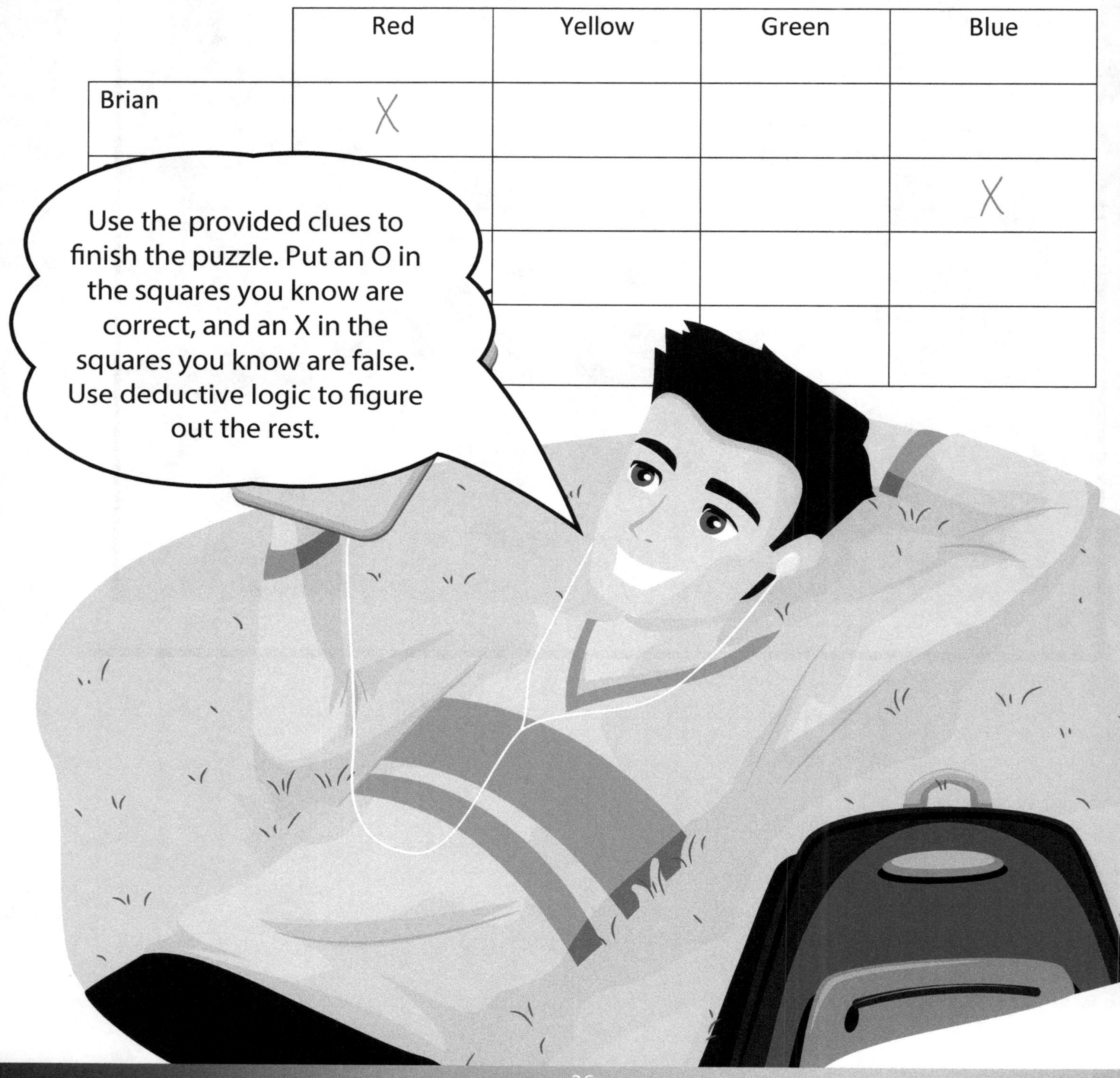

Use the provided clues to finish the puzzle. Put an O in the squares you know are correct, and an X in the squares you know are false. Use deductive logic to figure out the rest.

Puzzle 1

Four friends each have different favorite colors. What color is each friend's favorite?

1. Brian nor Greg like red.
2. Greg does not like blue.
3. Don's favorite color is yellow.

	Red	Yellow	Green	Blue
Brian				
Greg				
Ryan				
Don				

Puzzle 2

Michelle, Donna, Sabrina, and Julie have four different favorite cookies. Use the clues to find out which cookie each girl likes best.

1. Michelle is allergic to peanut butter and dislikes oatmeal.
2. Donna's favorite cookie is chocolate chip.
3. Sabrina loves oatmeal cookies.

	Chocolate Chip	Sugar	Oatmeal	Peanut Butter
Michelle				
Donna				
Sabrina				
Julie				

Puzzle 3

A van, a car, a pick-up truck, and a motorcycle are all in a parking lot. Use the clues below to determine the color of each vehicle.

1. The vehicle with 2 wheels is black.
2. The car is not white or grey.
3. The van is not white.

	Black	White	Red	Grey
Van				
Car				
Pick-Up Truck				
Motorcycle				

Puzzle 4

Four boys (Fred, Sam, Bob, and Carl) all have different pets (a fish, a bird, a dog, and a cat). Use the clues to find out who has which pet.

1. Fred's pet has fins.
2. Sam's pet does not have fur.
3. Carl has a cat.

	Fish	Bird	Dog	Cat
Fred				
Sam				
Bob				
Carl				

Puzzle 5

Five students in Miss Smith's class made an A+, each in a different subject. Use the clues below to determine which student made an A+ in each class.

1. Martin made an A+ in writing.
2. Edgar made a B in Science and Spelling.
3. The only student who made an A+ in Math was Katherine.
4. Gertrude made a C in Spelling.

	Writing	Math	Reading	Spelling	Science
Martin					
Edgar					
Gertrude					
Henry					
Katherine					

Puzzle 6

Every baseball team in a league has a different jersey color. Use the clues below to determine what color each team wears.

1. The Bears wear gray jerseys.
2. The black jersey is worn by a team whose mascot can fly.
3. The Eagles wear green jerseys.
4. The Tigers wear either gray or blue jerseys.

	Black	Gray	White	Blue	Green
Bears					
Hornets					
Eagles					
Bulldogs					
Tigers					

Puzzle 7

A circus has 5 acts. Use the clues to determine in what order the acts take the ring.

1. The clowns start the show.
2. The dancing dogs take the ring immediately after the elephants.
3. The elephants are the third act.
4. The trapeze act is not the last act.

	First	Second	Third	Fourth	Fifth
Clown					
Trapeze					
Tiger Tamer					
Dancing Dogs					
Elephants					

Puzzle 8

Four students (Amy, Cathy, Frank, and James) were the leaders of four teams (Red, Black, Green, and Purple). Each team competed in field day games. Use the clues below to determine who was the team captain and which team won first, second, third, and fourth place.

1. Amy was the captain of the red team and did not finish last.
2. The team that placed first wore black jerseys.
3. The purple team placed third with James as captain.
4. Cathy's team did not place 4th.

	Red Captain	Black Captain	Green Captain	Purple Captain
Amy				
Cathy				
Frank				
James				

1st	2nd	3rd	4th

1st				
2nd				
3rd				
4th				

Puzzle 9

Mrs. Johnson names a Student of the Month and allows them to bring their pet to class for a day. During January, February, March, and April, the students named as student of the month were Sally, Drew, Scott, and Holly. The animals brought to class were a hamster, fish, turtle, and dog.

1. The dog belongs to a student whose name starts with "S."
2. Sally was Student of the Month in January.
3. Scott owns a fish.
4. Drew has a pet with fur and was Student of the Month in April.
5. Holly was Student of the Month in February.

	January	February	March	April	Hamster	Fish	Turtle	Dog
Sally								
Drew								
Scott								
Holly								
Hamster								
Fish								
Turtle								
Dog								

Puzzle 10

Four students (John, Jeremy, Josh, and Jacob) have different last names (Smith, Scott, Stewart, and Shaw) and participate in different sports (soccer, football, basketball, and baseball). Use the clues below to determine each student's last name and sport.

1. John Shaw plays soccer.
2. Jeremy Stewart does not play basketball.
3. The player with last name Scott plays football.
4. Josh plays basketball
5. Jacob plays football.

	Smith	Scott	Stewart	Shaw	Soccer	Football	Basketball	Baseball
John								
Jeremy								
Josh								
Jacob								

	Smith	Scott	Stewart	Shaw
Soccer				
Football				
Basketball				
Baseball				

PiCross

How to: Picross

Use logic to turn these numbers into an image.

Each number means an unbroken line of black squares, and they appear in the same order as the numbers. Each row goes from left to right, and each column goes from top to bottom.

Every unbroken line of black squares is separated by at LEAST one empty box. Use this to your advantage!

	1 1	2	3	2	1 1
1					
1					
5					
1 1					
1 1					

Here are some hints...

A row of 0 has no black squares.

See if you can do the biggest numbers first. That will make the rest of the puzzle easier.

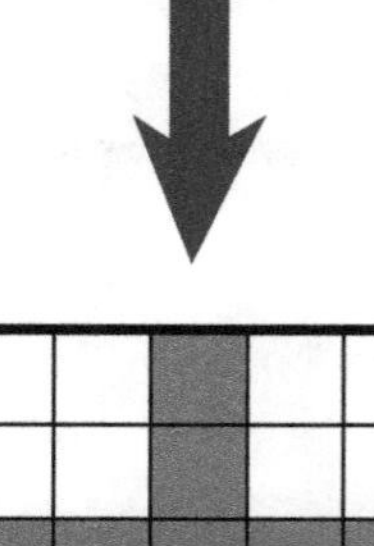

Puzzle 1

	1	3	2 2	3	1
1					
3					
2 2					
3					
1					

Puzzle 2

	2	1 3	3 1	1 3	2
3					
1 1 1					
5					
1 1					
3					

Puzzle 3

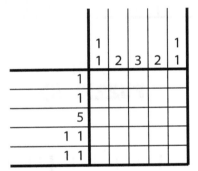

	1 1	2	3	2	1 1
1					
1					
5					
1 1					
1 1					

Puzzle 4

	2	2 1	1	2 1	2
1 1					
1 1					
1 1					
1 1					
3					

Puzzle 5

	1 1	1 1 1	1 1	1 1 1	1 1
1 1					
1 1 1					
1 1					
1 1 1					
1 1					

Puzzle 6

	3	1 2	1 1 1	2 1	3
3					
1 2					
1 1 1					
2 1					
3					

Puzzle 7

	1 1 1 1	1 1	10	1 1	1 1 1 1	1 1 1 1	1 1	10	1 1	1 1 1 1
1 1 6										
1 1										
6 1 1										
1 1										
1 1										
1 1										
1 1 6										
1 1										
6 1 1										
1 1										

Puzzle 8

	4	1 2 1	1 2 1	1 2 1	4 4	4 4	1 2 1	1 2 1	1 2 1	4
4										
1 2 1										
1 2 1										
1 2 1										
4 4										
4 4										
1 2 1										
1 2 1										
1 2 1										
4										

Puzzle 9

	8	2 2	1 4 1	1 2 2 1	1 1 2 1 1	1 1 2 1 1	1 2 2 1	1 4 1	2 2	8
8										
2 2										
1 4 1										
1 2 2 1										
1 1 2 1 1										
1 1 2 1 1										
1 2 2 1										
1 4 1										
2 2										
8										

Puzzle 10

	4	1 1	1 1	1 1	2 2 2	1 2 2 1	1 1	1 1	1 1	4
2 2										
1 2 1										
1 1 1										
1 1 1										
1 2 1										
1 1 1										
1 1 1										
1 1 1										
2 1										
2										

Puzzle 11

	3 3	1 1 1 1	10	1 1	1 2 1	1 2 1	1 1	10	1 1 1 1	3 3
3 3										
1 1 1 1										
10										
1 1										
1 2 1										
1 2 1										
1 1										
10										
1 1 1 1										
3 3										

Puzzle 12

	1 1 1 1	1 1 1 1	1 2 1	2 1 1 2	1 2 1	1 2 1	2 1 1 2	1 2 1	1 1 1 1	1 1 1 1
1 1 1 1										
1 1 1 1										
1 2 1										
2 1 1 2										
1 2 1										
1 2 1										
2 1 1 2										
1 2 1										
1 1 1 1										
1 1 1 1										

Puzzle 13

	2 2	1 2 1	3 2 3	1 1 1 1	2 2 2	2 2 2	1 1 1 1	3 2 3	1 2 1	2 2
2 2										
1 2 1										
3 2 3										
1 1 1 1										
2 2 2										
2 2 2										
1 1 1 1										
3 2 3										
1 2 1										
2 2										

Puzzle 14

	4	1 1	1 1	1 1 1 1	1 3 1	2 5	3 2 3	8	6	4
4										
1 3										
1 3										
1 1 3										
1 4										
1 6										
1 3 3										
1 5										
1 3										
4										

Puzzle 15

Column	Clues
1	1
2	1 1 1 1
3	2
4	1
5	1 1 1 1
6	2 1
7	1 1 2 2 1
8	7 1
9	6 4 1
10	1 4 **11**
11	5 8 4
12	1 5 6 1
13	4 3 1
14	3 1 1
15	1 1 3 1
16	1 1 1 1
17	1 1
18	2
19	1 1 1 1
20	1

Row	Clues
1	1
2	1 3 1 1
3	1
4	1 2 1
5	3
6	2 1 1
7	1 4 1
8	1 1 2
9	5 1
10	1 4 1 1
11	6
12	1 2 5
13	6 2
14	1 9 1
15	1 6 2 1
16	8
17	2
18	**16**
19	3 2 3
20	0

Puzzle 16

Column	Clues
1	1 1
2	8 1
3	12 1
4	1 4 3 2
5	16 1
6	3 11 2
7	2 8 1
8	2 10 2
9	2 4 4
10	4 4
11	4 4
12	4 4
13	10 2
14	8 1
15	11 2
16	16 1
17	3 1 4 3 2
18	2 12 1
19	2 8 1
20	2 1 1

Row	Clues
1	0
2	2 2
3	5 5
4	5 5
5	1 1
6	1 1 1 1
7	4 4
8	1 2 1 2 1 2 1
9	4 6 4
10	18
11	18
12	8 8
13	3 4 4 3
14	2 4 4 2
15	7 7
16	7 7
17	18
18	4
19	1 1 6 1 1
20	20

Puzzle 17

			1	2																
		2	7	2			2			1		1			2	2				
		2	2	5	**11**		9		2	4	3	6		2	7	7	3	5	8	
	1	3	1	3	6	**16**	1	**19**	**17**	**10**	6	1	8	9	1	3	**11**	**11**	4	6
4 4 3																				
1 2 2 1 5																				
1 2 1 2 1 3																				
8 3																				
9 3																				
2 2 3 3																				
1 2 2 2																				
7 3																				
9 6																				
1 **16**																				
17																				
16																				
14																				
15																				
15																				
6 2 3																				
3 3 3 3																				
3 3 3																				
3 2 3																				
3																				

Puzzle 18

1. 1
2. 1
3. 1 2
4. 7 2
5. 7 2
6. 16
7. 1 7 7
8. 2 6 10
9. 10 1
10. 6
11. 1 3 3
12. 2 6
13. 1 3 7
14. 1 7 3
15. 1 1 13
16. 2 6 2
17. 2 6 2
18. 7 1
19. 1 3 1
20. 1

Row clues (top to bottom):

1. 2
2. 2 1 2
3. 3 1 1 2
4. 7 1
5. 7 1 1
6. 9 3
7. 8 1 2
8. 8 2 2
9. 6 5
10. 2 1 1 7
11. 1 2 1 7
12. 1 1 1 9
13. 2 3 1 5
14. 2 3 2 3
15. 5 2 1
16. 4 2 1
17. 3 2 1
18. 2 3 4
19. 2 5
20. 2 4

Puzzle 19

						4														
					6	2	9	9				5	6				9	5		
	1	1	1	5	3	1	1	1	**13**	7	6	1	2	**10**	6	6	1	5	9	**10**
0																				
0																				
3																				
1 5 2																				
9 4																				
8 7																				
2 **14**																				
2 **14**																				
11 2																				
12 2																				
13 2																				
1 2 2 1 2																				
1 1 1 1 1																				
2 1 1 1 1																				
1 1 1																				
1 1 1																				
1 2 1																				
1 2																				
0																				
0																				

Puzzle 20

	6	3 2 3	2 2 2	1 2 1	3 2 3	2 3 2 3 2	1 8 1	2 2 2	1 2 1	20	20	1 2 1	2 2 2	1 8 1	2 3 2 3 2	3 2 3	1 2 1	2 2 2	3 2 3	6
6																				
3 2 3																				
2 2 2																				
2 2 2																				
1 2 2 2 1																				
2 1 2 1 2																				
1 2 2 2 1																				
2 1 2 1 2																				
1 1 2 1 1																				
20																				
20																				
1 1 2 1 1																				
2 1 2 1 2																				
1 2 2 2 1																				
2 1 2 1 2																				
1 2 2 2 1																				
2 2 2																				
2 2 2																				
3 2 3																				
6																				

Puzzle 21

Column	Clue
1	4
2	1 3 1
3	1 1 9 3
4	1 3 2 1
5	1 2 2 2
6	1 1 3 2
7	2 1 1 2
8	1 2 2
9	1 2 1 1 1
10	1 3 1
11	1 3 1
12	1 2 1 1 1
13	1 2 2
14	2 1 1 2
15	1 1 3 2
16	1 2 2 2
17	1 3 2 1
18	1 1 9 3
19	1 3 1
20	4

Row clues (top to bottom):

Row	Clue
1	4 4
2	1 2 2 1
3	1 1 8 1 1
4	2 4 4 2
5	1 2 2 1
6	3 3
7	1 1
8	1 3 3 1
9	1 2 1 1 2 1
10	1 4 4 1
11	1 1 1 1
12	1 1
13	1 1
14	2 2
15	2 4 2
16	1 2 1
17	1 1 2 1 1
18	1 2 1 1 2 1
19	1 2 2 1
20	2 6 2

Masyu

How to: Masyu

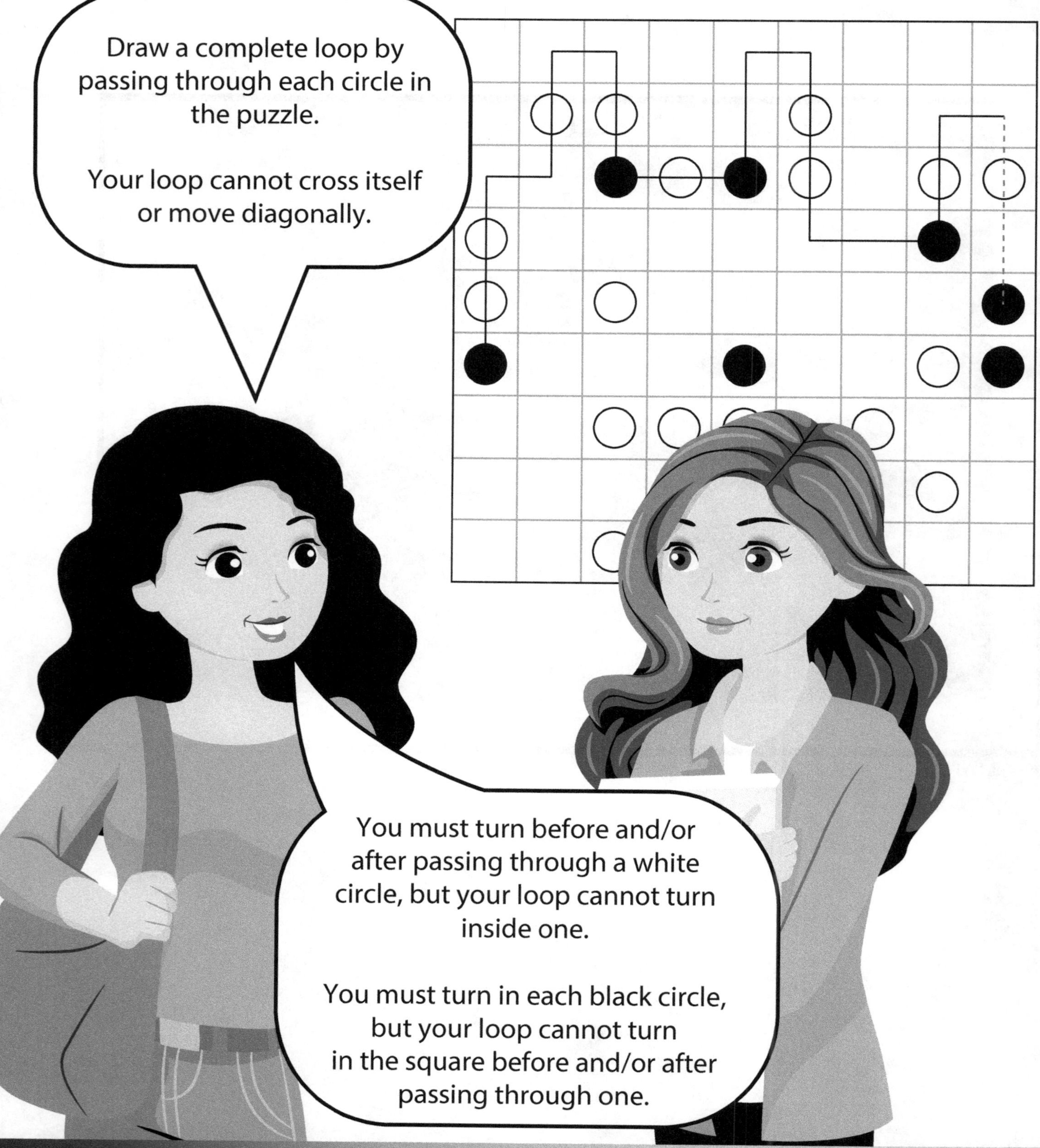
Draw a complete loop by passing through each circle in the puzzle.
Your loop cannot cross itself or move diagonally.
You must turn before and/or after passing through a white circle, but your loop cannot turn inside one.
You must turn in each black circle, but your loop cannot turn in the square before and/or after passing through one.

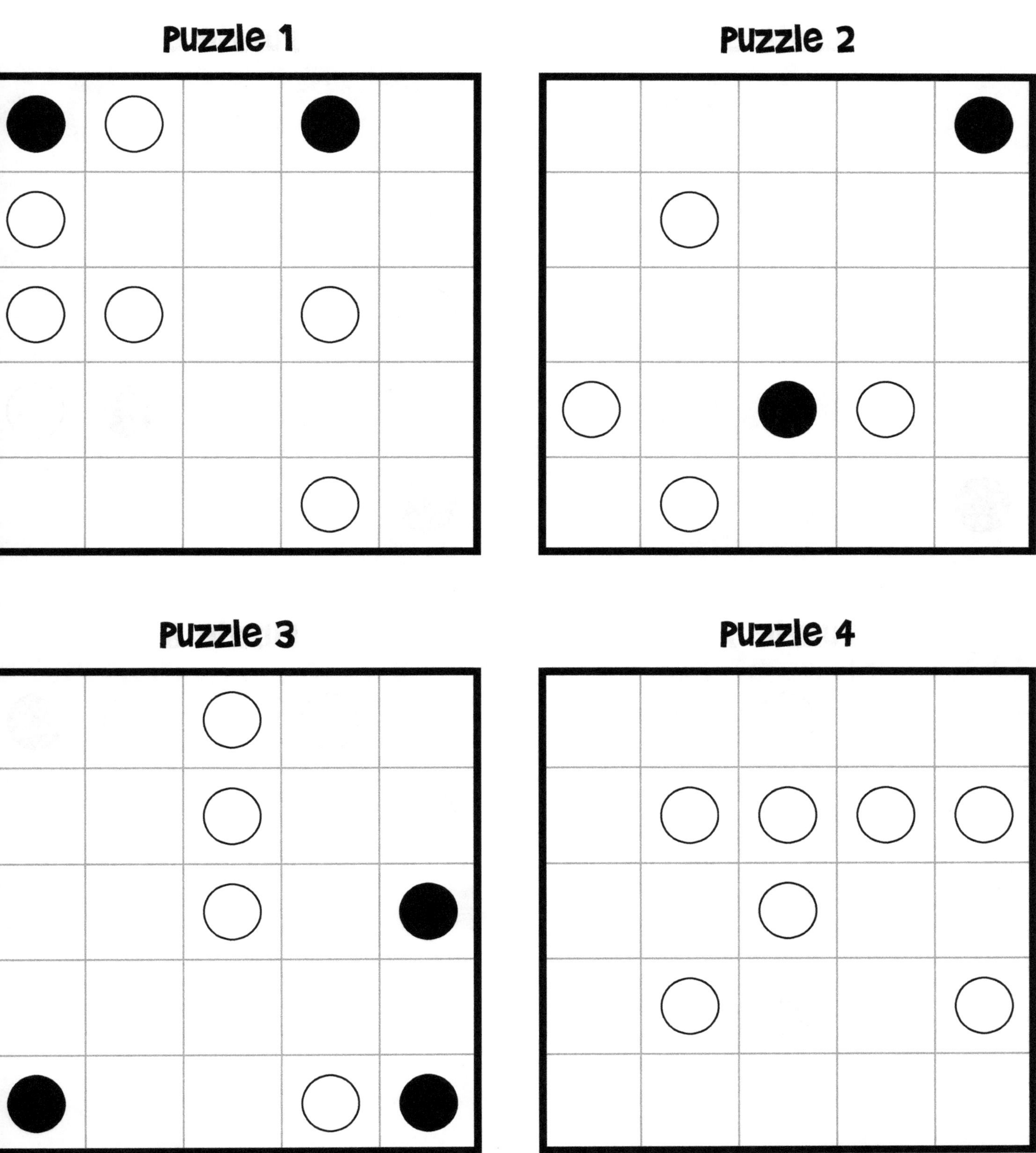
Puzzle 1
Puzzle 2
Puzzle 3
Puzzle 4

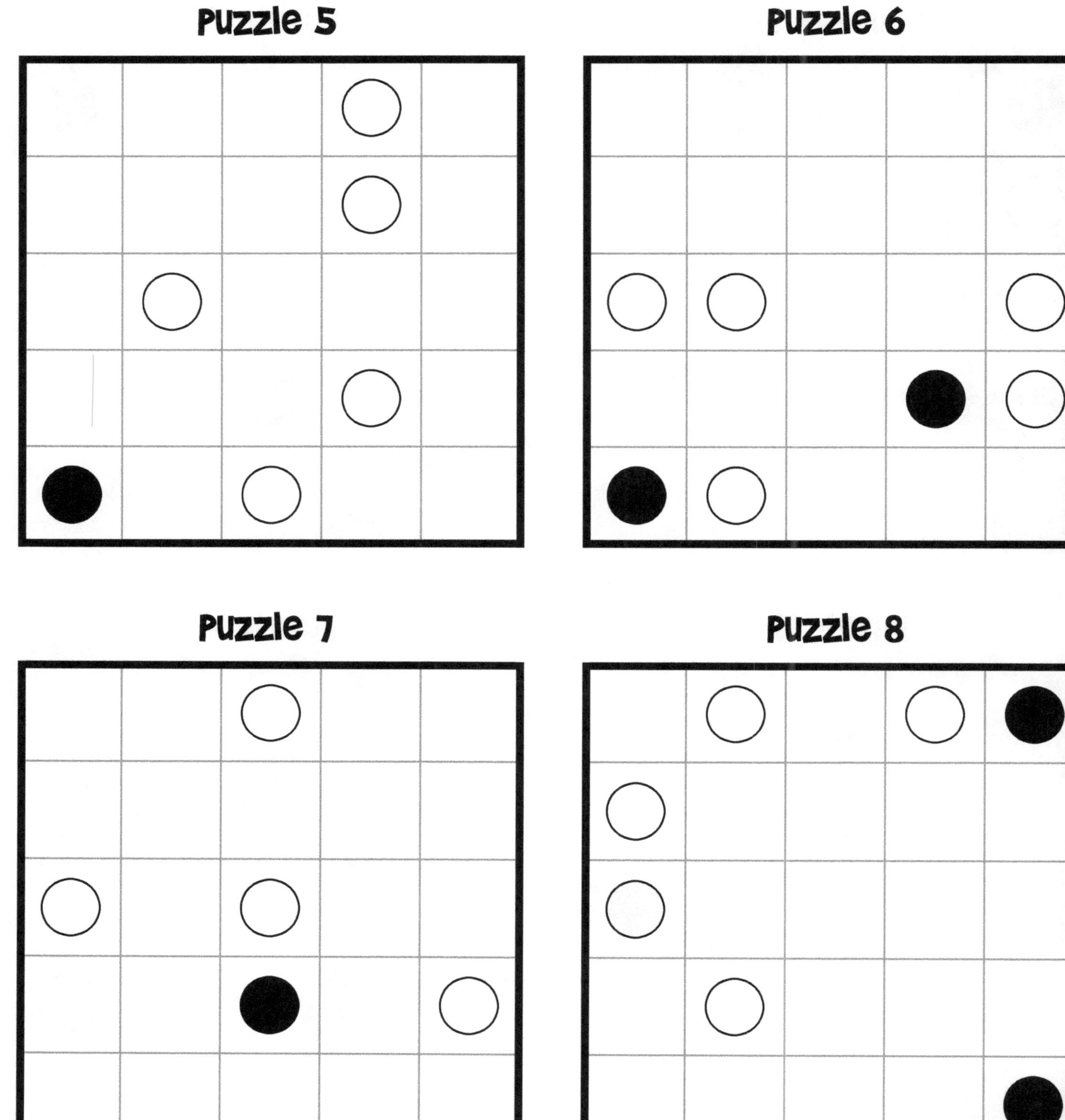
Puzzle 5
Puzzle 6
Puzzle 7
Puzzle 8

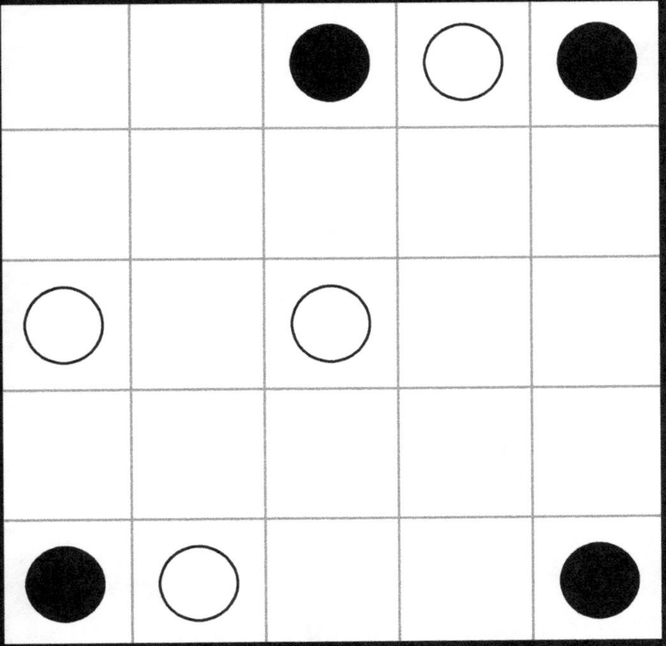

Puzzle 10

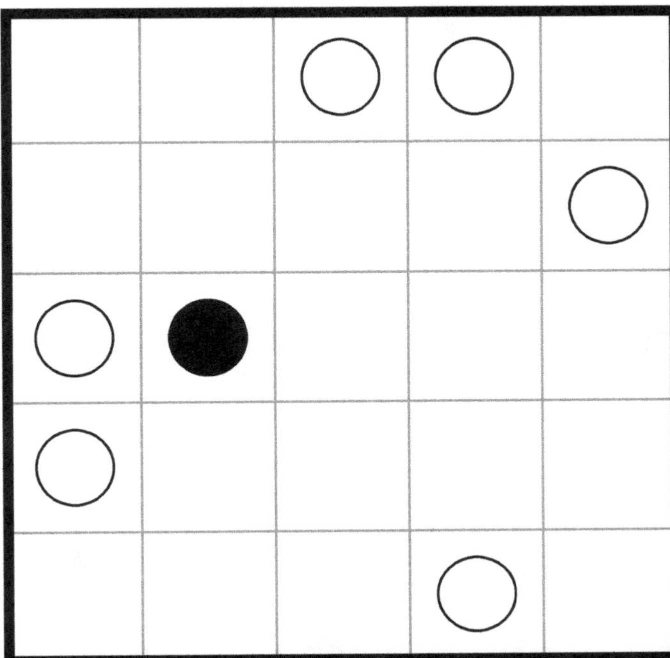

Puzzle 11

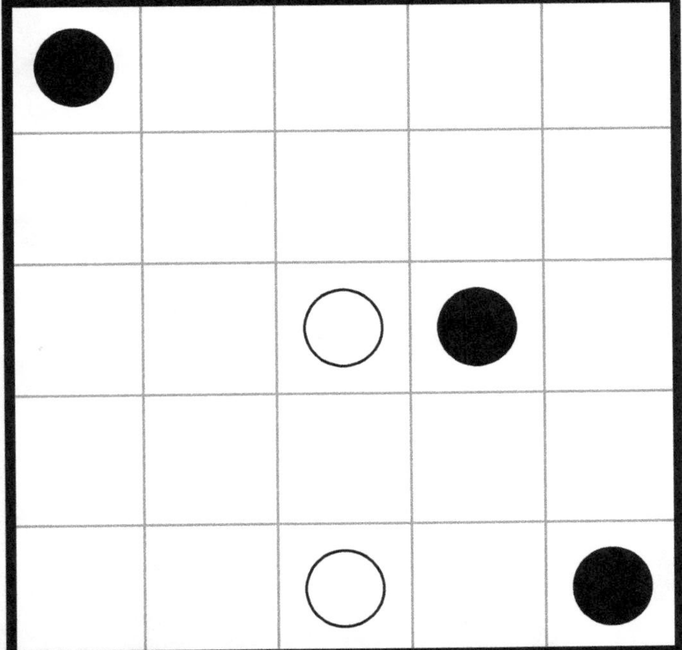

Puzzle 12

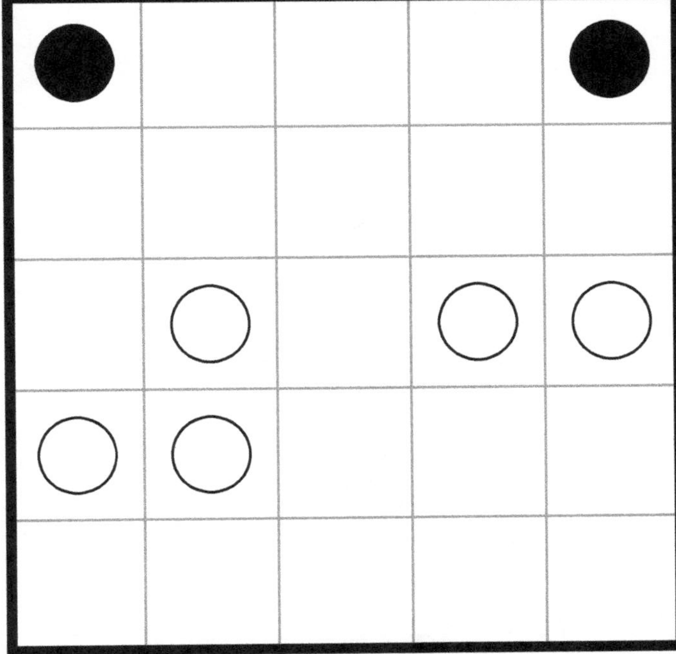

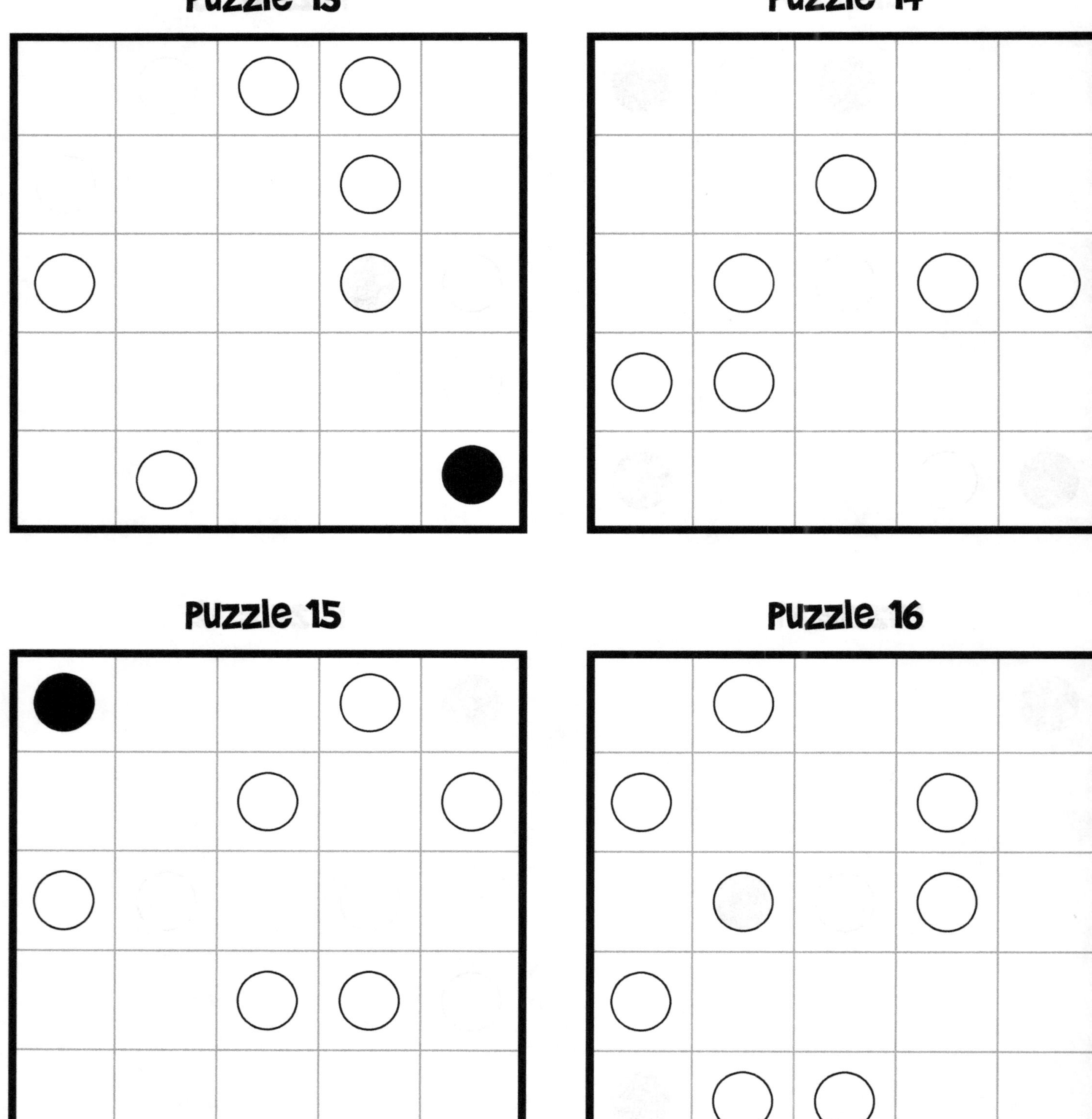

Puzzle 13
Puzzle 14
Puzzle 15
Puzzle 16

Puzzle 17

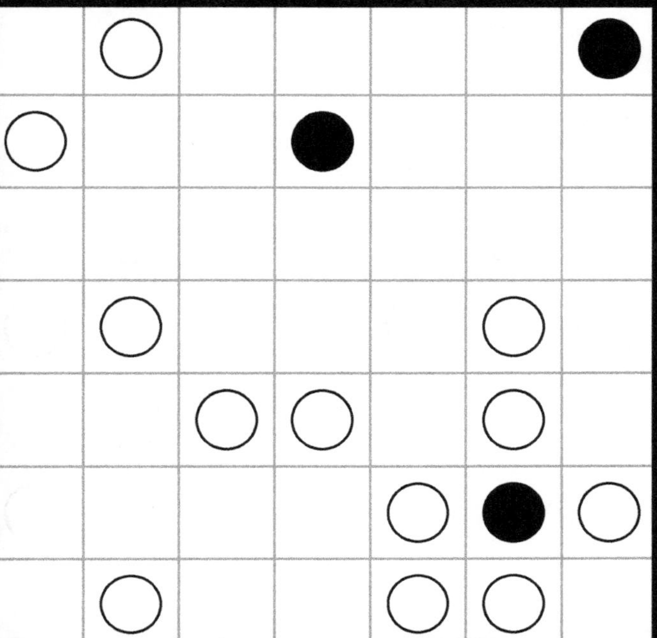

Puzzle 18

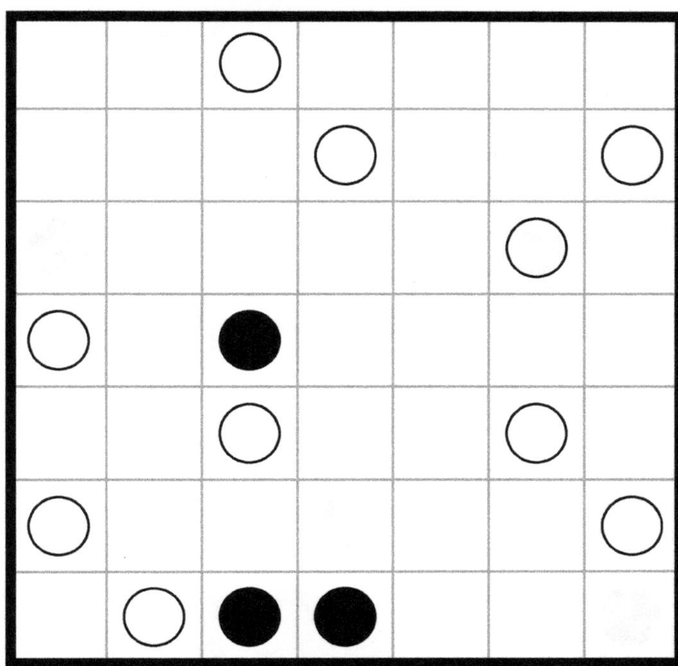

Puzzle 19

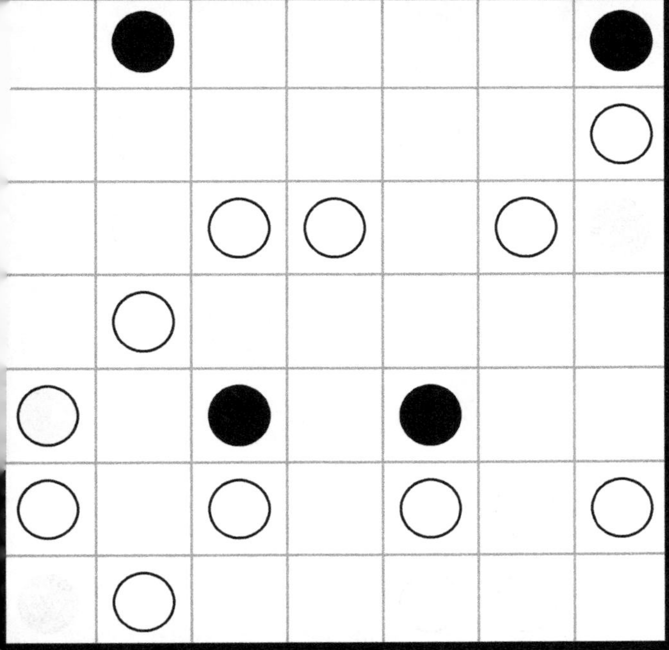

Puzzle 20

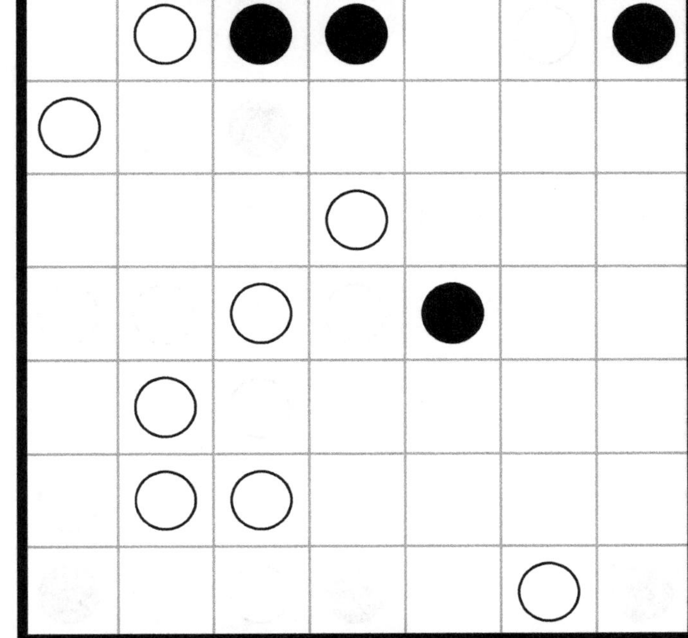

Puzzle 21

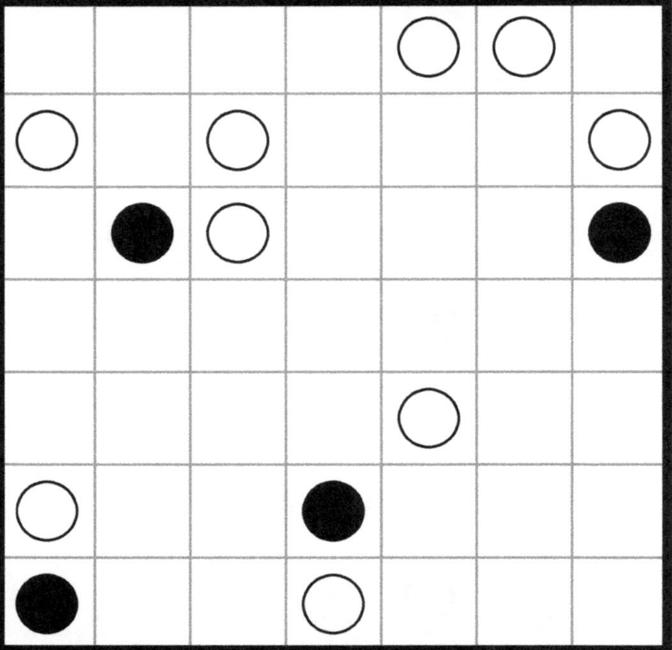

Puzzle 22

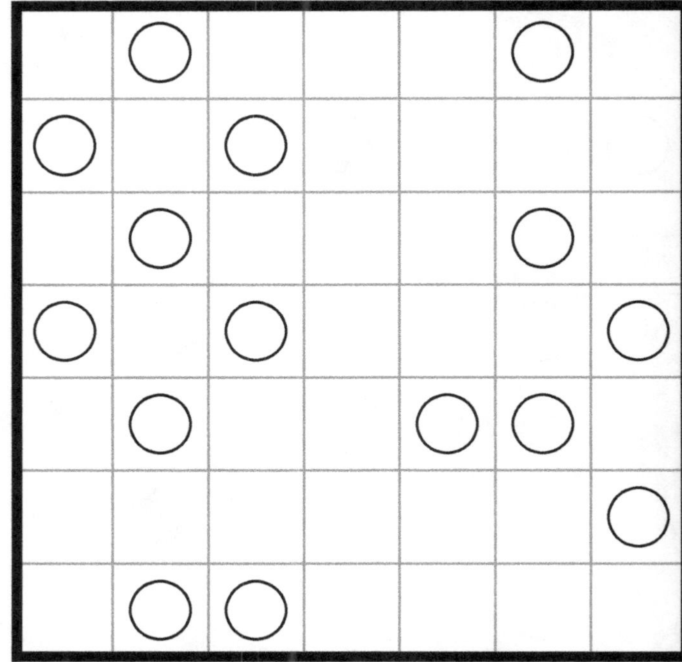

Puzzle 23

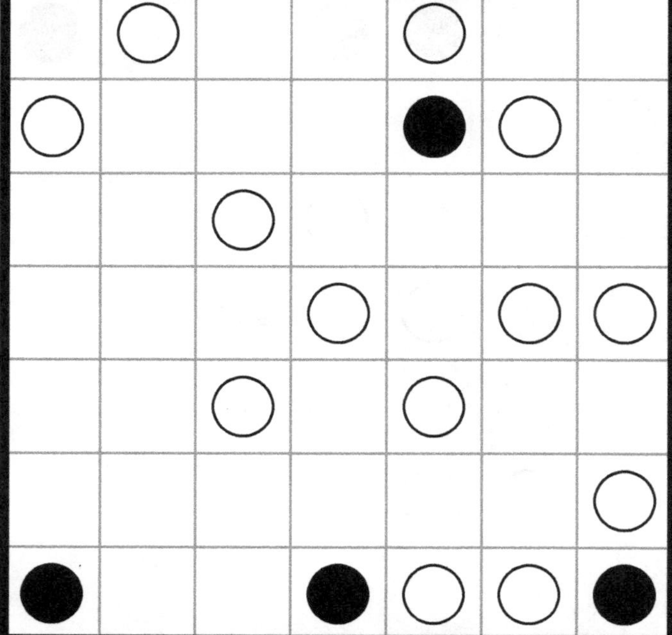

Puzzle 24

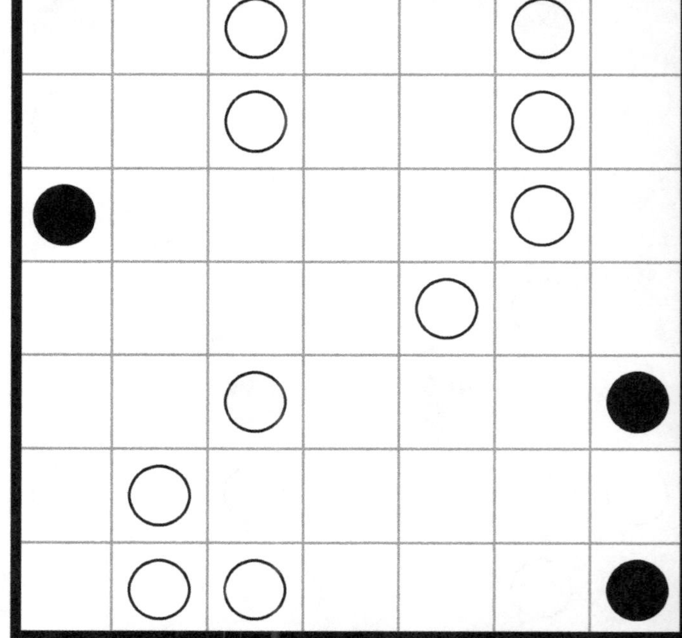

Puzzle 25

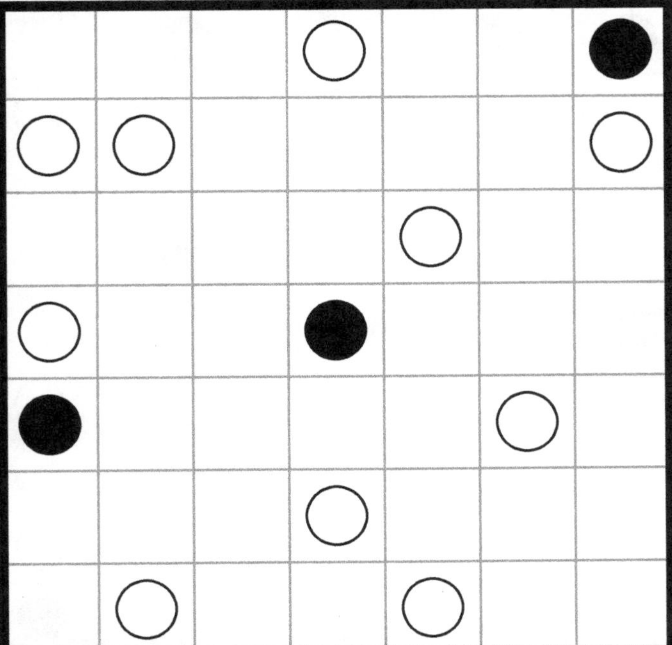

Puzzle 26

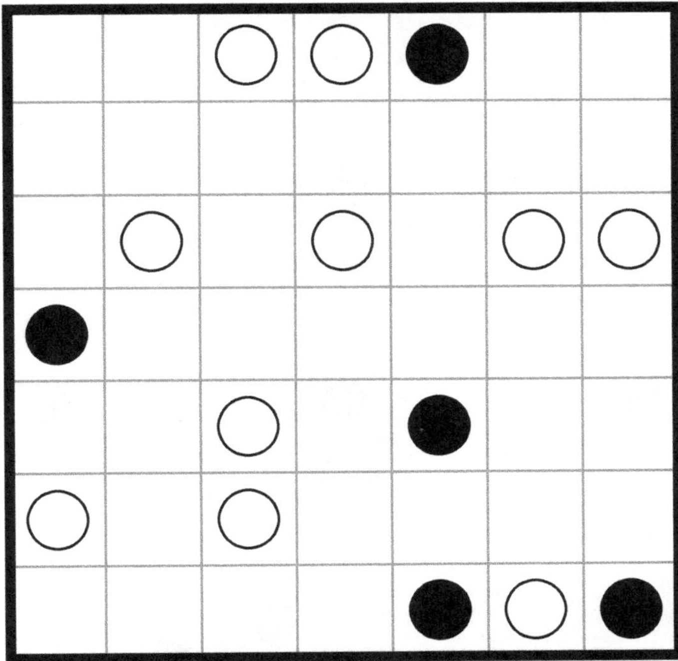

Puzzle 27

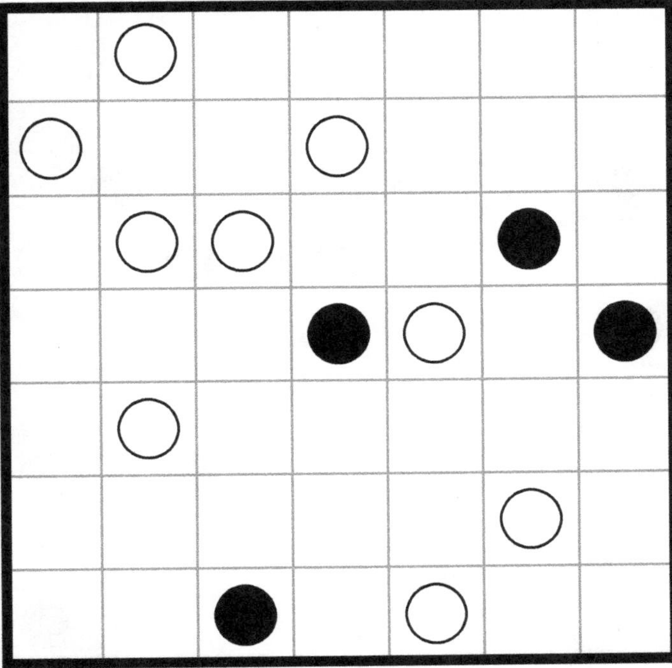

Puzzle 28

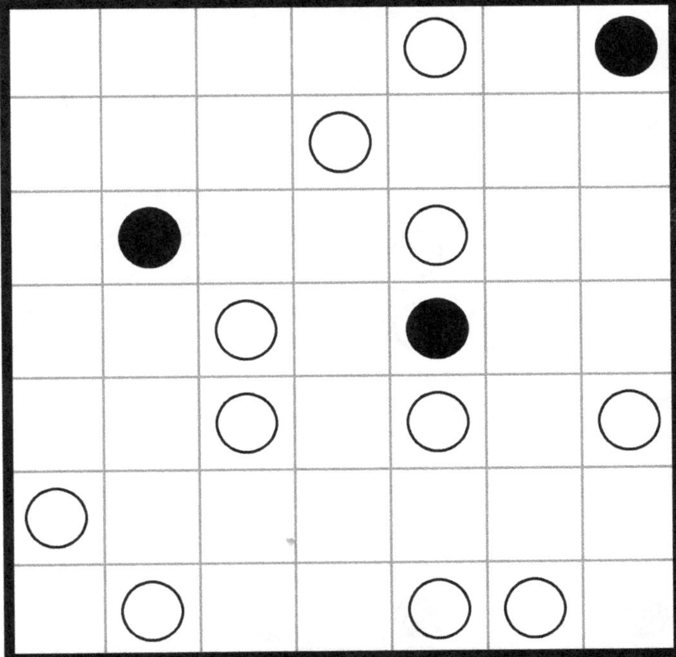

Puzzle 29

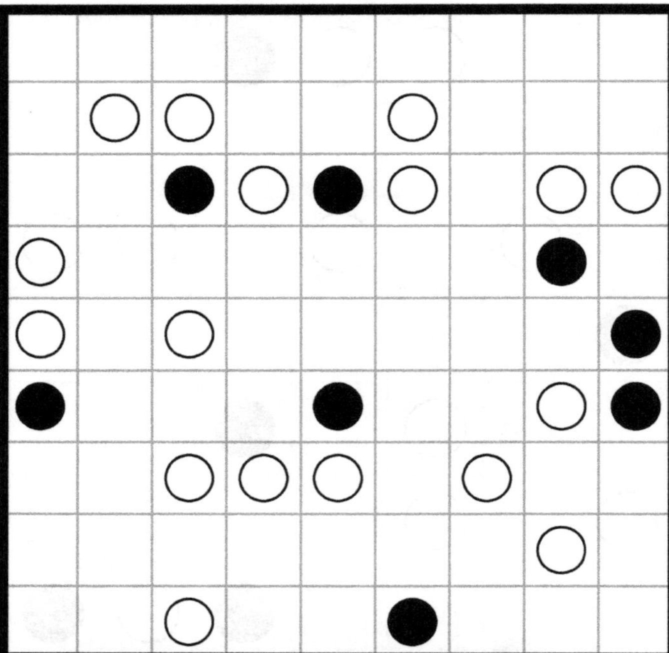

Puzzle 30

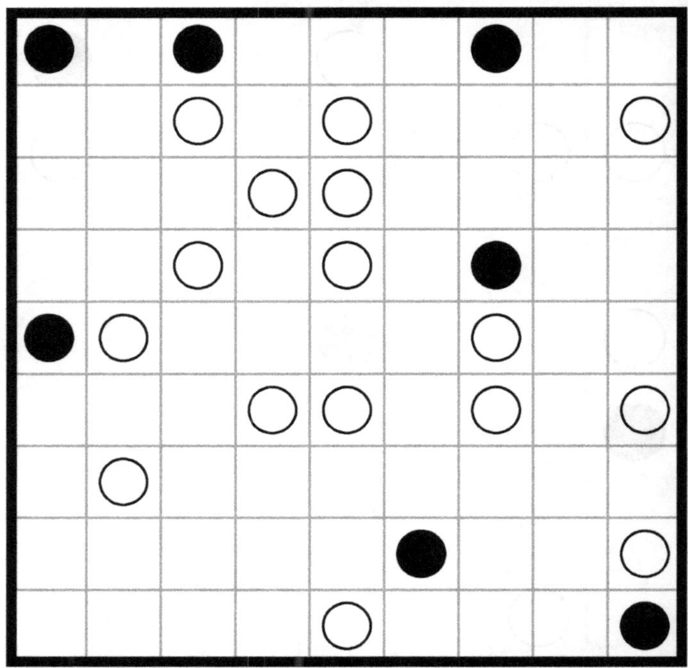

Puzzle 31

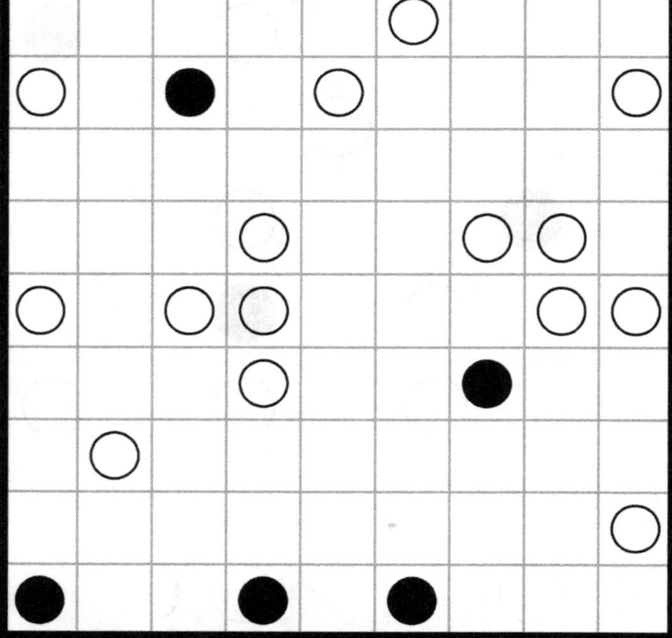

Puzzle 32

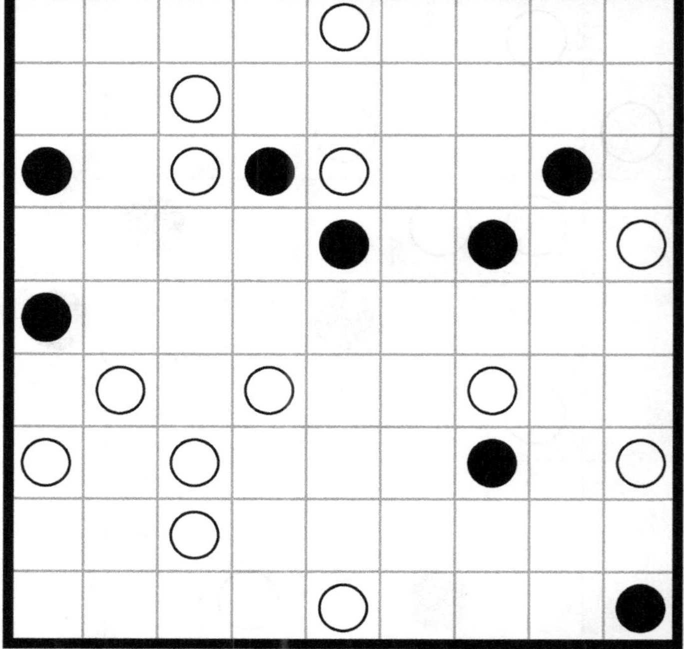

Puzzle 33

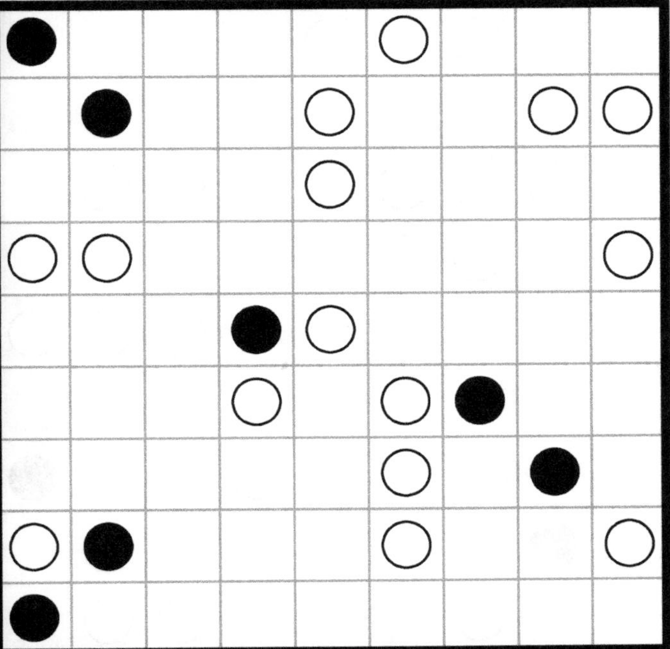

Puzzle 34

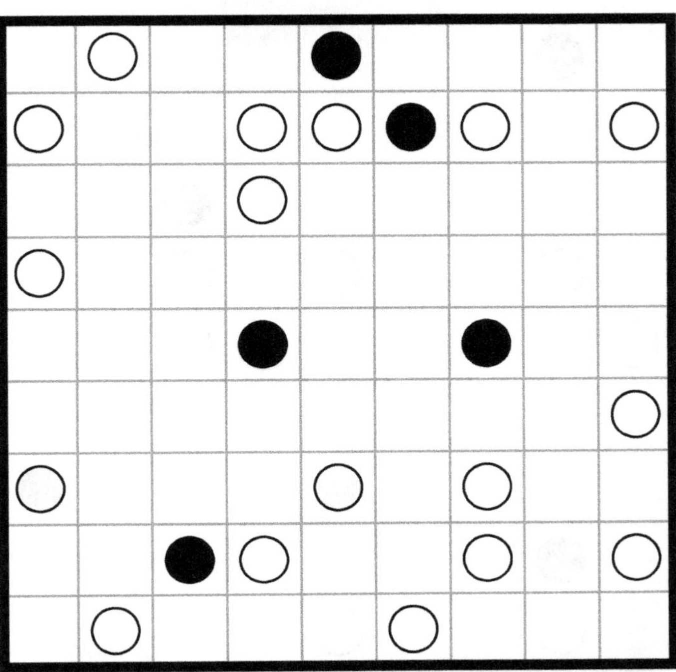

Puzzle 35

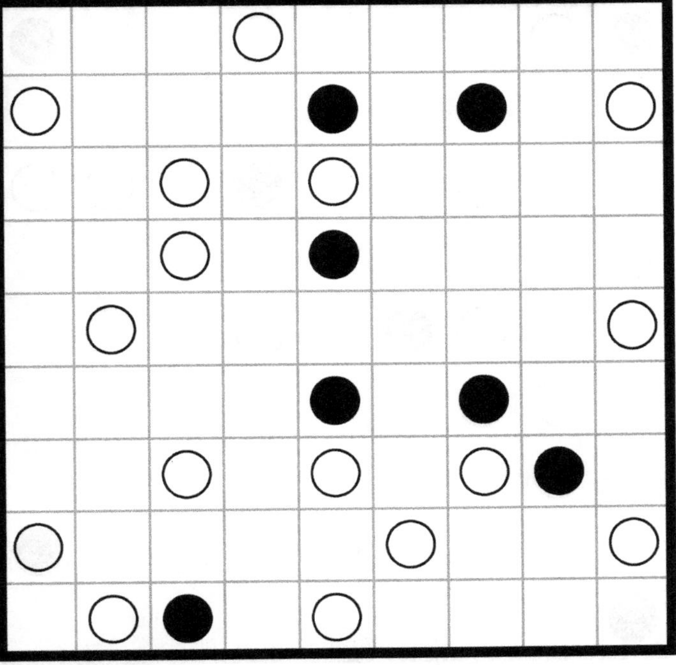

Puzzle 36

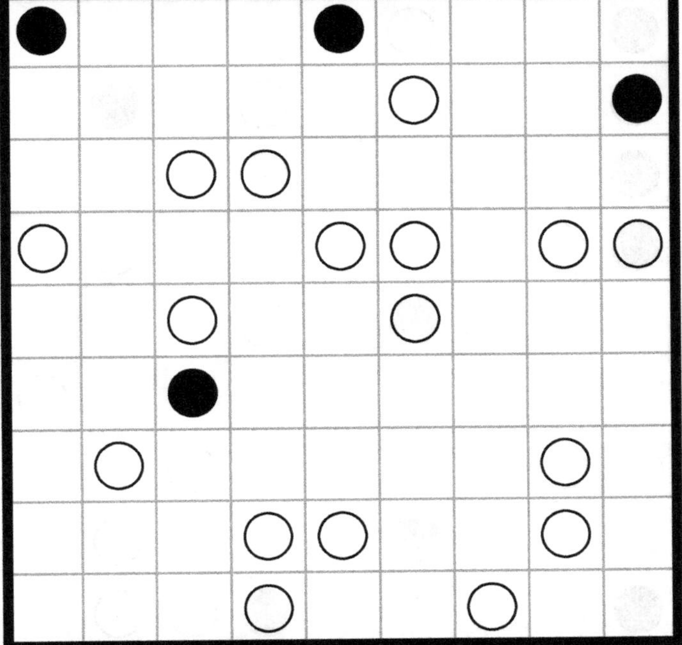

Puzzle 37

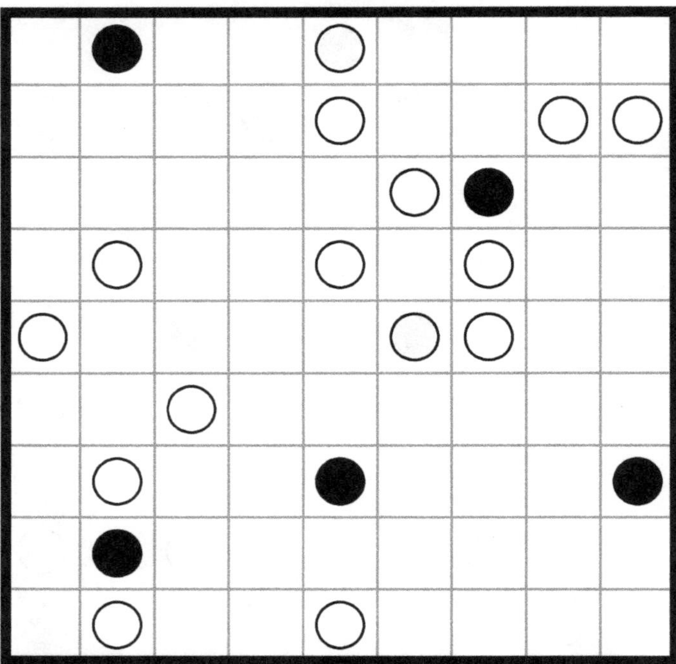

Puzzle 38

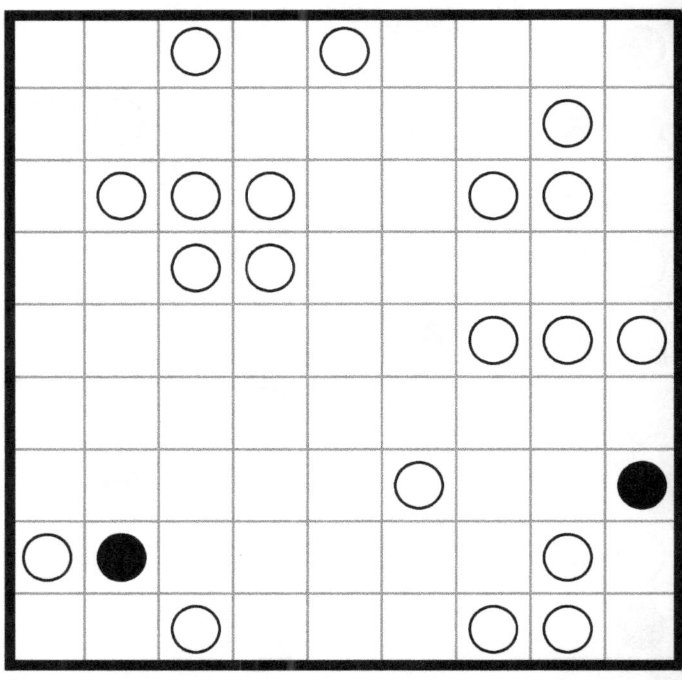

Puzzle 39

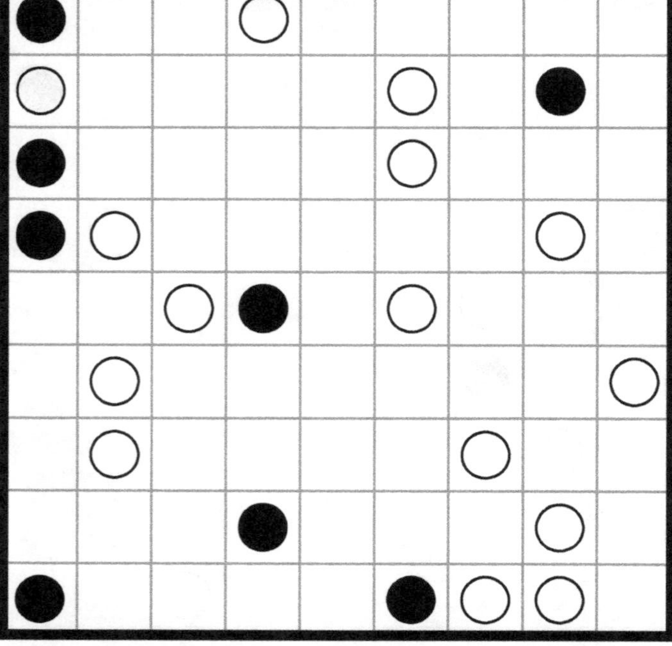

Puzzle 40

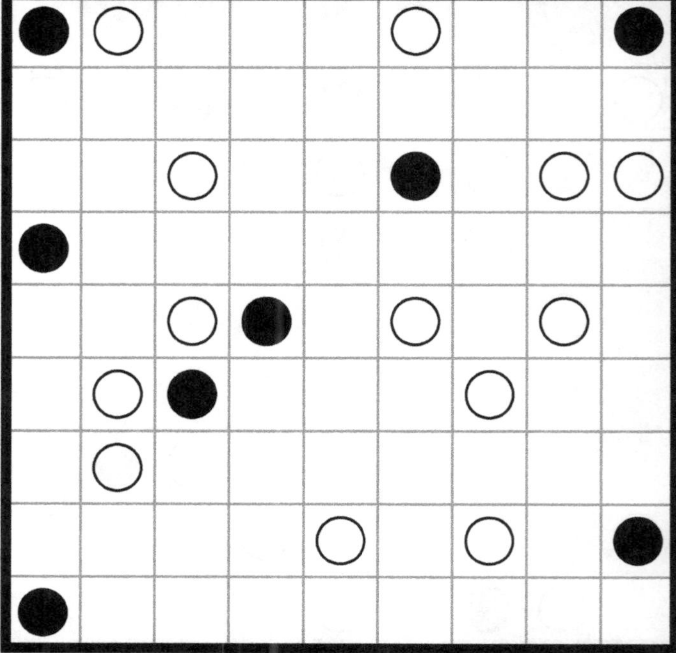

Matchsticks

How to: Matchsticks

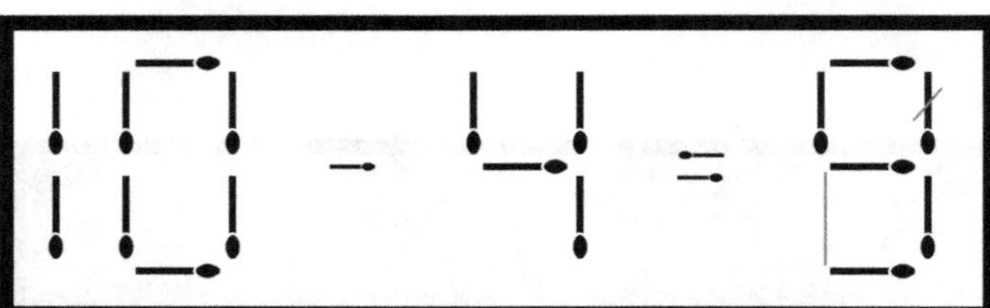

10 - 4 = 9 ✗

10 - 4 = 6 ✓

Move only 1 line to make a true mathematical equation.
Sometimes you might need to move a matchstick from an addition sign, or onto a subtraction sign!

Ready? Let's go!

Puzzle 1

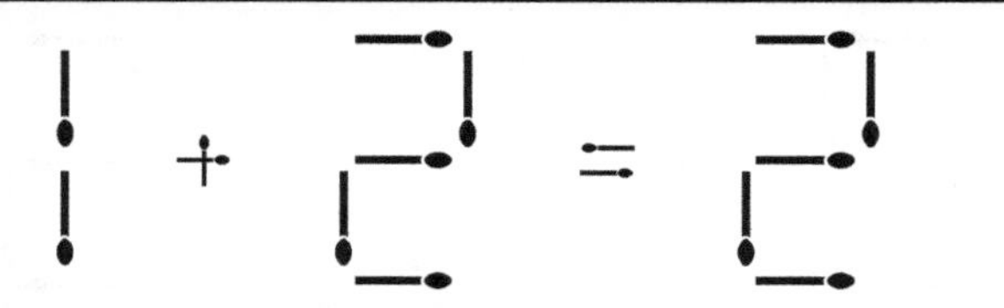

Puzzle 2

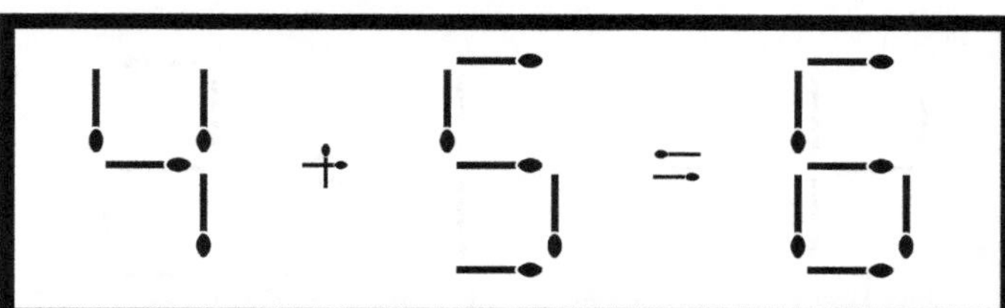

Puzzle 3

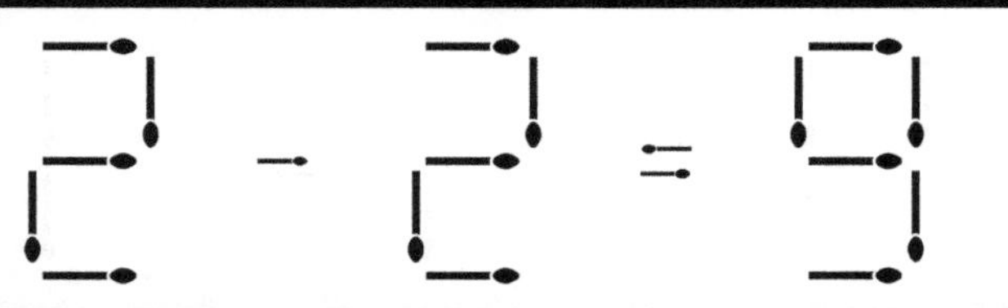

Puzzle 4

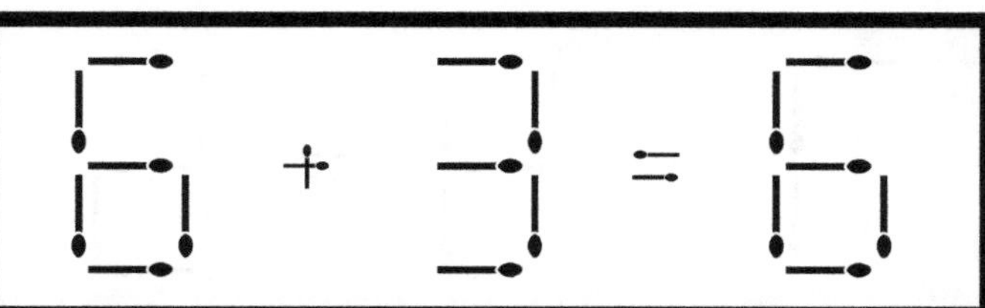

Puzzle 5

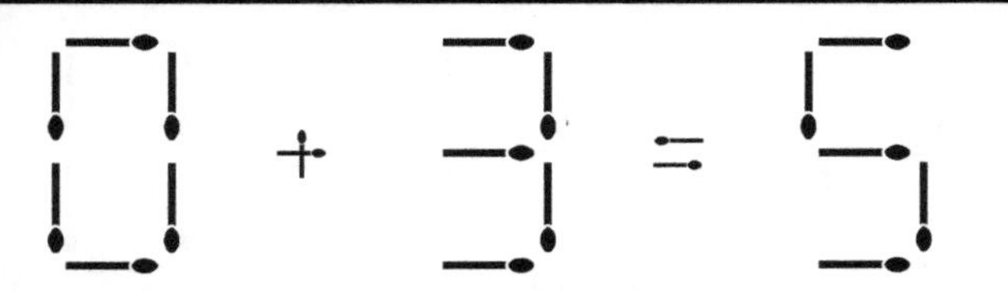

Puzzle 6

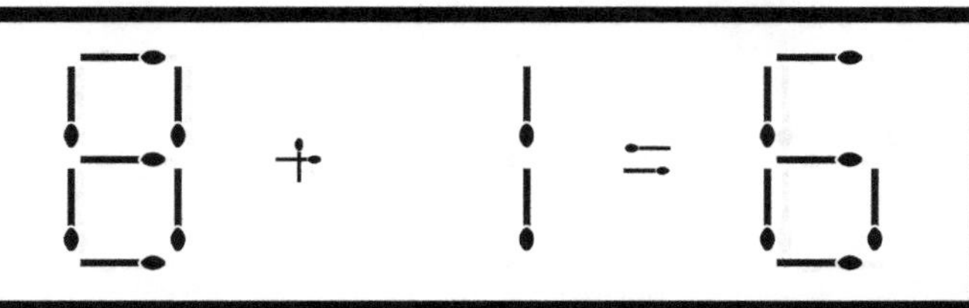

Puzzle 7

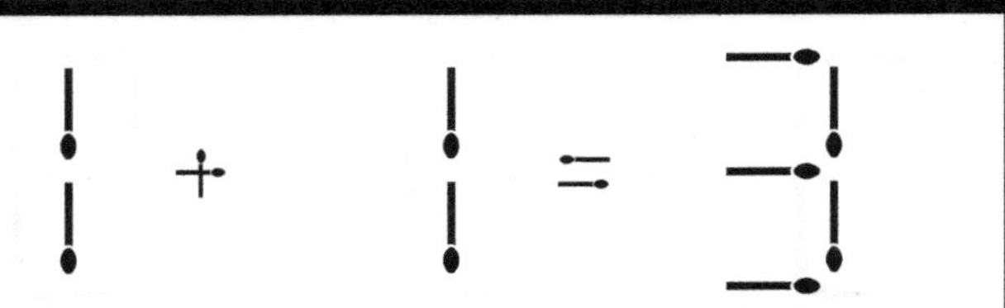

Puzzle 8

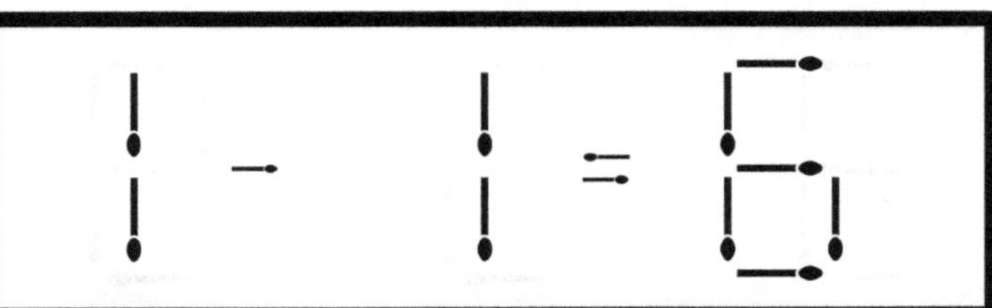

Puzzle 9

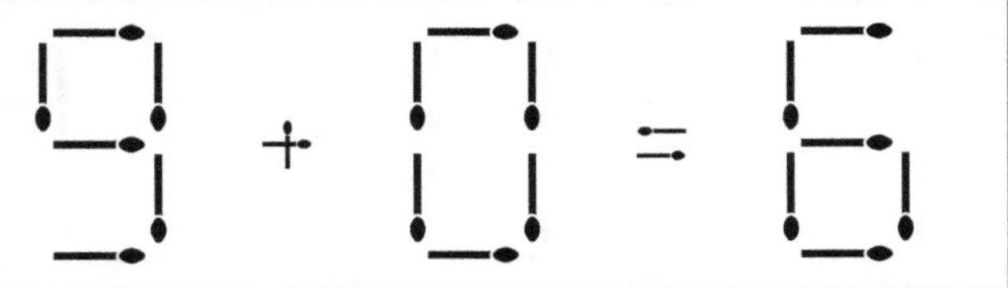

Puzzle 10

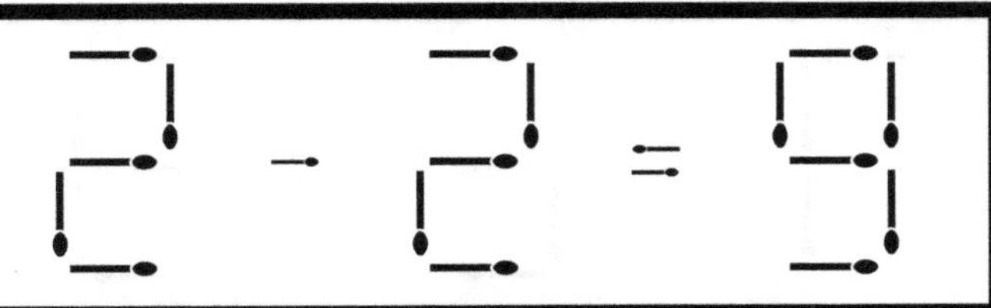

Puzzle 11

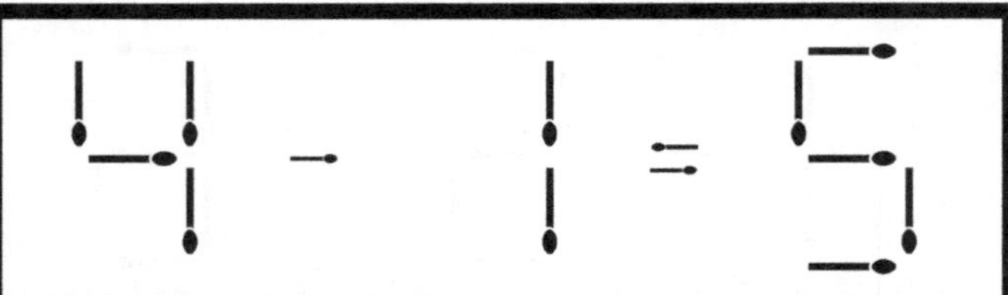

Puzzle 12

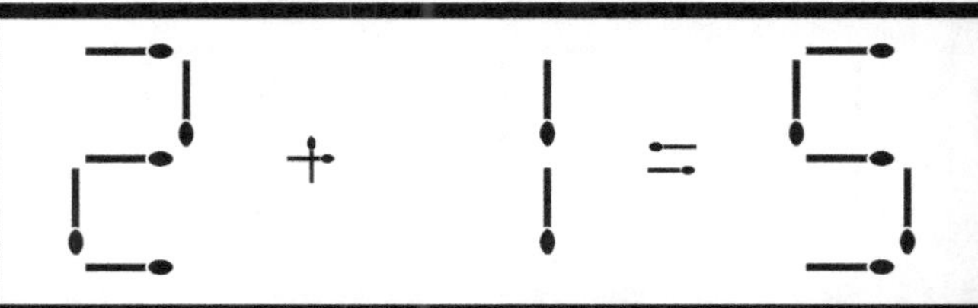

Puzzle 13

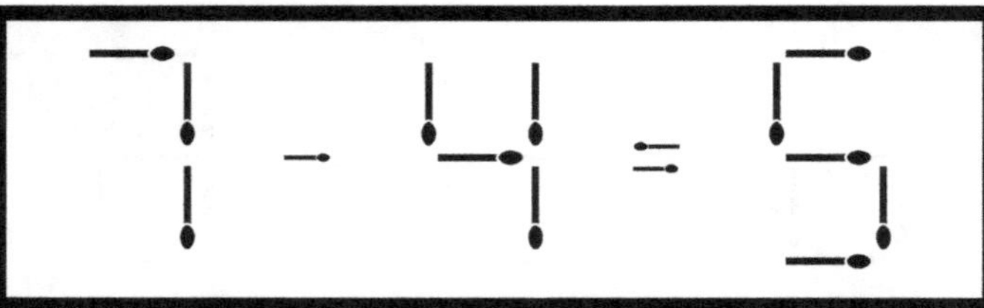

Puzzle 14

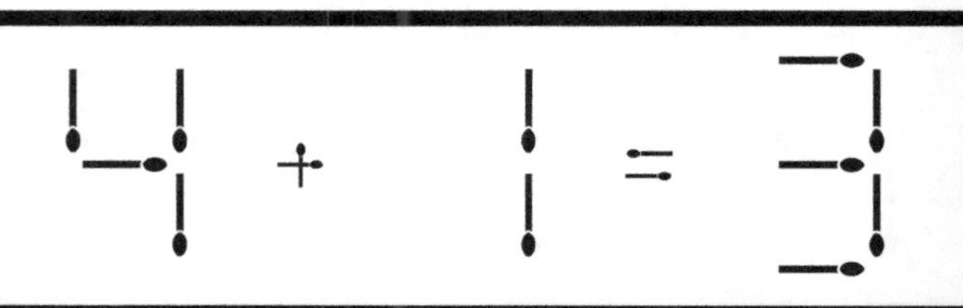

Puzzle 15

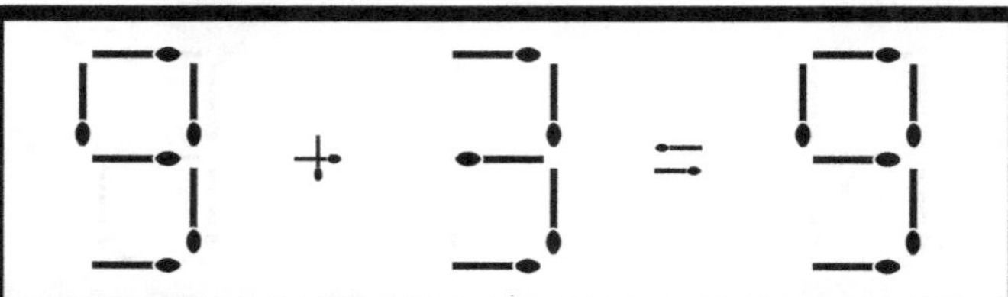

Puzzle 16

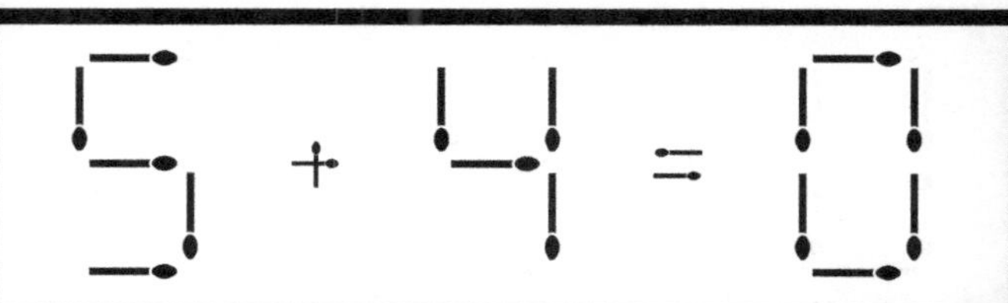

Puzzle 17

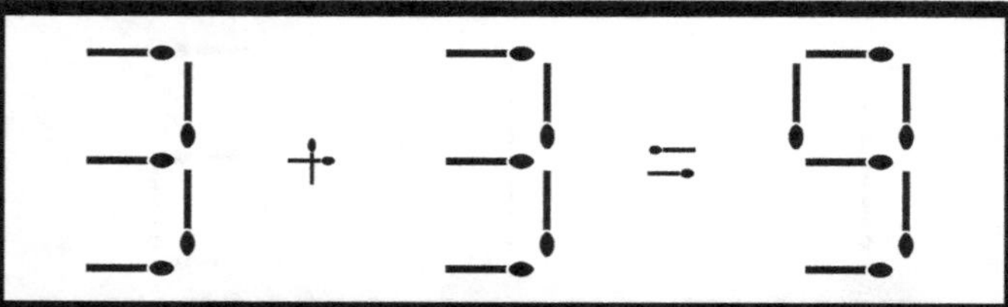

Puzzle 18

Puzzle 19

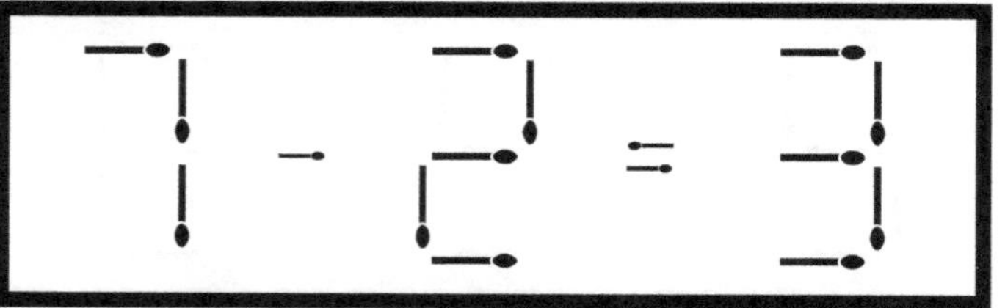

Puzzle 20

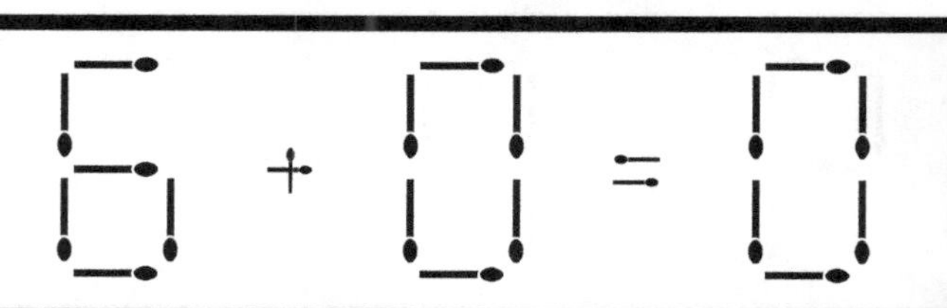

Puzzle 21

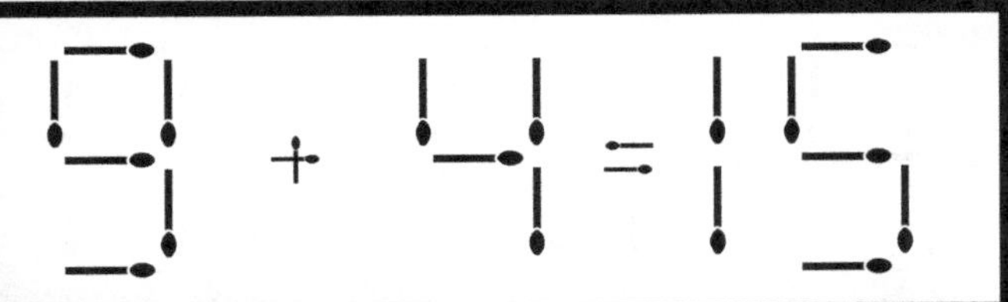

Puzzle 22

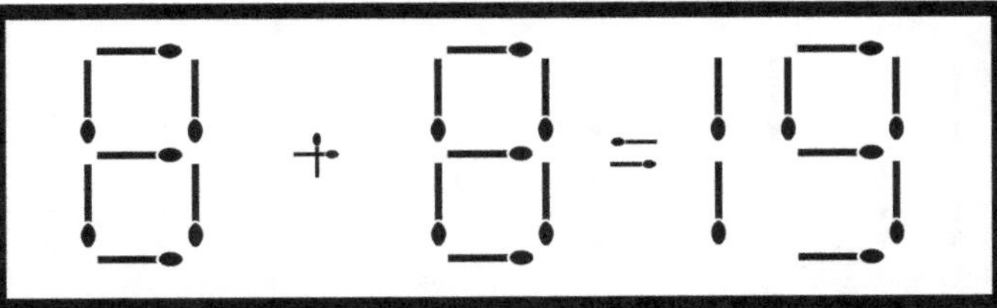

Puzzle 23

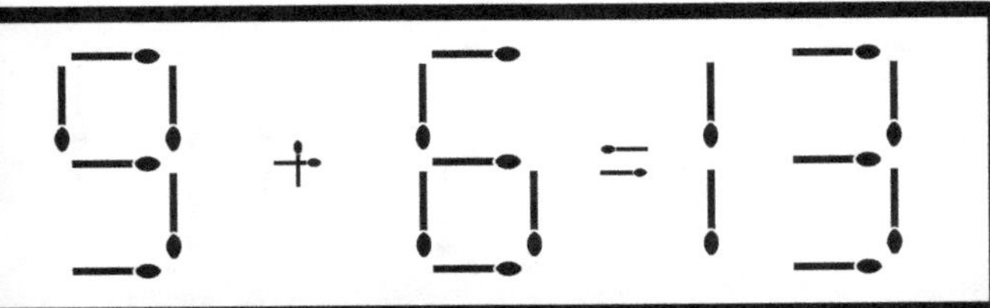

Puzzle 24

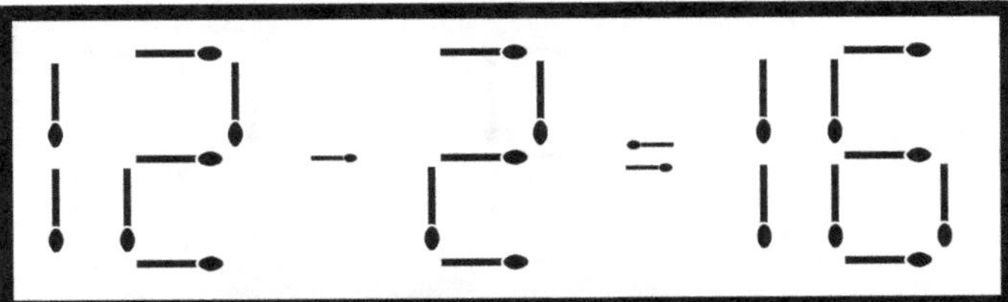

Puzzle 25

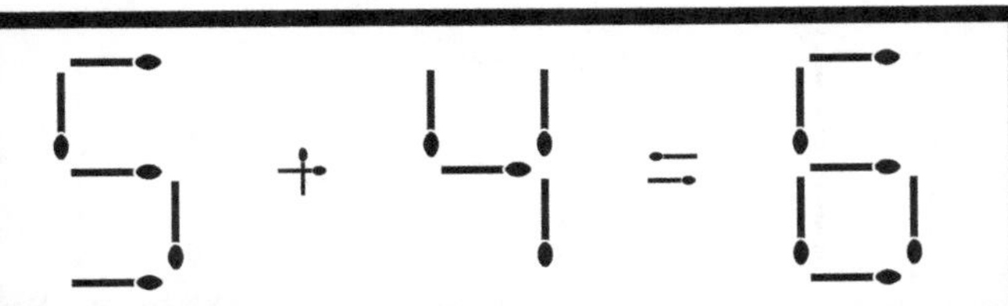

Puzzle 26

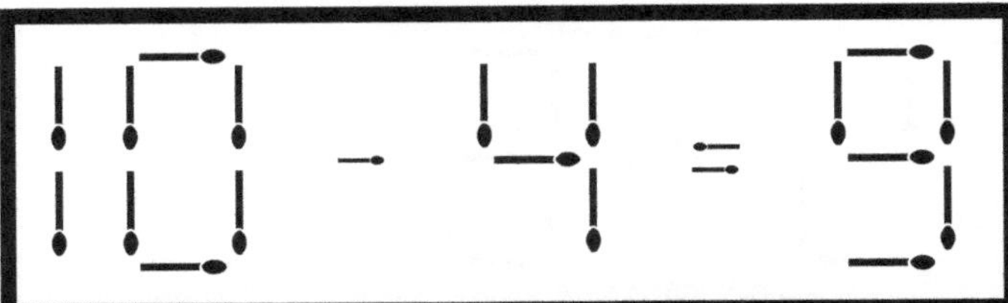

Puzzle 27

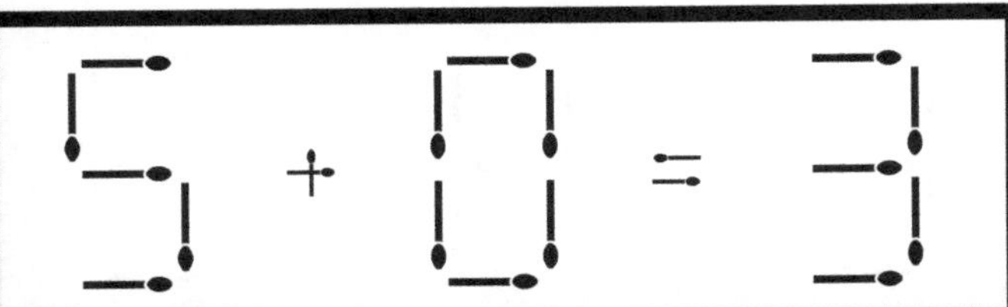

Puzzle 28

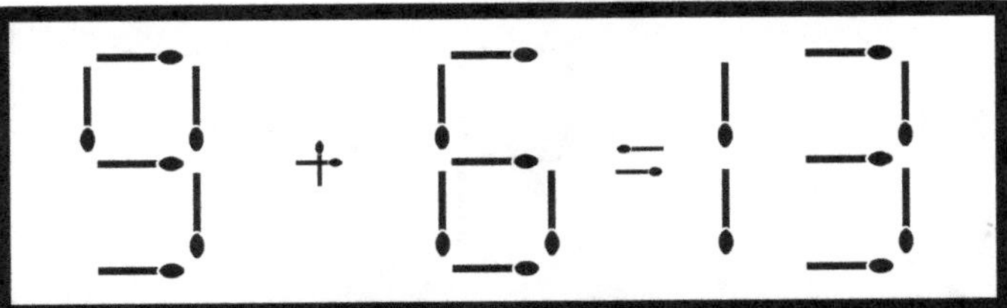

Puzzle 29

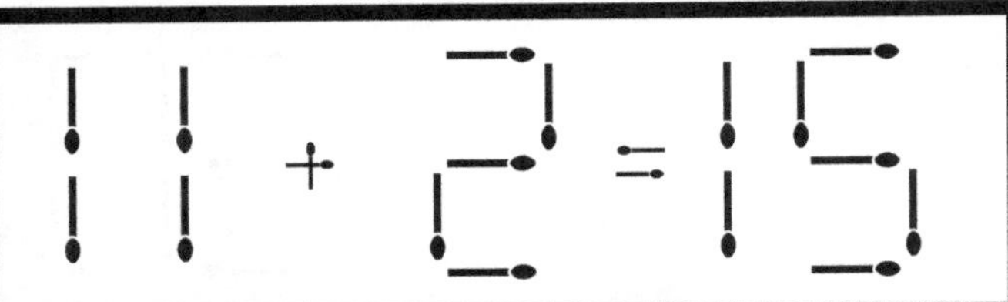

Puzzle 30

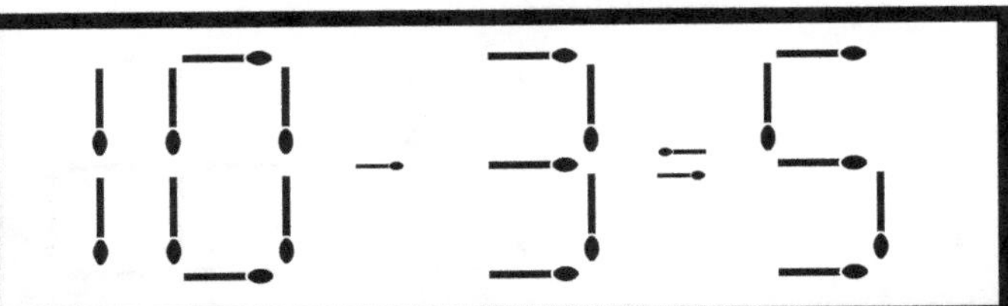

Puzzle 31

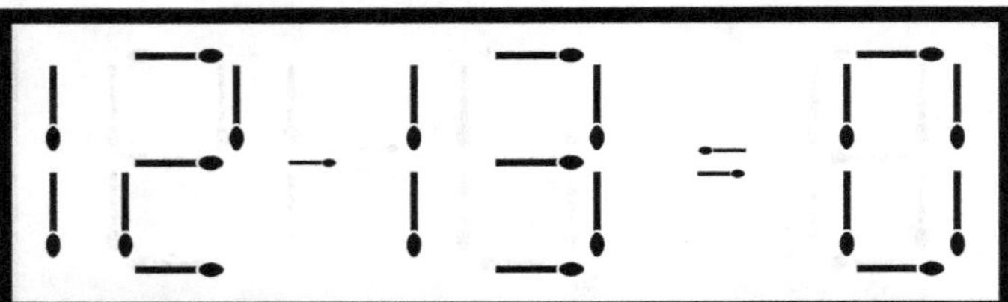

Puzzle 32

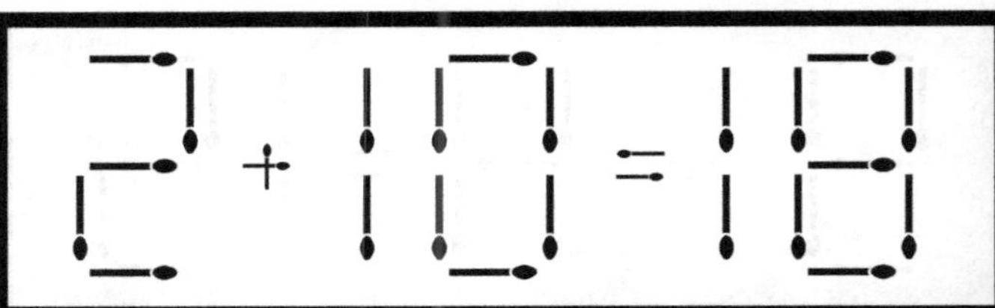

Puzzle 33

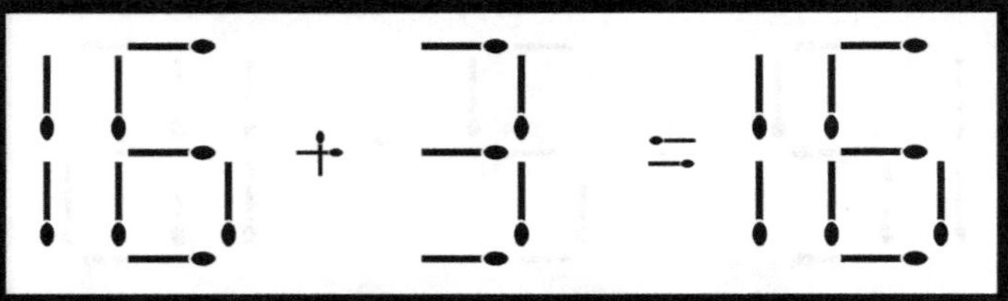

Puzzle 34

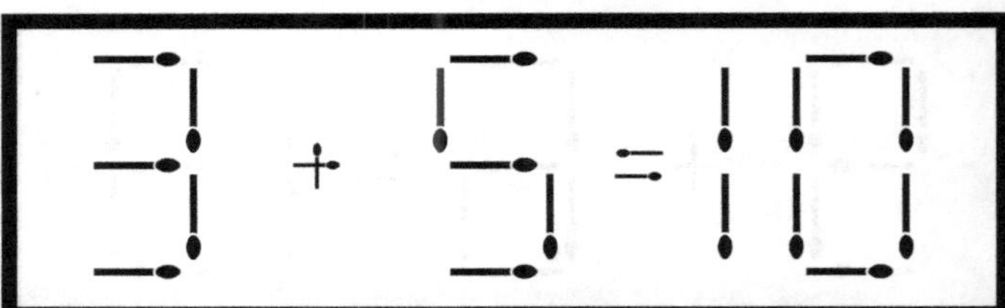

Puzzle 35

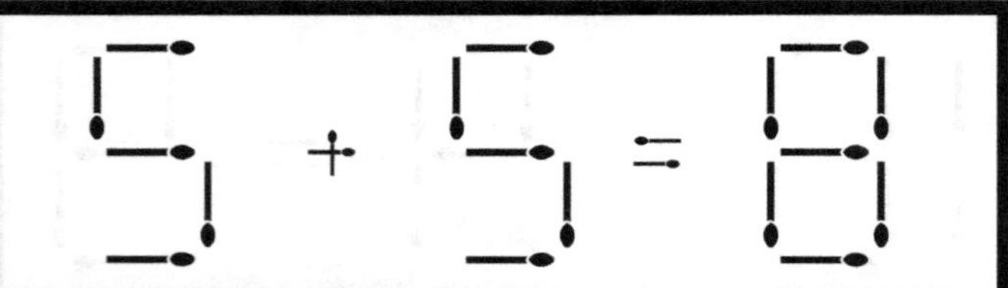

Puzzle 36

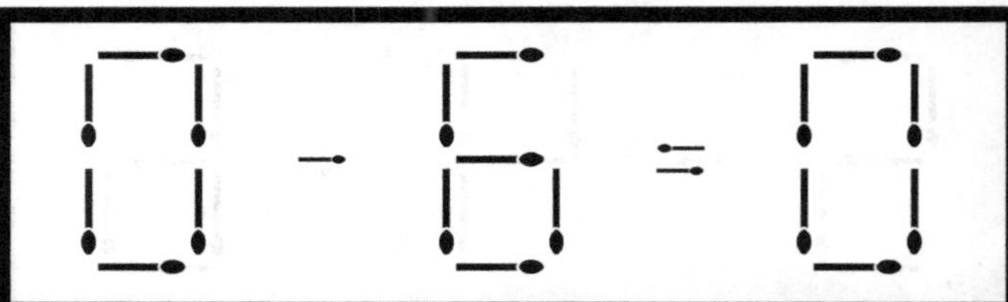

Puzzle 37

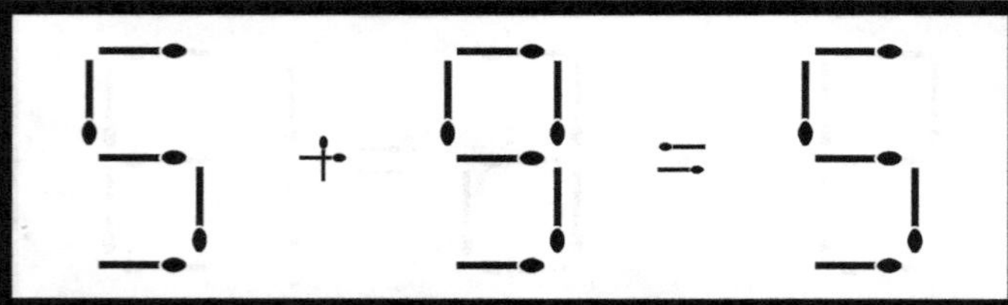

Puzzle 38

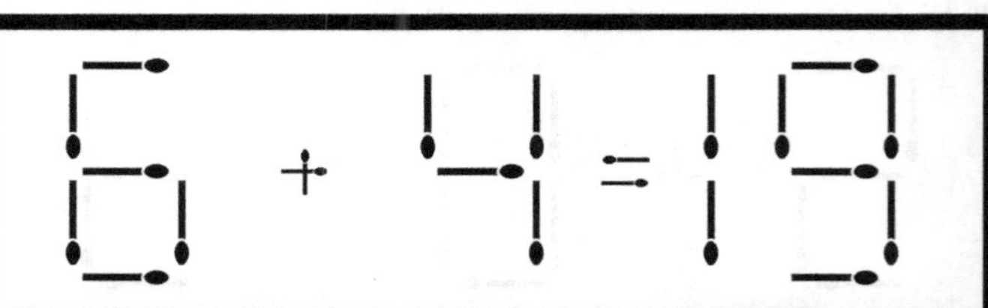

Puzzle 39

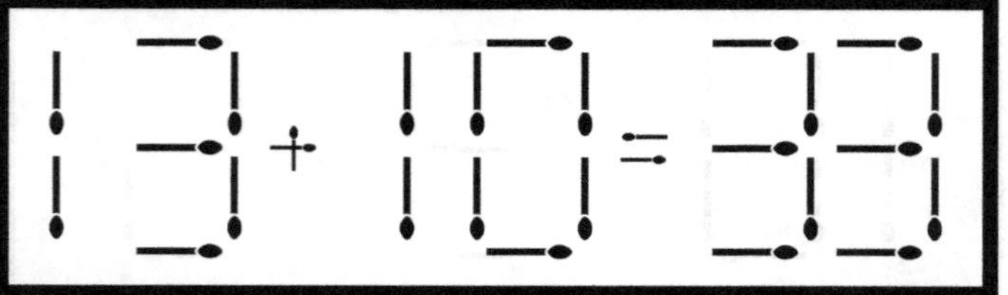

Puzzle 40

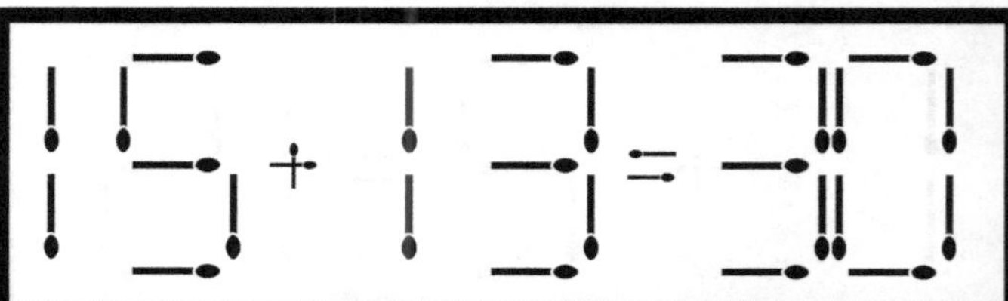

Puzzle 41

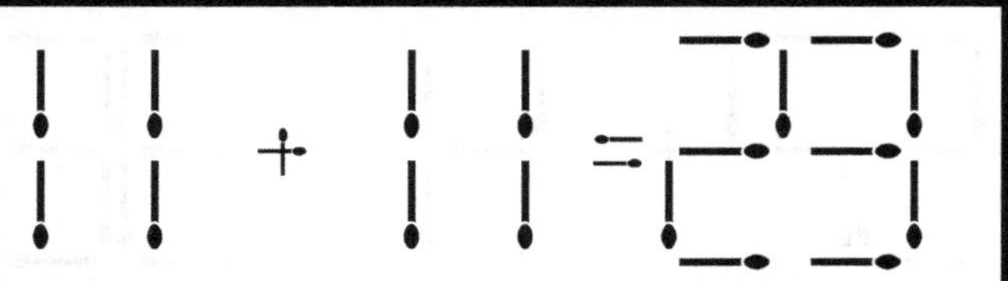

Puzzle 42

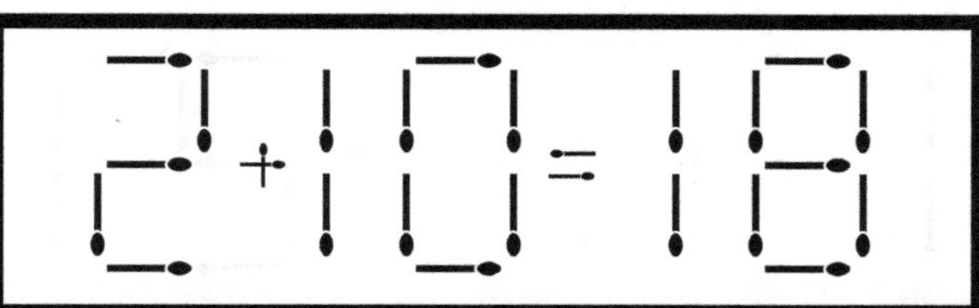

Puzzle 43

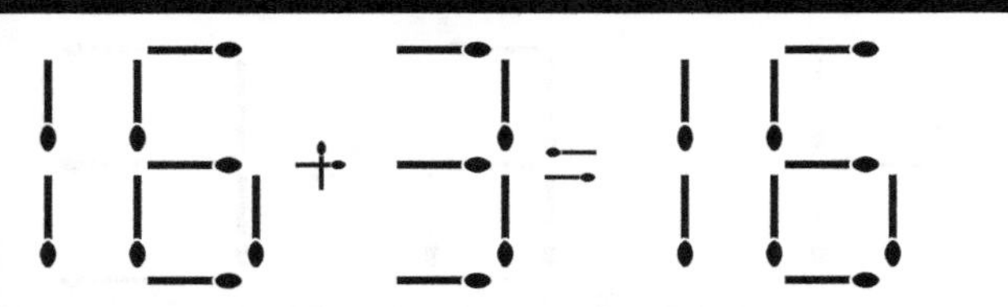

Puzzle 44

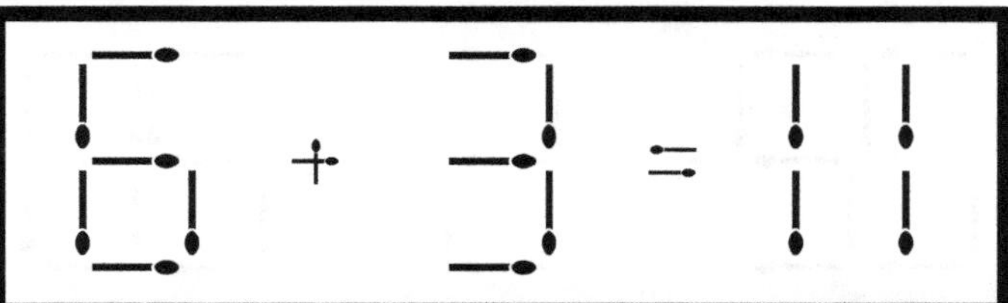

Puzzle 45

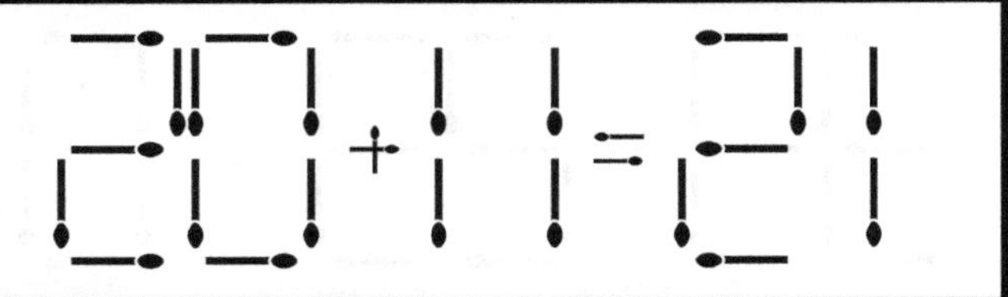

Puzzle 46

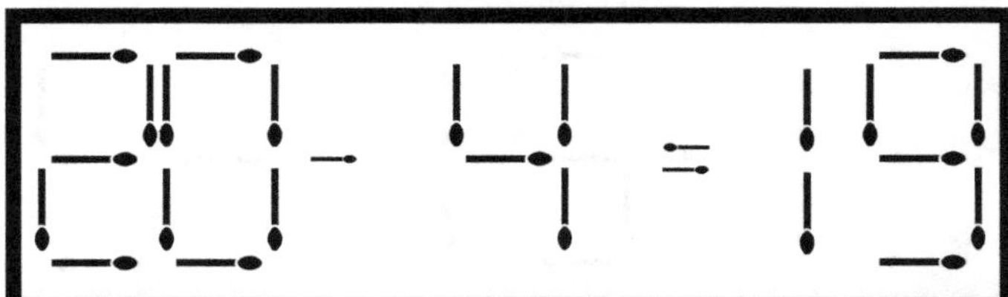

Puzzle 47

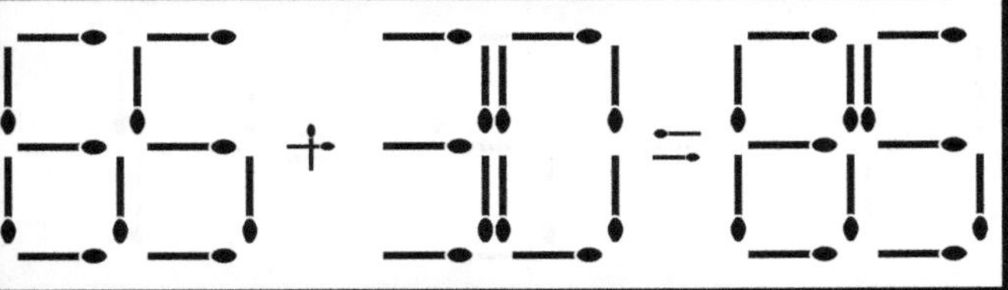

Puzzle 48

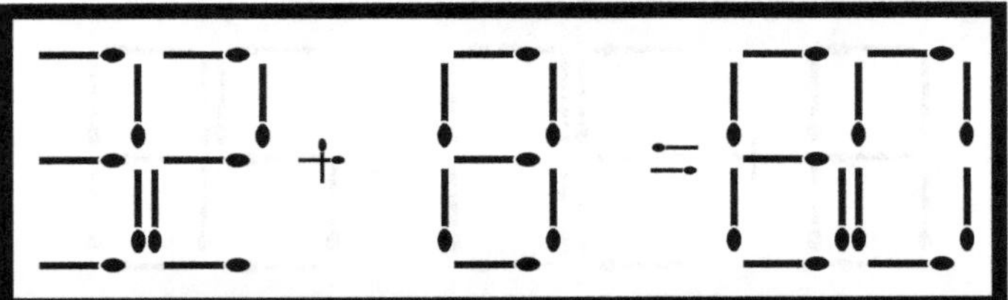

Puzzle 49

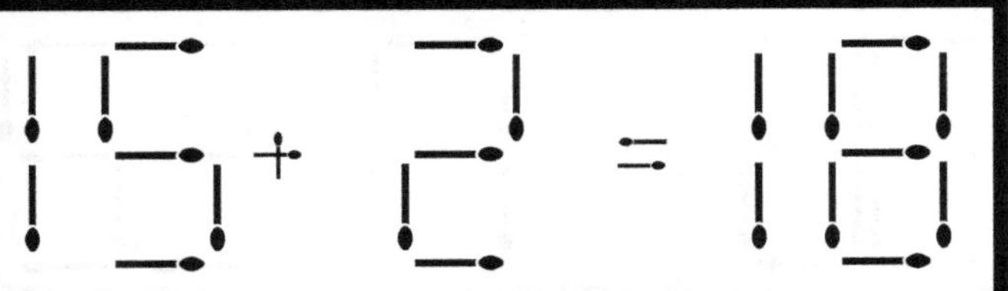

Puzzle 50

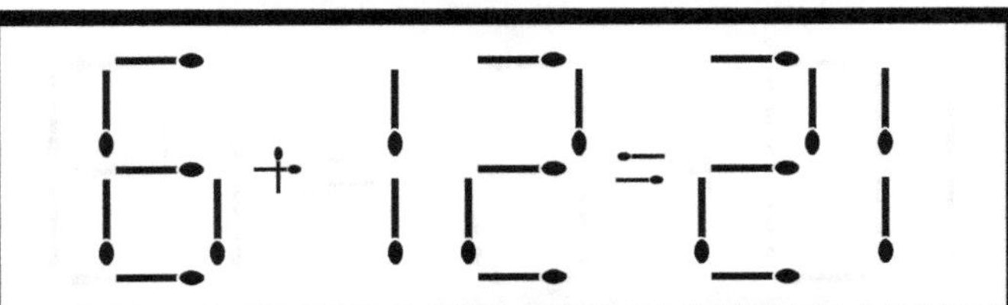

Puzzle 51

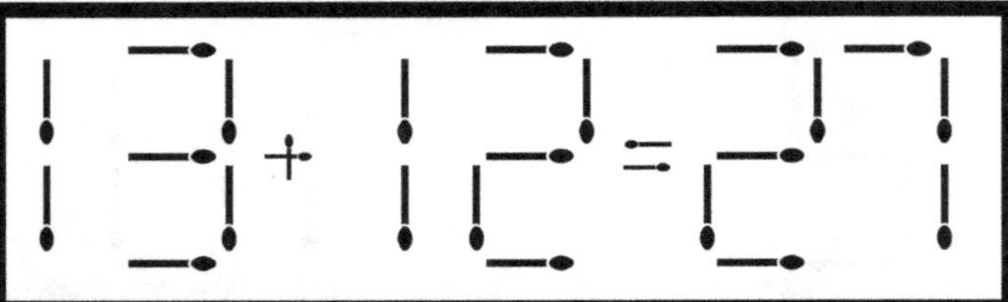

Puzzle 52

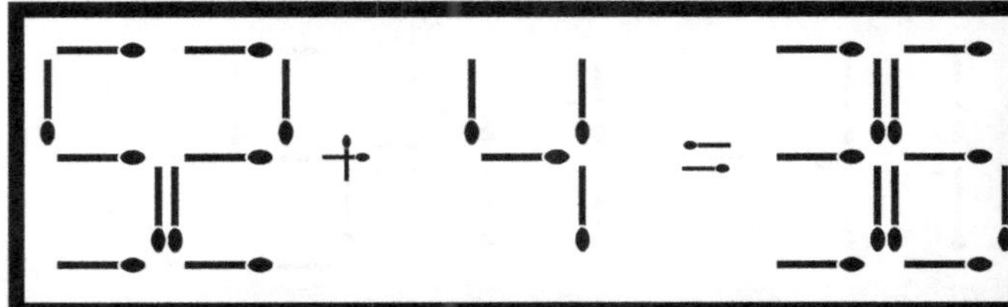

Puzzle 53

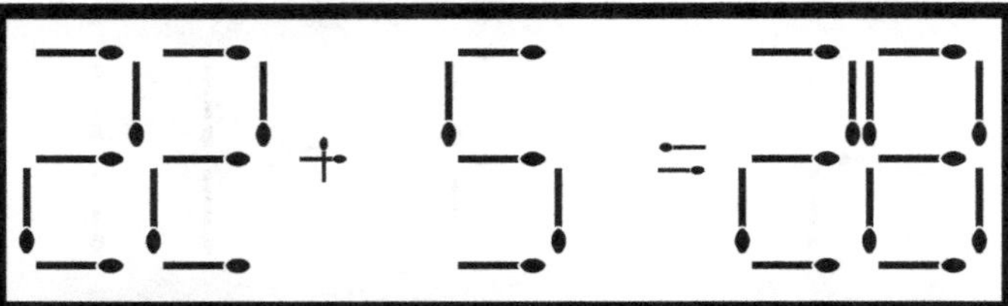

Puzzle 54

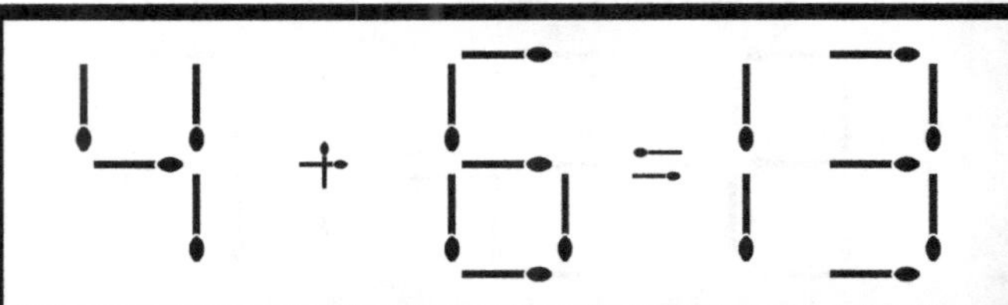

Puzzle 55

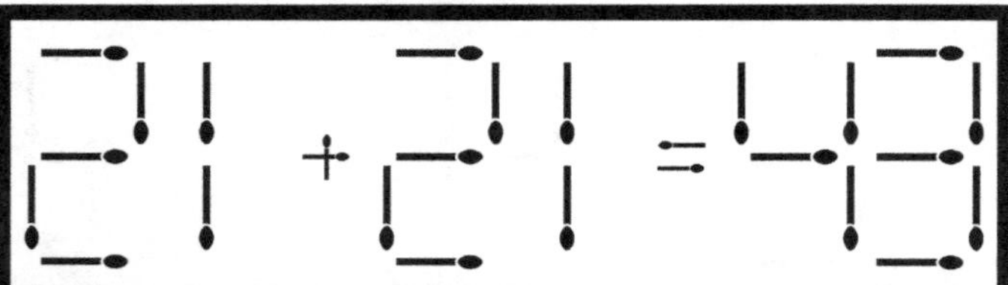

Puzzle 56

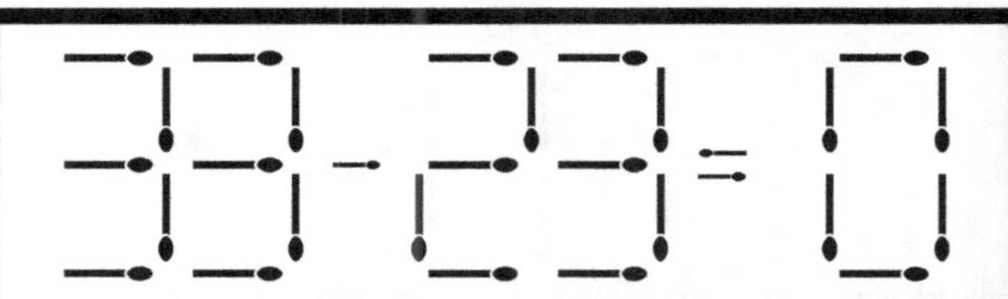

Puzzle 57

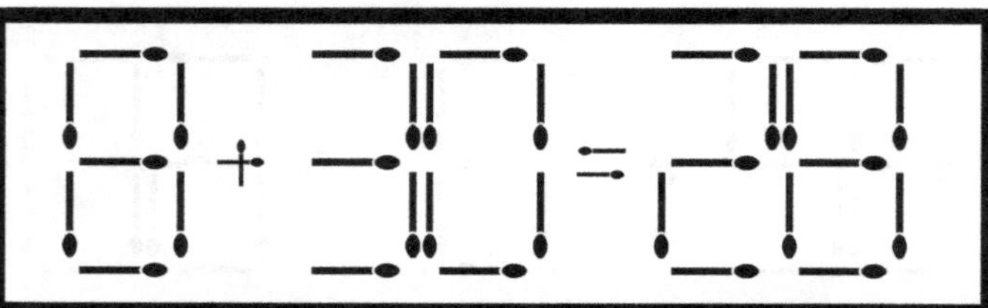

Puzzle 58

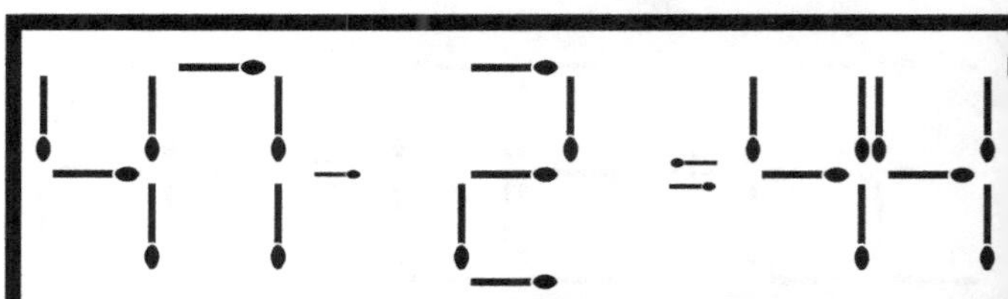

Puzzle 59

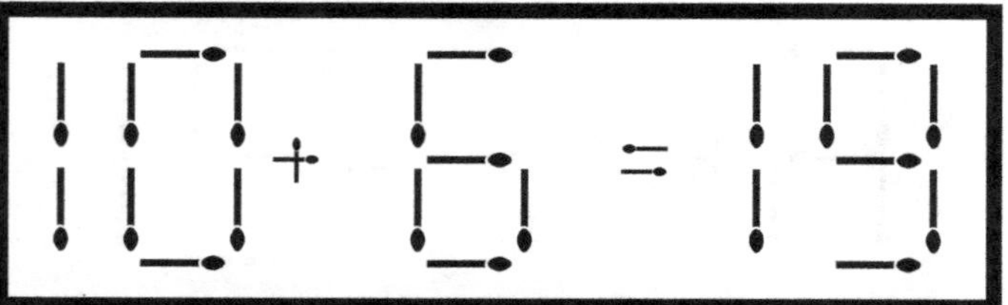

Puzzle 60

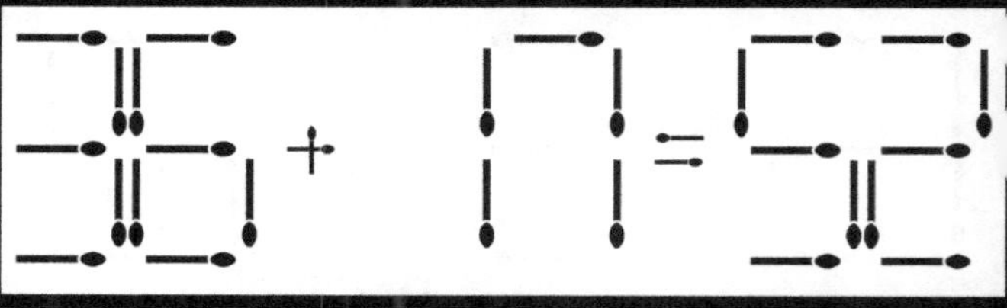

Puzzle 61

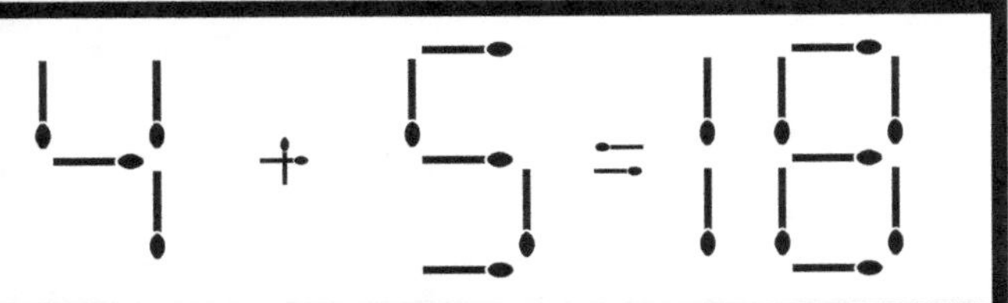

Puzzle 62

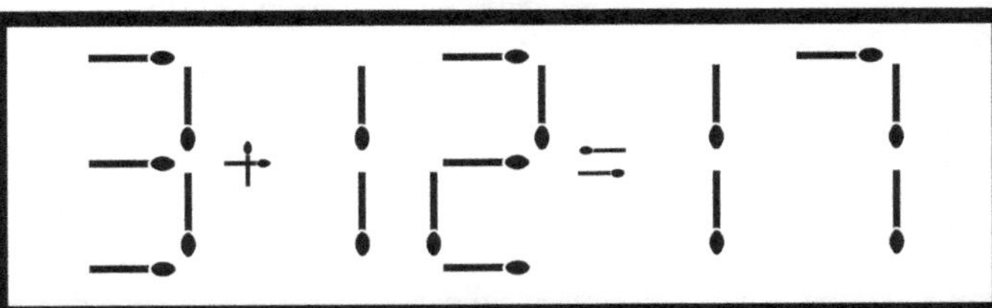

Puzzle 63

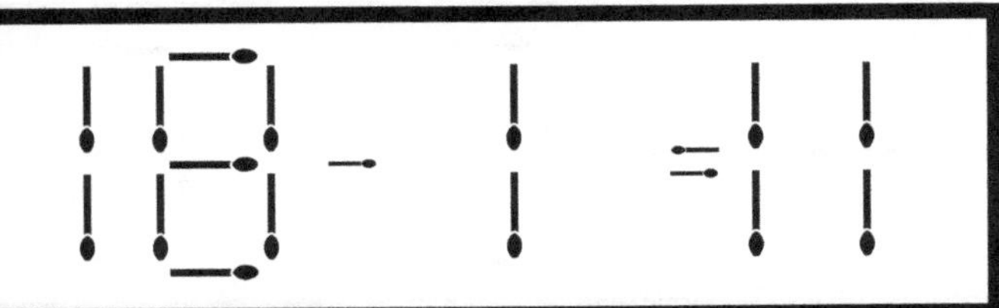

Puzzle 64

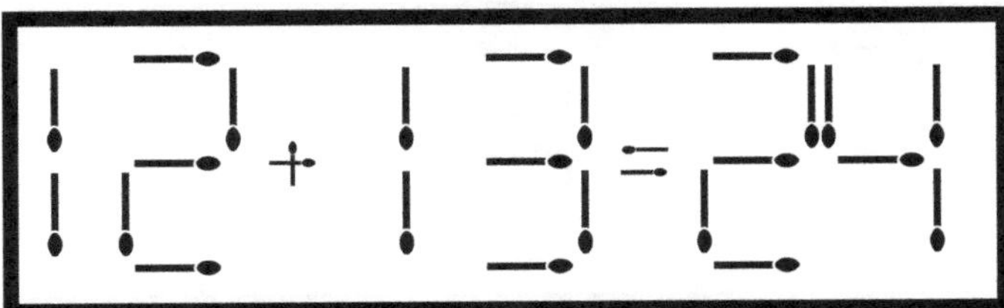

Puzzle 65

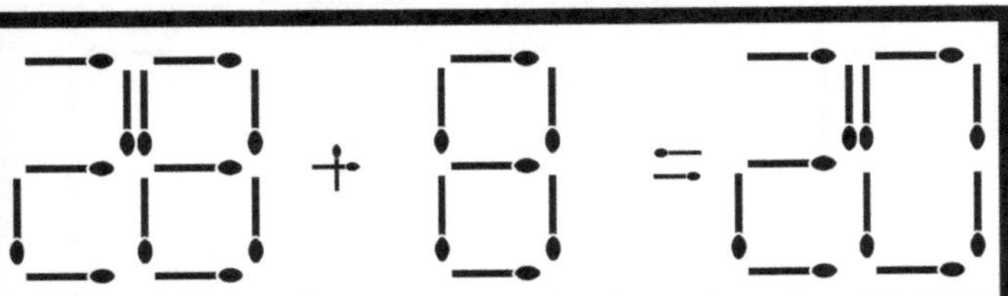

Puzzle 66

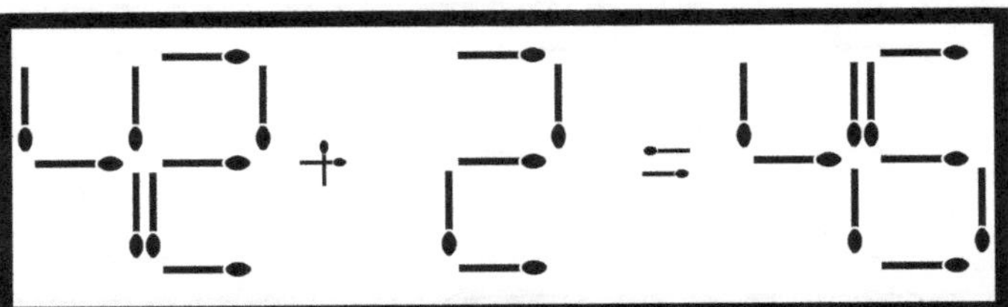

Puzzle 67

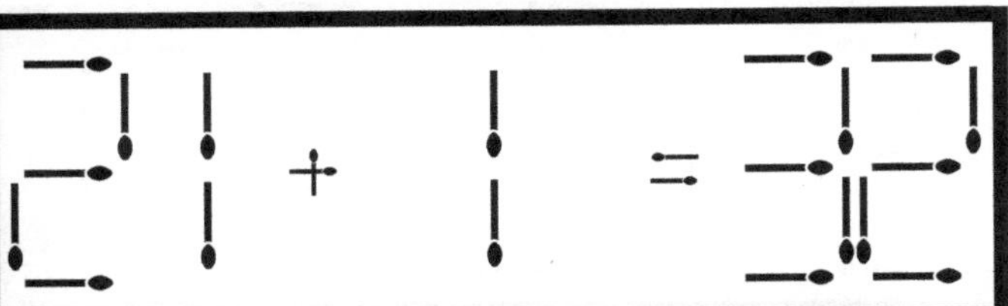

Puzzle 68

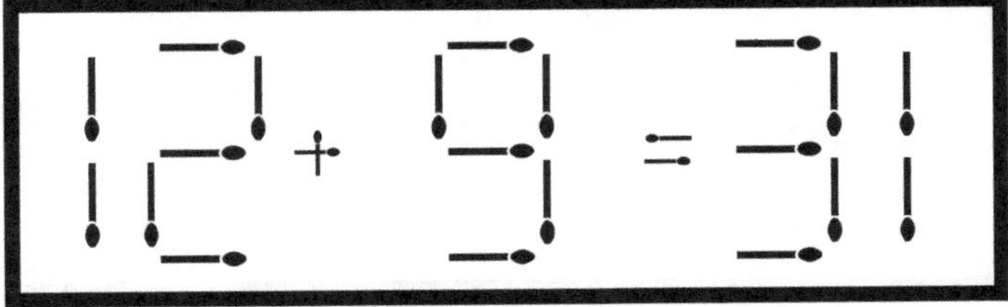

Puzzle 69

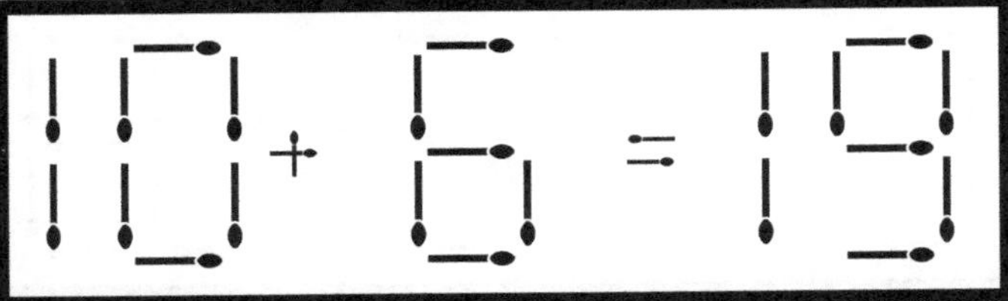

Puzzle 70

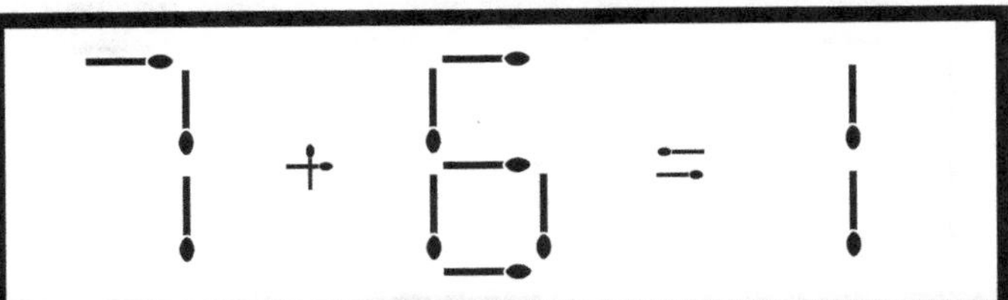

Puzzle 71

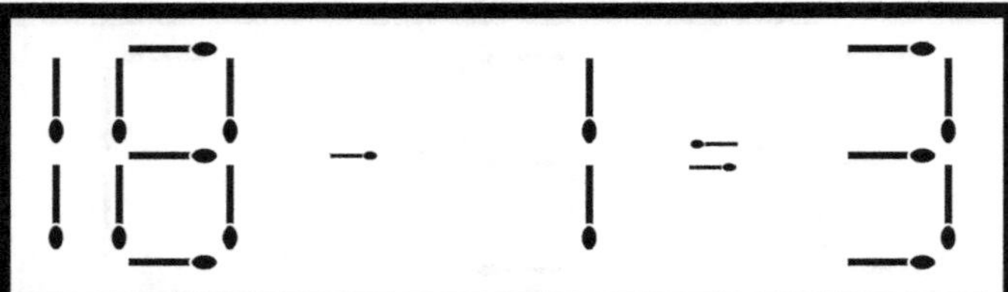

Puzzle 72

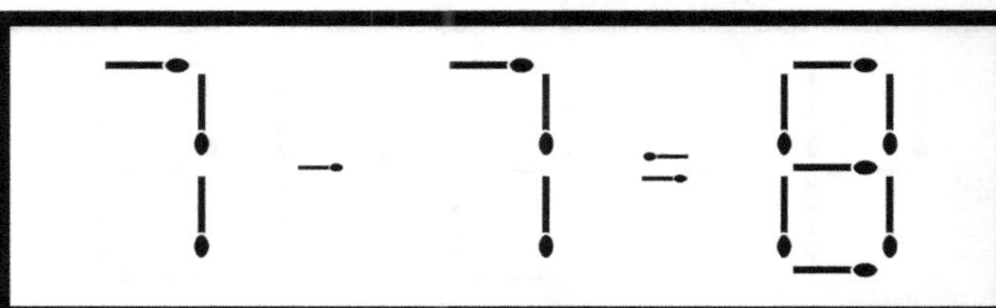

Puzzle 73

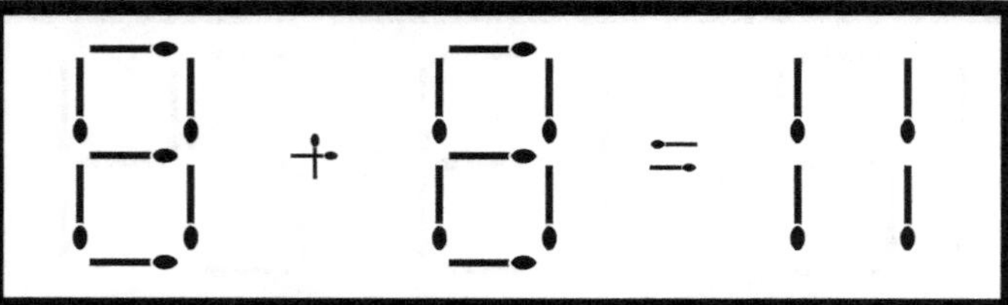

Puzzle 74

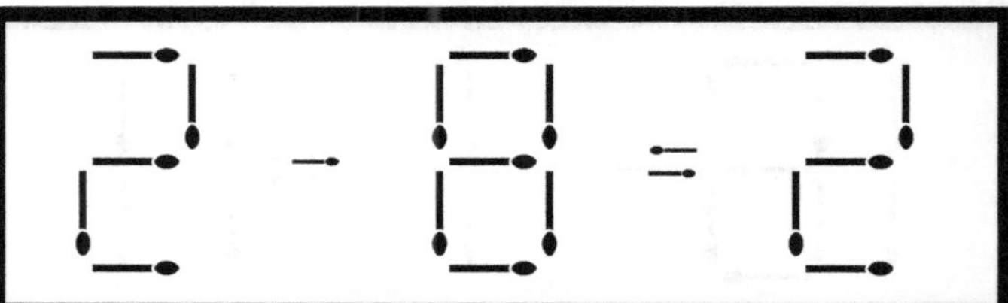

Puzzle 75

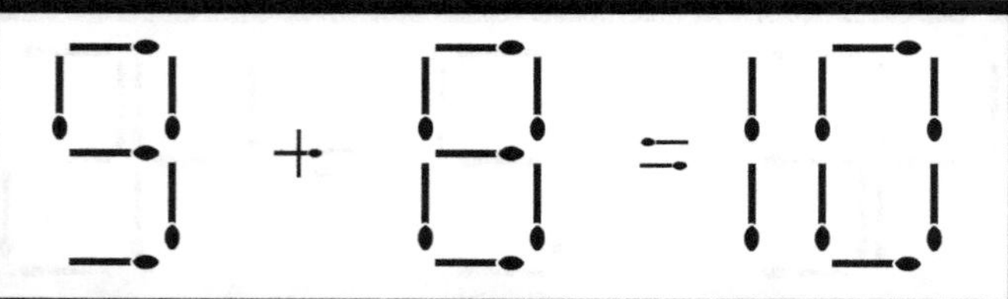

Puzzle 76

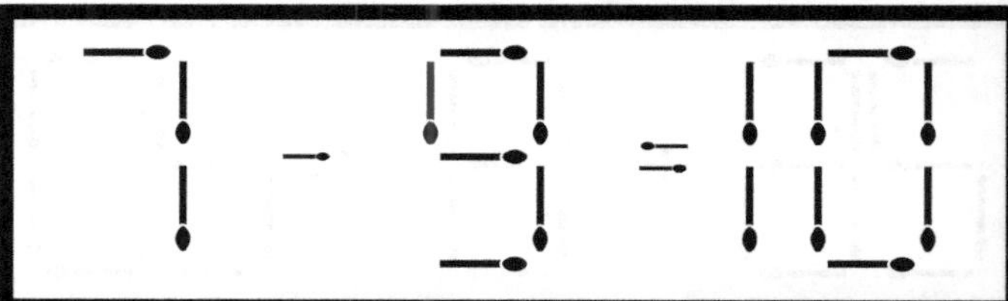

Puzzle 77

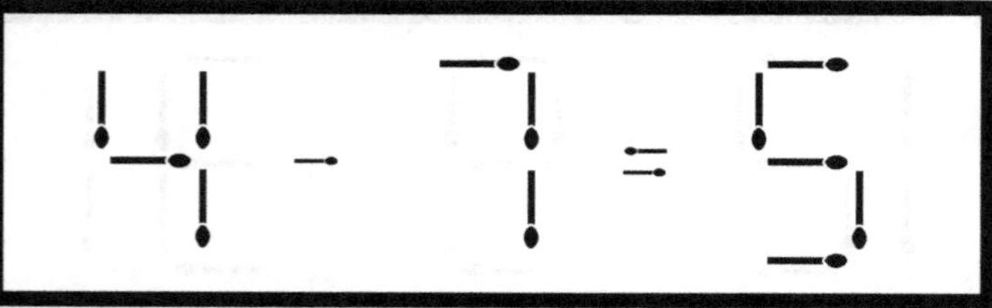

Puzzle 78

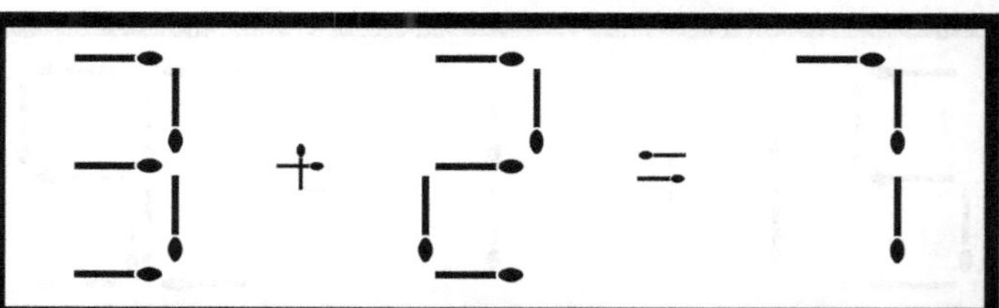

Puzzle 79

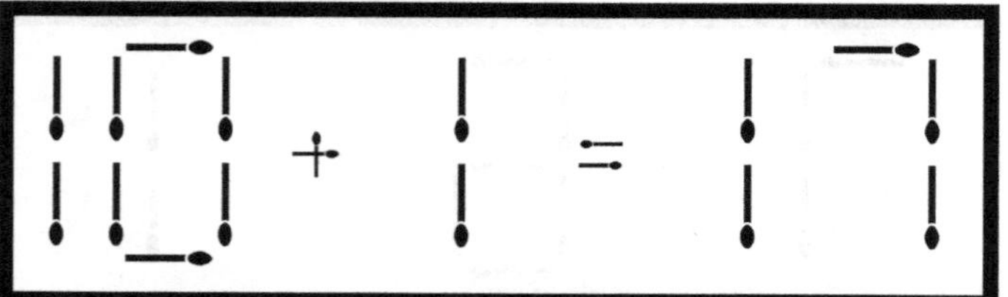

Puzzle 80

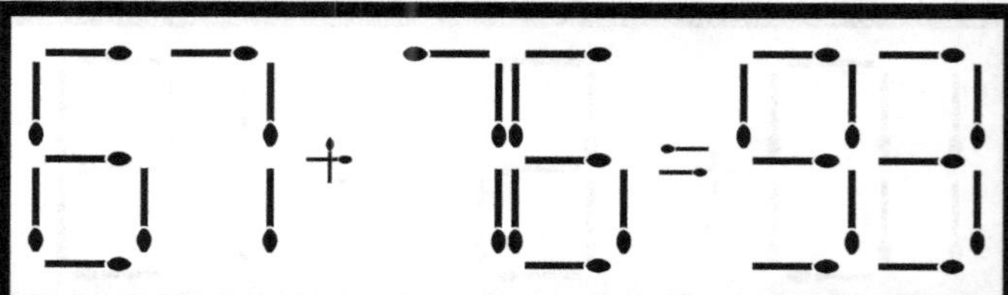

Puzzle 81

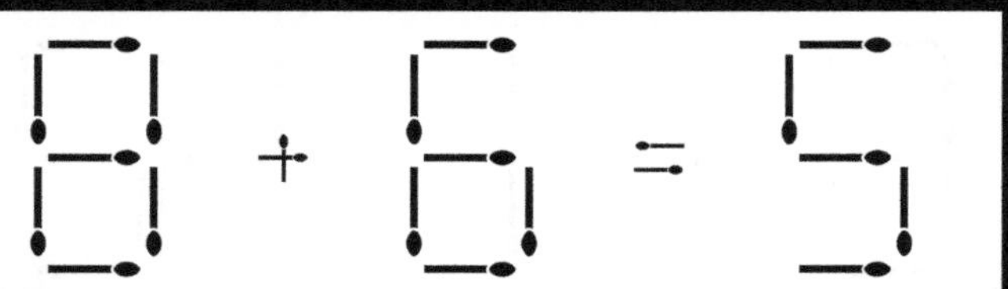

Puzzle 82

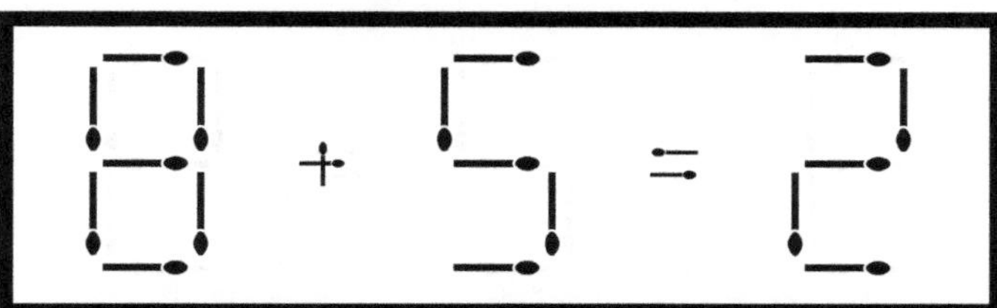

Puzzle 83

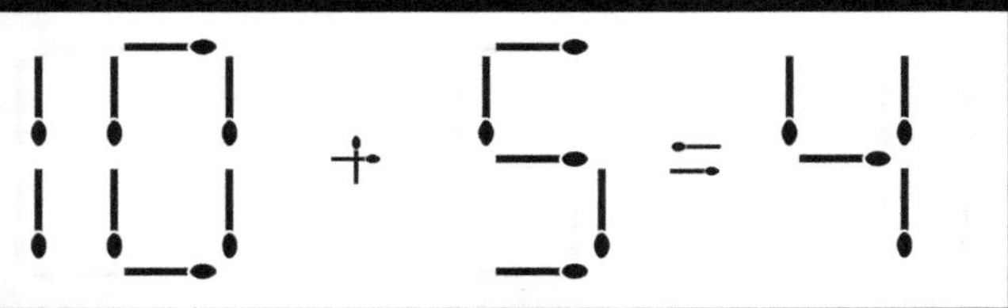

Puzzle 84

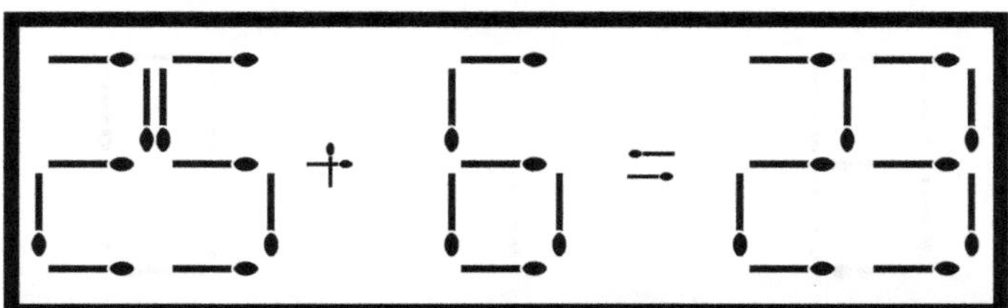

Puzzle 85

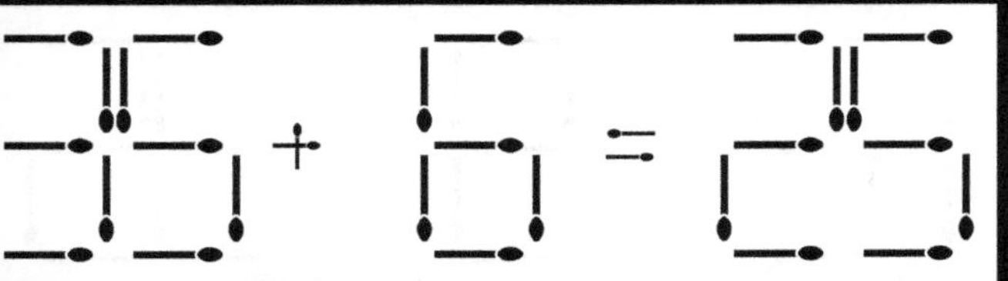

Puzzle 86

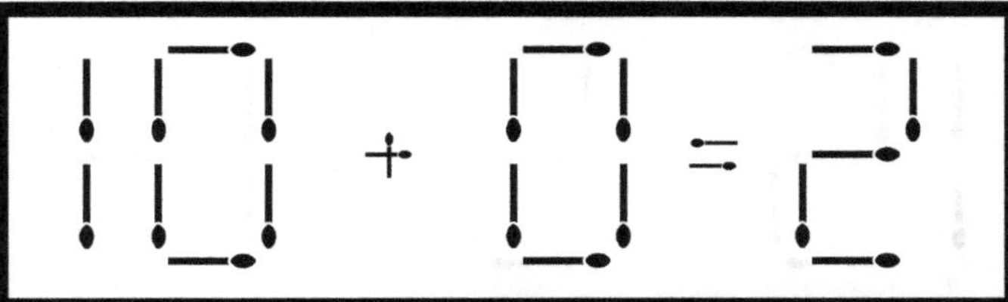

Puzzle 87

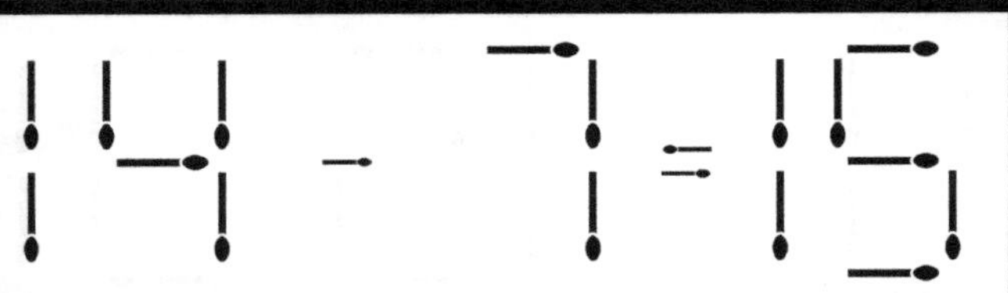

Puzzle 88

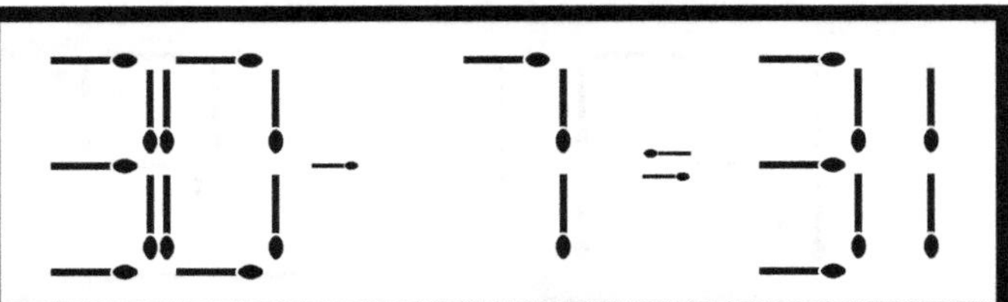

Puzzle 89

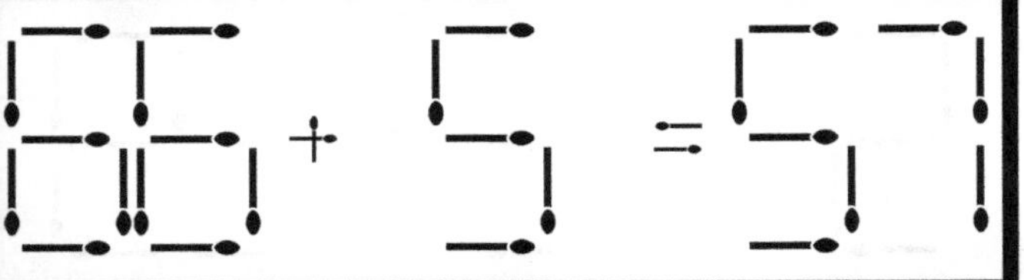

Puzzle 90

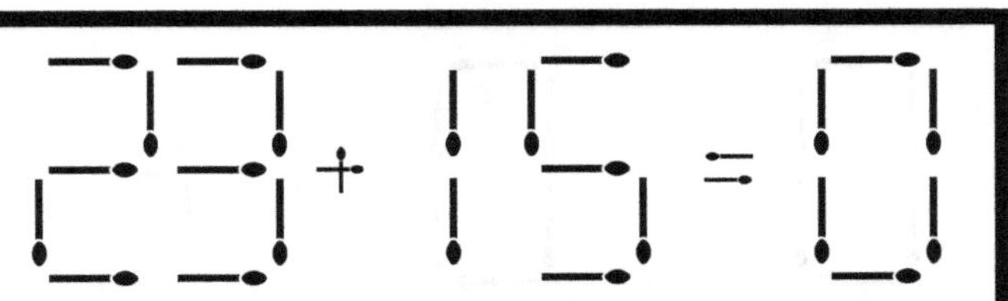

Puzzle 91

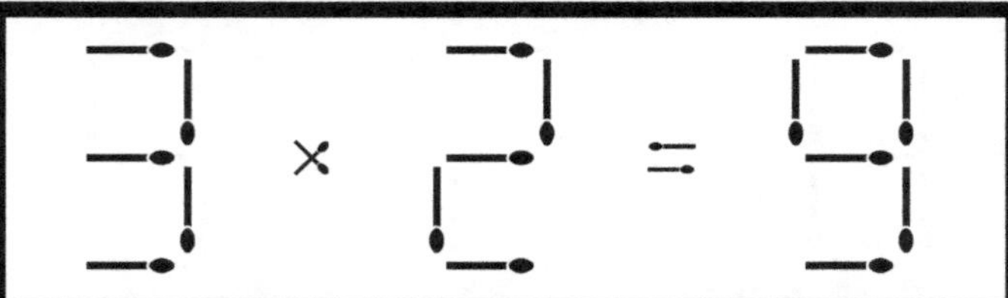

Puzzle 92

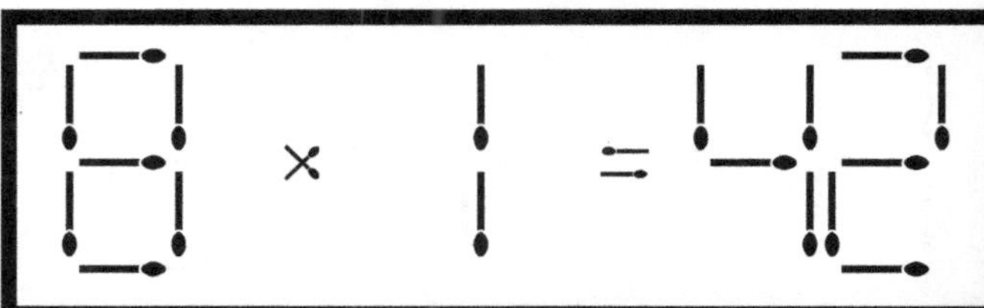

Puzzle 93

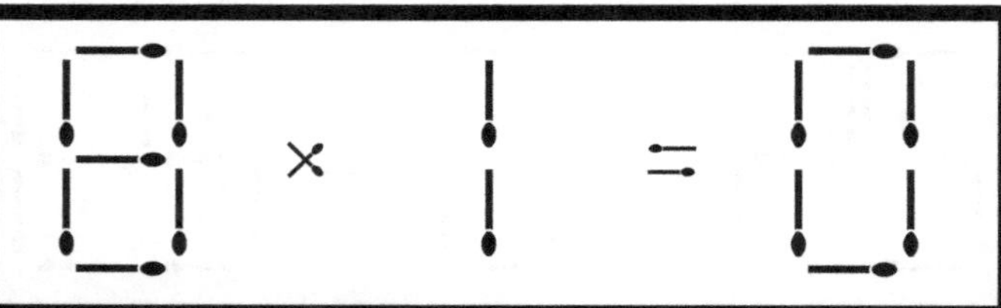

Puzzle 94

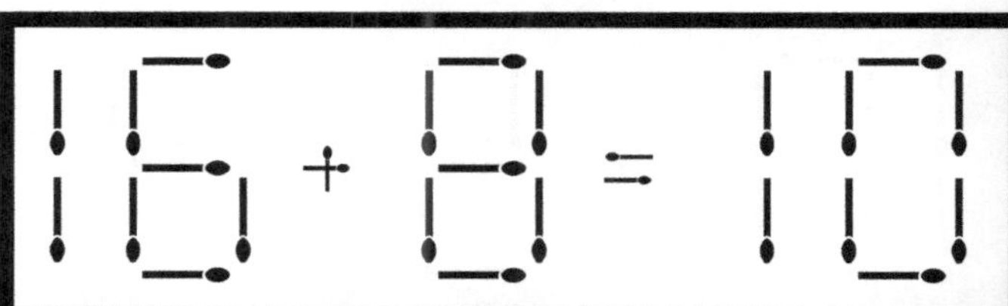

Puzzle 95

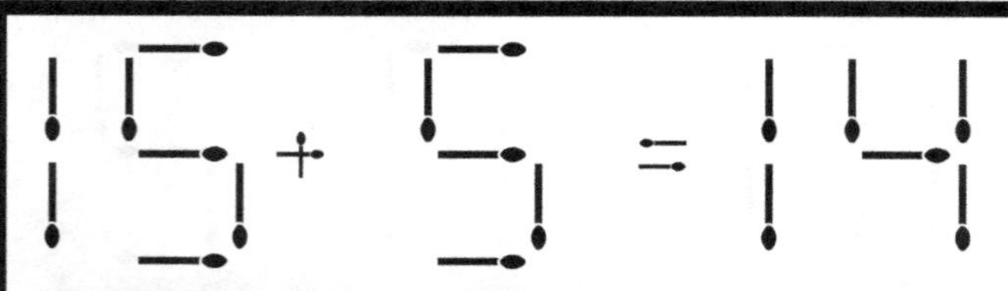

Puzzle 96

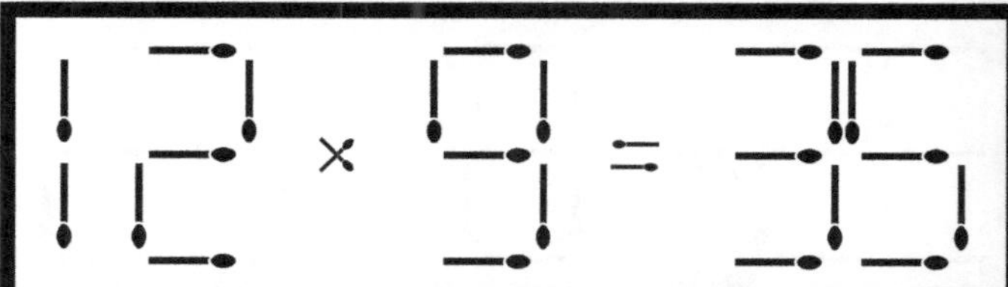

Puzzle 97

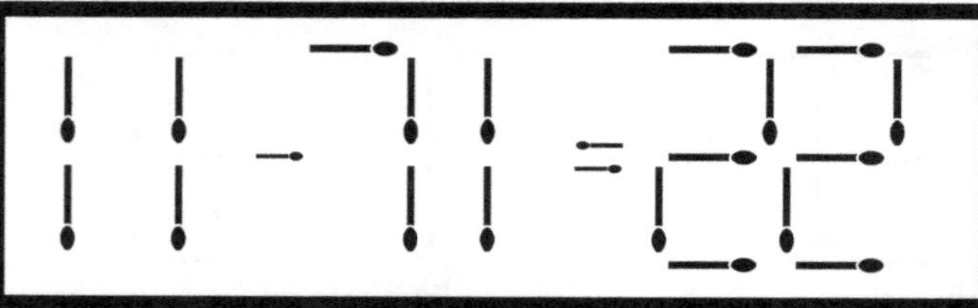

Puzzle 98

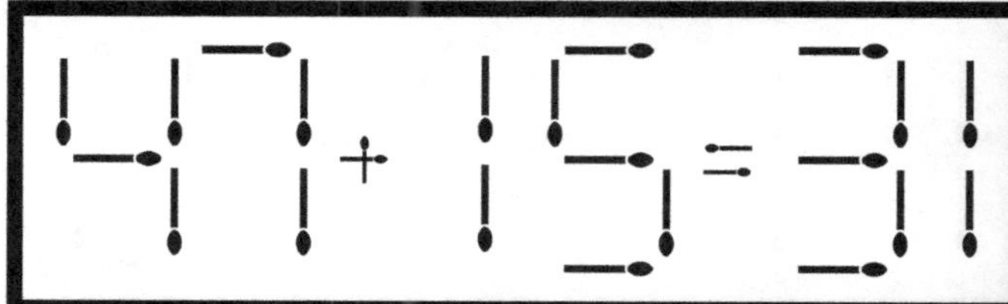

Puzzle 99

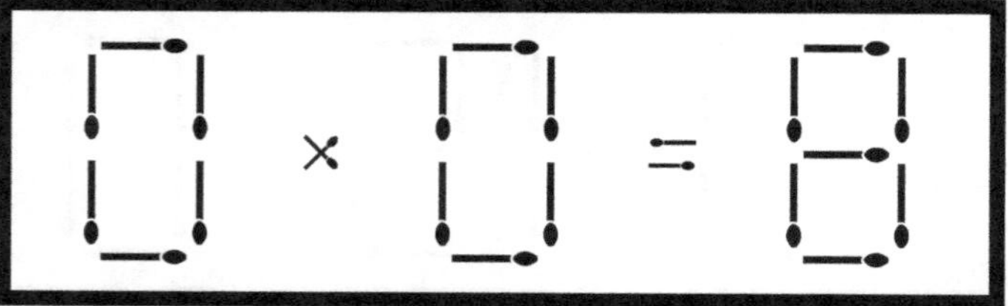

Puzzle 100

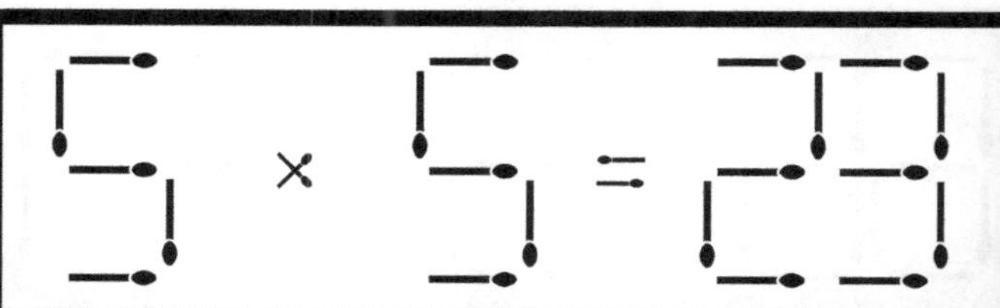

NumBerlinks

How to: Numberlinks

Connect each number with its pair using lines that do not cross. All spaces must have a line passing through them. You may not use diagonal lines.

1	2				3
4		2	1		
5					
			4	3	
			5		

Puzzle 1

			2
	1	3	
		2	
3			1

Puzzle 2

	1		3
	3		2
	2		
			1

Puzzle 3

			3
	2	1	
	1	2	3

Puzzle 4

1				
2	2			
		3		
3	1			

Puzzle 5

1	2				
3		4	1		
	4	3			
			2		

Puzzle 6

1		4		2	
3		5			
			5		
			1	4	
		3	2		

Puzzle 7

1	2				1
3	4				2
		4			3

Puzzle 8

5					3
			2	4	
5	4	2	3		
1					1

Puzzle 9

1	2				3
4		2	1		
5					
			4	3	
			5		

Puzzle 10

1					
1	4	3			
			2		
			3		
			4	2	

Puzzle 11

5					5
	3				
2			1		
3		4			
1				4	2

Puzzle 12

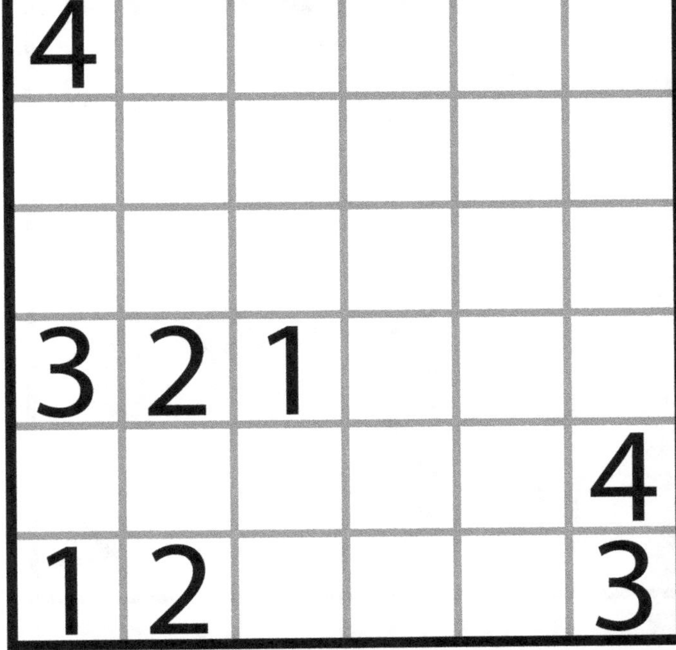

4					
3	2	1			
					4
1	2				3

Puzzle 13

1	2	3		5	4
			5		3
				4	
	1		2		

Puzzle 14

			4	2	1
		5			
				1	
	3				
4					
3				5	2

Puzzle 15

		1	3		3
	2	5			4
		5			
		2			
		1			4

Puzzle 16

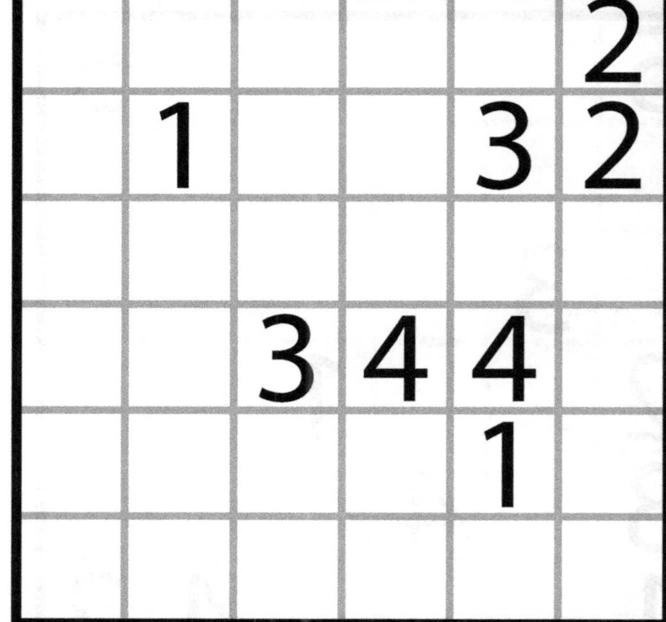

					2
	1			3	2
		3	4	4	
				1	

Puzzle 17

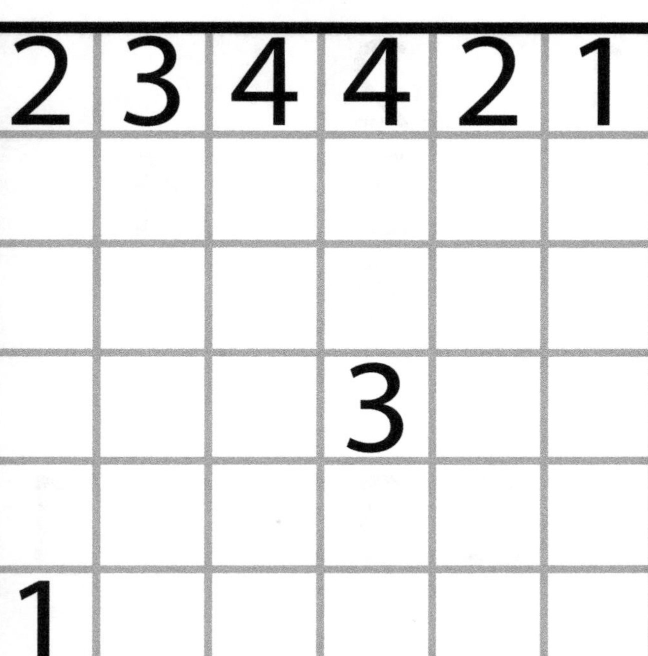

2	3	4	4	2	1
			3		
1					

Puzzle 18

1	2	3	4	5	
	1				5
2			3		4

Puzzle 19

1	2				
	3	4	4	3	
				1	
2					

Puzzle 20

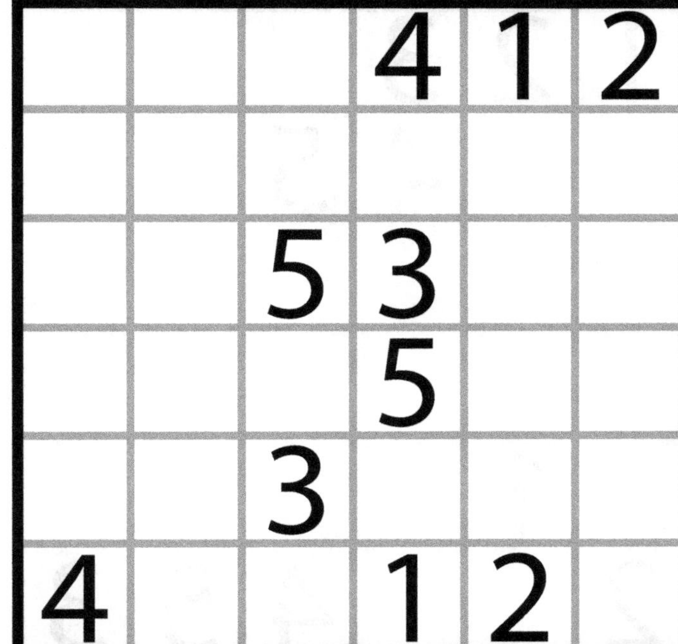

			4	1	2
		5	3		
			5		
		3			
4			1	2	

Puzzle 21

2	4			3	1
	3				
			4		
1					
				2	

Puzzle 22

1		2			
		3		4	
		4			
	2	3			1

Puzzle 23

1	2	3			
		4	5		
	1				
2			4	5	3

Puzzle 24

1	1	2	3	4	5
2					
3					
4					
5					

Numberlinks

Puzzle 25

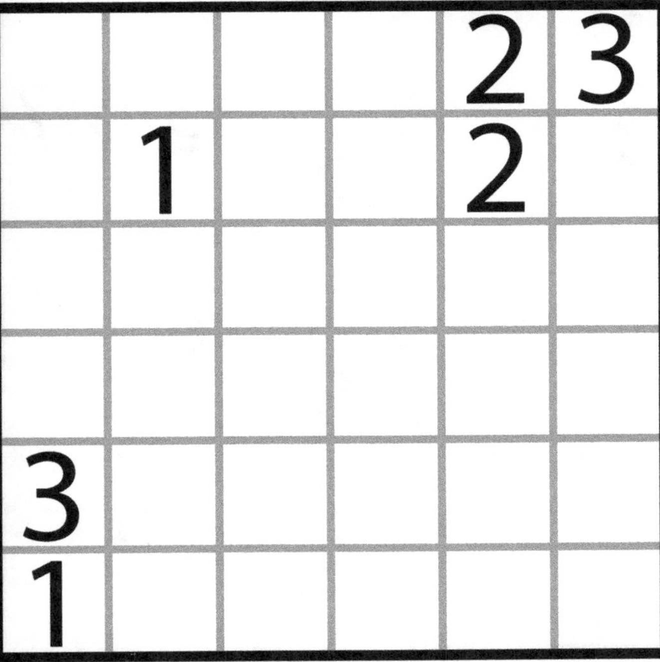

				2	3
	1			2	
3					
1					

Puzzle 26

1					
				3	
				4	
				2	
					4
1	2				3

Puzzle 27

1					
				2	
	3	4			
			4		
	1			3	
2					

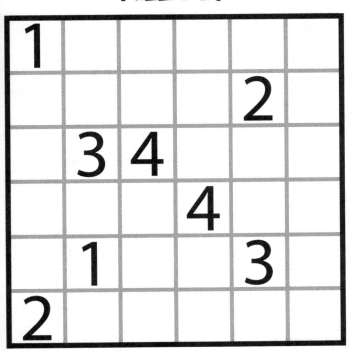

Puzzle 28

			2		
	2		4	3	
1		1			
		4			
	3				

Puzzle 29

1					2			
		3			4		6	4
					7			
				2	8			
						9		
	5				9			
						8	7	
1	3	5	6					

Puzzle 30

1			2					
3			4			5	6	7
4				2				
					7			
			3			6		
				8				
		1						
				8			5	

Puzzle 31

1	2	3			4			
					5		6	
		2		4				
7								
	8			5	9			
7		1						
3		8						
9					0	6	0	

Puzzle 32

		1	1					
	2			4	5	6	7	
	8	3						
					5			
	8				6	7	4	
	3		2					

Puzzle 33

1	2		3	5		6	7	8
			5	4		7		
								9
1	2			6			0	
				3	8			
	4				0			
			9					

Puzzle 34

1	2	3	1					6
					4		5	
					7		8	
		3						
		2			7			
						8		
5	4					6		

Puzzle 35

				4			6	7
1	2				5			
2	3		5					
								7
						6		
	3			1			4	

Puzzle 36

								1
	3		4	5				6
7			8					1
3								
7								
4	9			5				
	2	9						
			2	8			6	

Puzzle 37

1					2	3	2	
5			6				4	
	1							
5						3	4	
7		7		9			8	
6		8				9		

Puzzle 38

1	2	3	5	6		7	8	6
						7		
					5			
3			4					
	1		2	4			8	

Puzzle 39

	5	9	0	9	8			
							2	
		0						1
								2
6	5				3	4	3	
		7			4			
			8					
	6			7	1			

Puzzle 40

	1	2		4			5	
	3						6	5
						4		7
8								
				3			0	
9	0							
			2	1				
		8				6		
9								7

CryPtograms

How to: Cryptograms

ne from humble beginnings.
This is a decoding puzzle.
Decipher the quoted phrase by finding the substitute letters. Each puzzle will have a hint!
Sometimes it's about the person who said it, and others are about the quote itself.
Careful—sometimes the missing letter and its code letter could be the same.

Puzzle 1

Hint: A quote about carefree living from an American poet.

A	B	C	D	E	F	G	H	I	J	K	L	M	N	O	P	Q	R	S	T	U	V	W	X	Y	Z
Y	U	R	G	P	J	W	E	H	F	Z	S	O	K	Q	V	N	L	D	X	B	M	C	A	I	T

"S H M P H K X E P D B K D E H K P , D C H O

X E P D P Y , G L H K Z X E P C H S G Y H L ."

L Y S V E C Y S G Q P O P L D Q K

Puzzle 2

Hint: A lesson in patience.

A	B	C	D	E	F	G	H	I	J	K	L	M	N	O	P	Q	R	S	T	U	V	W	X	Y	Z
	F	H	V	L	T		A	Y		C		W	E	I	N		S	X		O	G	D	U		P

"J M M B S L J Q J H A Y L G L W L E Q X S L R O Y S L

Q Y W L ."

W J K J J E B L M I O

Puzzle 3

Hint: What is life about?

A	B	C	D	E	F	G	H	I	J	K	L	M	N	O	P	Q	R	S	T	U	V	W	X	Y	Z
L	C		A		V	I	R		X	Q		Z		N		G			O	Y		M	P		S

"T U V W U K B ' O L C N Y O V U B A U B I

F N Y E K W T V . T U V W U K L C N Y O D E W L O U B I

F N Y E K W T V ."

I W N E I W C W E B L E A K R L M

Puzzle 4

Hint: Owning up to these can increase your quality of life.

A	B	C	D	E	F	G	H	I	J	K	L	M	N	O	P	Q	R	S	T	U	V	W	X	Y	Z
	T	F			J		Y		L		I		K		Z	E				Q	D		V	A	U

"X W G N S R C G S P C S I M S A G J H P B W D S T I C ,

W J H K C Y S G N Y C F H Q P S B C N H

S O X W N N Y C X ."

T P Q F C I C C

Puzzle 5

Hint: This quoted author, famous for writing a magical trilogy of books, has insight on paths.

A	B	C	D	E	F	G	H	I	J	K	L	M	N	O	P	Q	R	S	T	U	V	W	X	Y	Z
	T	Q	I		G	F		U		P		X				E		B		N			D	W	L

"S R M A J J M Z R B H Y Z R Y A S I H O

A O H J R B M."

C . O . O . M R J P U H S

Puzzle 6

Hint: One of the world's most famous scientists encourages us to think outside the box.

A	B	C	D	E	F	G	H	I	J	K	L	M	N	O	P	Q	R	S	T	U	V	W	X	Y	Z
J		K	L				P		T		D		O	I		X	N	B		Q			U		A

"F P G F N Q G B Z H O I Y Z O F G D D Z H G O K G

Z B O I F S O I M D G L H G V Q F Z E J H Z O J F Z I O."

J D V G N F G Z O B F G Z O

Puzzle 7

Hint: This ancient Greek philosopher knows the value of practice.

A	B	C	D	E	F	G	H	I	J	K	L	M	N	O	P	Q	R	S	T	U	V	W	X	Y	Z
F			W		X		A	D		N			O		K	I	B		E	M			P		U

"Y T T W A F G D E H X T B Q S W F E V T M E A

Q F N S F J J E A S W D X X S B S O R S ."

F B D H E T E J S

Puzzle 8

Hint: A reminder to take bold risks from a US President.

A	B	C	D	E	F	G	H	I	J	K	L	M	N	O	P	Q	R	S	T	U	V	W	X	Y	Z
	F	S			Z	X	J			G				M		W	V			L	I	Y		E	

"P J M K C Y J M N R V C P M Z R D O T D K C V R F O E

S R U R S J D C I C X V C R P O E ."

A M J U Z . G C U U C N E

Puzzle 9

Hint: Learning prepares you for the future.

A	B	C	D	E	F	G	H	I	J	K	L	M	N	O	P	Q	R	S	T	U	V	W	X	Y	Z
F	Z		W	A		M		T	U		B		L					P		Y		S			

" W V G O F P D R J   D Q   P M W   B R Q P   L R H W K A G X

H W F L R J   H M D O M   C R G   O F J   G Q W   P R

O M F J E W   P M W   H R K X V . "

J W X Q R J   B F J V W X F

Puzzle 10

Hint: An apple famously fell on this man's head.

A	B	C	D	E	F	G	H	I	J	K	L	M	N	O	P	Q	R	S	T	U	V	W	X	Y	Z
	T	B		A			W		O		F				I	R			G		J				Q

" M W L G   Z N A V   U I   P U V G   B N P A   C N M Y . "

H V L L B   Y A M G N Y

Puzzle 11

Hint: An Eastern philosopher encourages reading.

A	B	C	D	E	F	G	H	I	J	K	L	M	N	O	P	Q	R	S	T	U	V	W	X	Y	Z
	O		X	I		W			T			J		V			S		G		D		F		

" Y V K   M B L L V G   V A I L   B   O V V N   R P G U V K G

Z I B S L P L W   H V J I G U P L W . "

M V L E K M P K H

Puzzle 12

Hint: A lesson in peacefully winning battles from a famous US President.

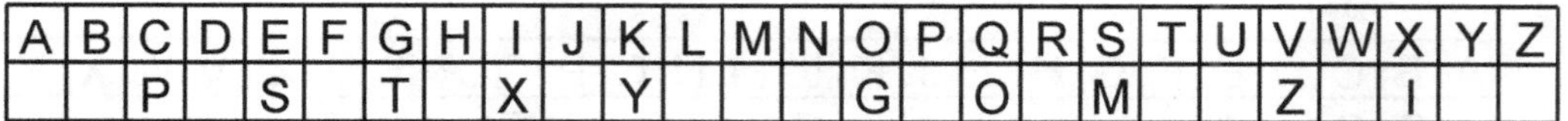

A	B	C	D	E	F	G	H	I	J	K	L	M	N	O	P	Q	R	S	T	U	V	W	X	Y	Z
		P		S		T		X		Y				G		O		M			Z		I		

" D G   X   A G E   D S M E W G N   L N   S A S L X S M

J C S A   X   L R Y S   E C S L   L N   U W X S A D M ? "

R K W R C R L   V X A P G V A

Puzzle 13

Hint: This famous woman is a self-made billionaire, and knows a thing or two about the benefits of studying.

A	B	C	D	E	F	G	H	I	J	K	L	M	N	O	P	Q	R	S	T	U	V	W	X	Y	Z
O	V				N		W			F		C				G			E	K					R

"S L K P O E Y X M Y D E W S F S I E X K M Z X P F Y M B

E W S J X A Z L , O H O D D H X A E E X N A S S L X C ."

X H A O W J Y M N A S I

Puzzle 14

Hint: A reminder that your day is what you make of it.

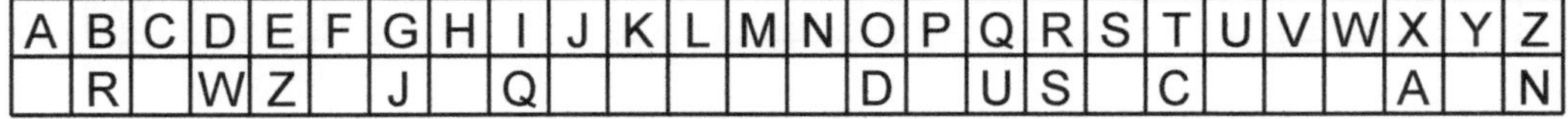

A	B	C	D	E	F	G	H	I	J	K	L	M	N	O	P	Q	R	S	T	U	V	W	X	Y	Z
	R		W	Z		J		Q					D			U	S		C				A		N

"B H K D L W I W B I Q V G D E B C H T P D S

B V L G G I W Q V Y D V Q C Q D G ."

X Q K K Q B E B S C T L S X B S W

Puzzle 15

Hint: Fun hobbies are a good example of this.

A	B	C	D	E	F	G	H	I	J	K	L	M	N	O	P	Q	R	S	T	U	V	W	X	Y	Z
	Q			J	L		C		F			N	W			K				Z	S		E		

" V C J   V O N J   D Y Z   J W F Y D   M X P V O W T

O P   W Y V   M X P V J I   V O N J . "

Q J A V A X W I   A Z P P J R R

Puzzle 16

Hint: A famous comedian talks about ways to improve the world.

A	B	C	D	E	F	G	H	I	J	K	L	M	N	O	P	Q	R	S	T	U	V	W	X	Y	Z
	G	D		I		T		Y		Q			U				C	B	N		R		W		

" J I   U I I Z   P V C I   Q Y U Z U I B B ,   P V C I

D V P E M B B Y V U ,   P V C I   X V F ,   P V C I

S M L T K N I C . "

I S S I U   Z I T I U I C I B

Puzzle 17

Hint: Trees come from humble beginnings.

A	B	C	D	E	F	G	H	I	J	K	L	M	N	O	P	Q	R	S	T	U	V	W	X	Y	Z
		N		J			G		C			X		L			S		P		H		K		

" T S L X   D   O X D A A   O J J B   D   X I W G P U
P S Y V F   X D U   W S L E . "

D J O N G U A Y O

Puzzle 18

Hint: Motivation from an electric man.

A	B	C	D	E	F	G	H	I	J	K	L	M	N	O	P	Q	R	S	T	U	V	W	X	Y	Z
X		Z			S				I	N			H	Y				J		C					O

" K S   V W   P K P   X G G   D E W   D E K H M J   V W
X U W   Z X A X F G W   Y S ,   V W   V Y C G P   G K D W U X G G L
X J D Y C H P   Y C U J W G B W J . "

D E Y Q X J   X .   W P K J Y H

Puzzle 19

Hint: When this happens, try again.

A	B	C	D	E	F	G	H	I	J	K	L	M	N	O	P	Q	R	S	T	U	V	W	X	Y	Z
F					J			L					W		T		N			B				V	

"J F L E B N H   L I   I L S T E V   K X H   C T T C N K B W L K V

K C   R H O L W   F O F L W ,   K X L I   K L S H

S C N H   L W K H E E L O H W K E V ."

X H W N V   J C N G

Puzzle 20

Hint: A good reason to have a sunny outlook on life.

A	B	C	D	E	F	G	H	I	J	K	L	M	N	O	P	Q	R	S	T	U	V	W	X	Y	Z
		O		D			U						A	H			V		J			S			

"Y D D F   Q H W V   L B O D   J H   J U D   G W A G U K A D

B A E   Q H W   O B A A H J   G D D   B   G U B E H S ."

U D M D A   Y D M M D V

Math Squares

How to: Math Squares

Fill in the missing numbers to complete each number sentence.
They're all equations. The trick is to use both rows and columns to figure out the missing numbers.
Sometimes the order of operations will matter.
Remember to multiply and divide before adding and subtracting!

Puzzle 1

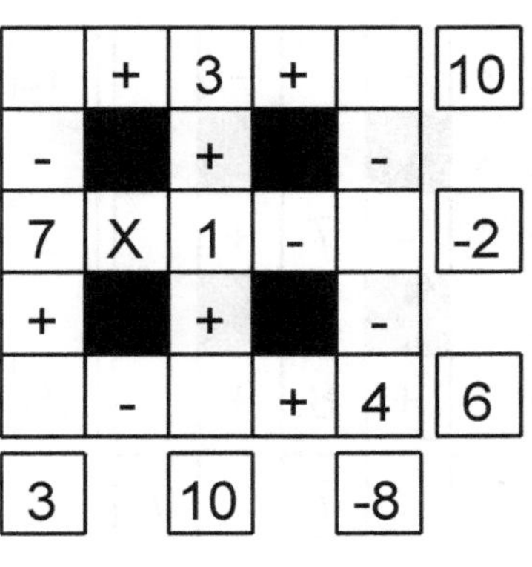

Puzzle 2

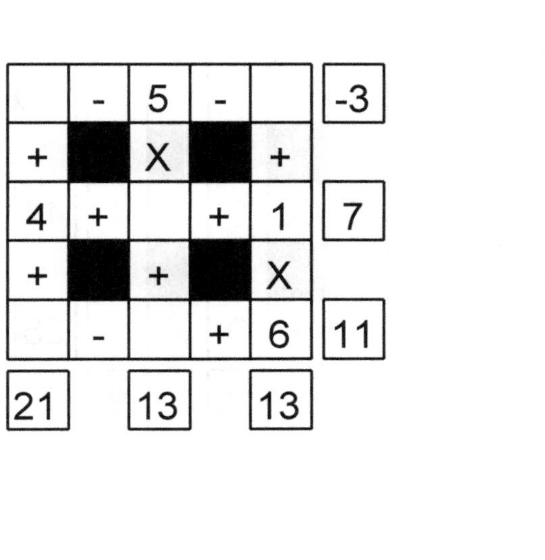

Puzzle 3

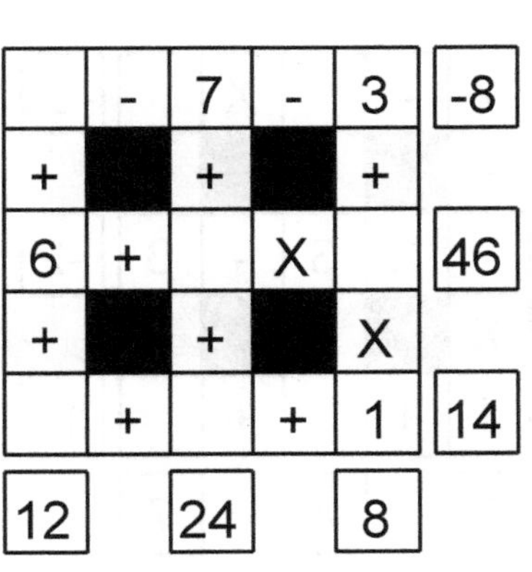

Puzzle 4

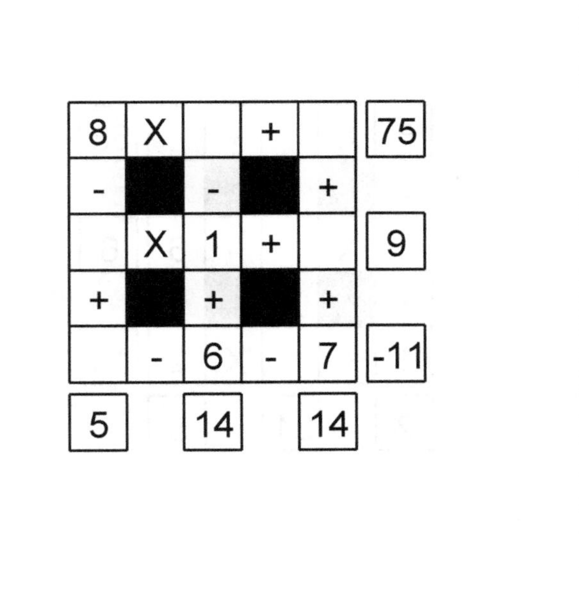

Puzzle 5

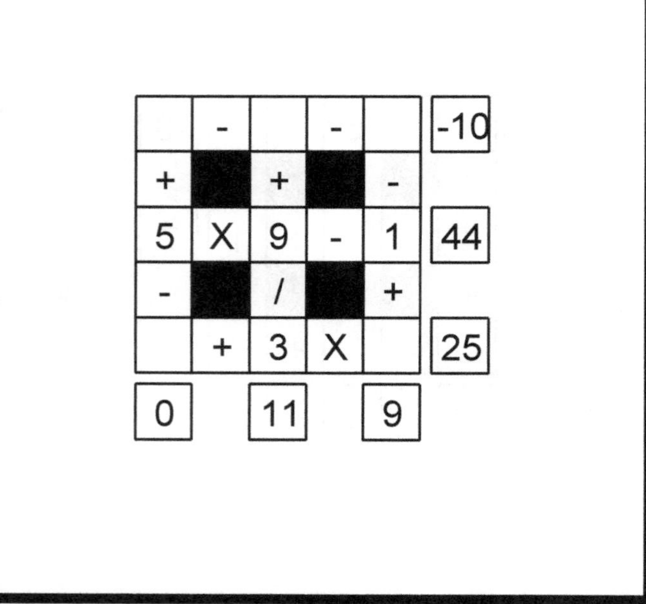

Puzzle 6

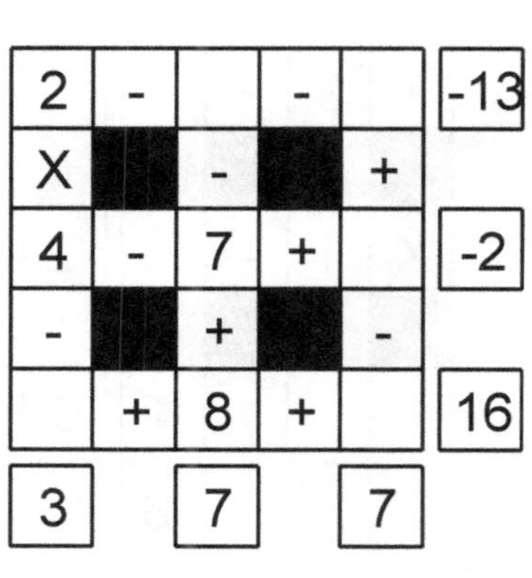

Puzzle 7

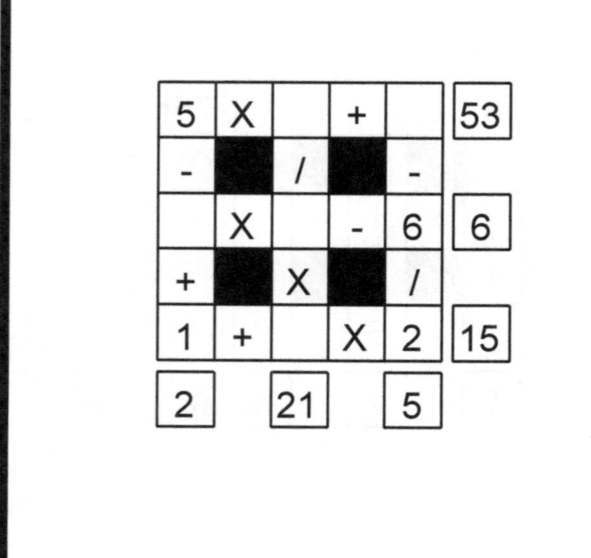

Puzzle 8

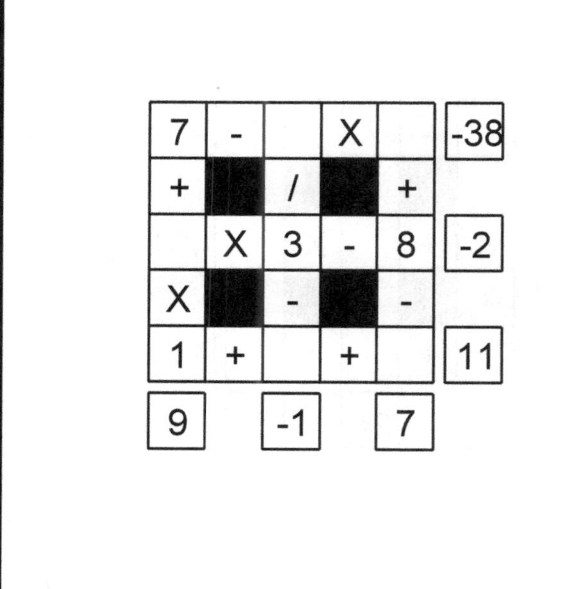

Puzzle 9

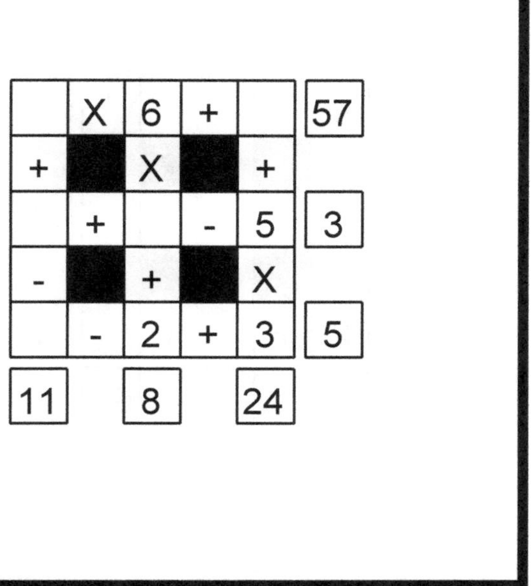

Puzzle 10

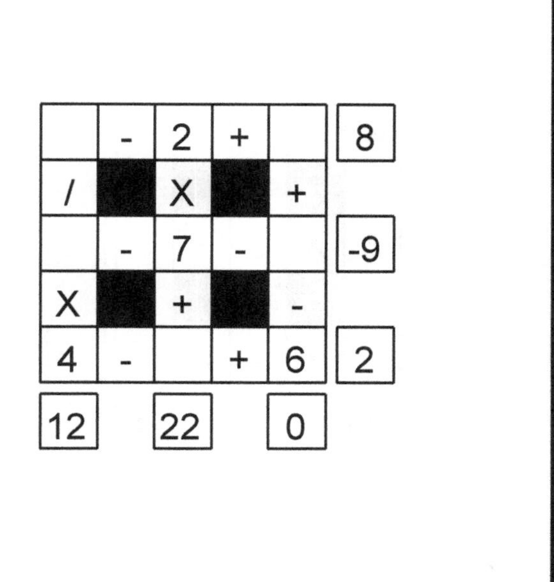

Puzzle 11

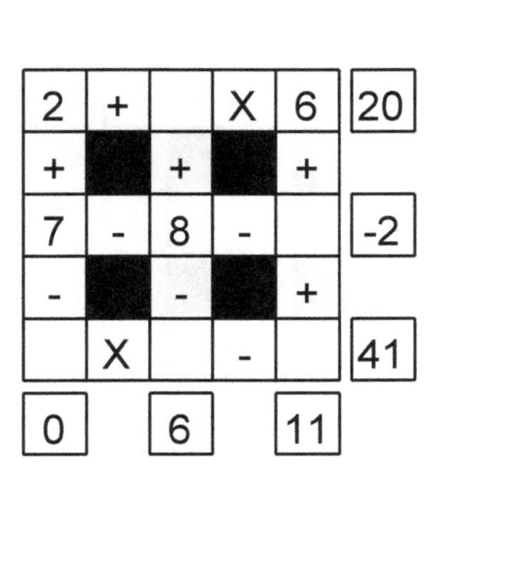

Puzzle 12

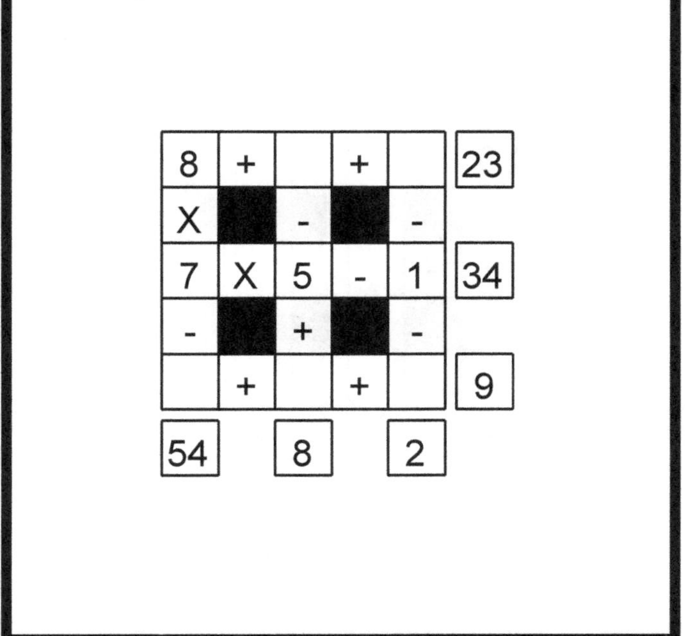

Puzzle 13

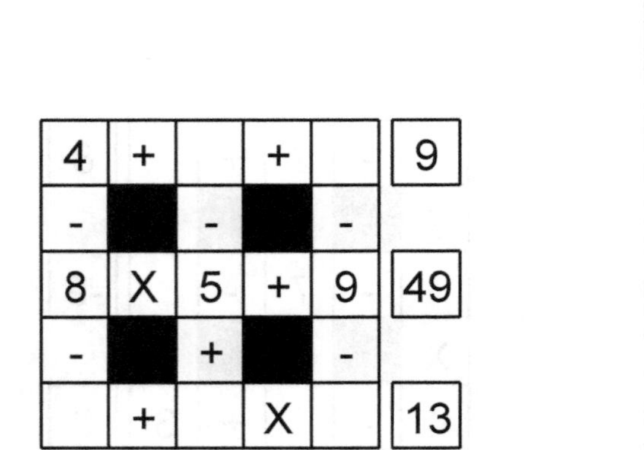

Puzzle 14

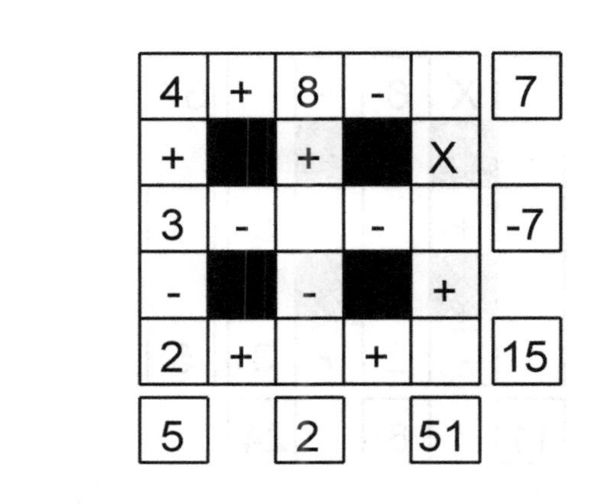

Puzzle 15

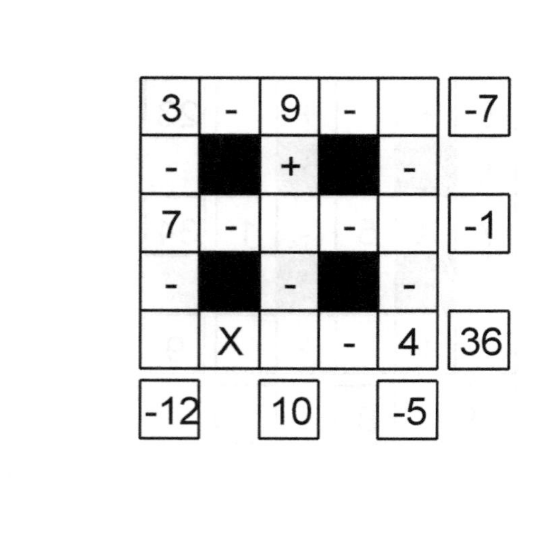

Puzzle 16

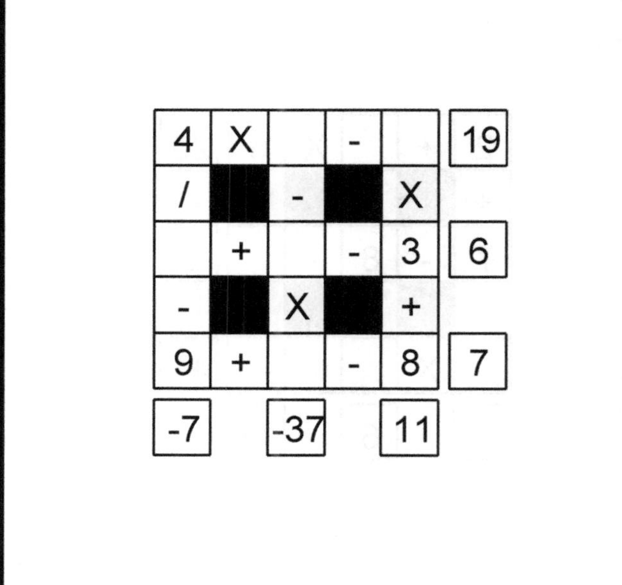

Puzzle 17

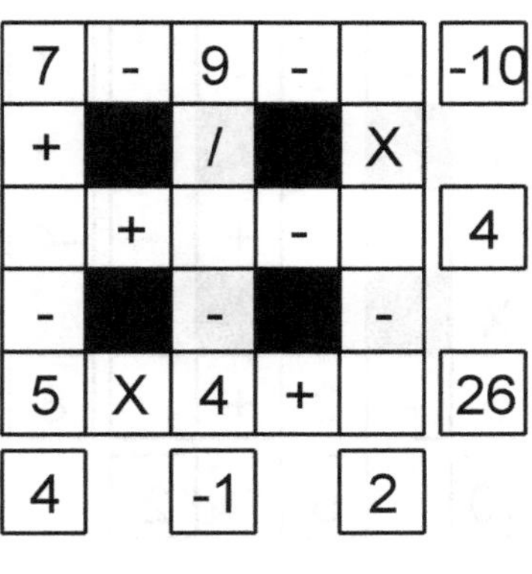

7	-	9	-		-10
+		/		X	
	+		-		4
-		-		-	
5	X	4	+		26
4		-1		2	

Puzzle 18

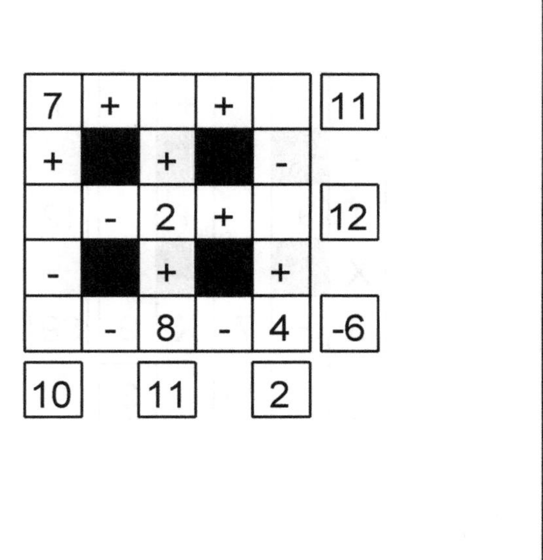

7	+		+		11
+		+		-	
	-	2	+		12
-		+		+	
	-	8	-	4	-6
10		11		2	

Puzzle 19

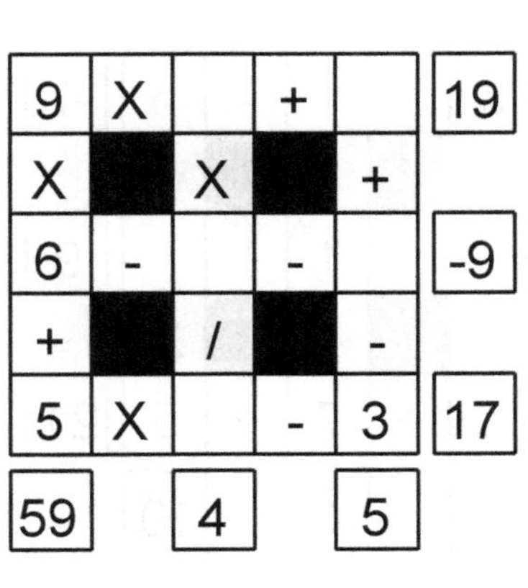

9	X		+		19
X		X		+	
6	-		-		-9
+		/		-	
5	X		-	3	17
59		4		5	

Puzzle 20

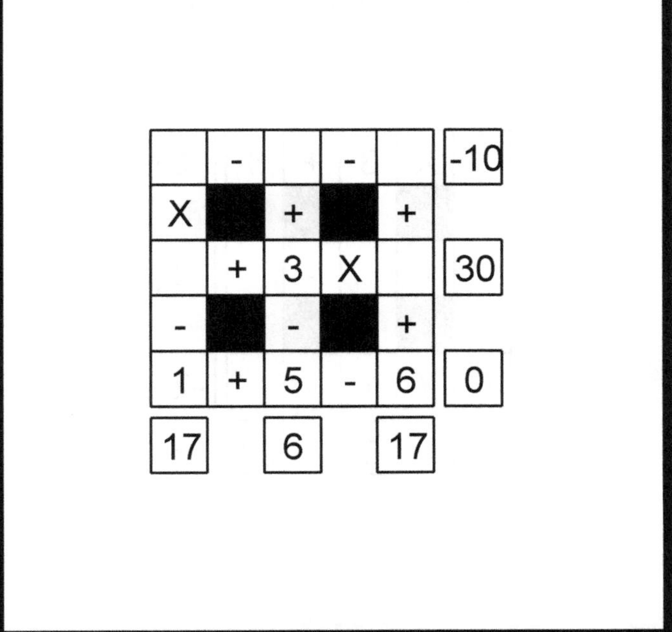

	-		-		-10
X		+		+	
	+	3	X		30
-		-		+	
1	+	5	-	6	0
17		6		17	

Math Squares

Puzzle 21

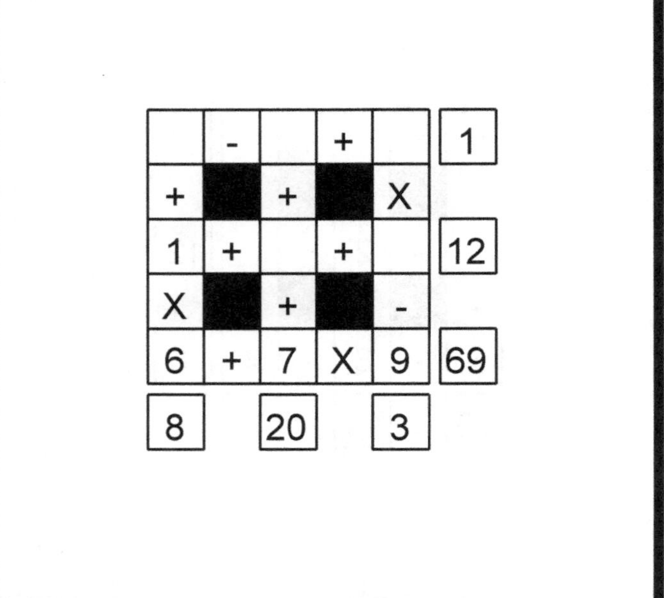

	-		+		1
+		+		X	
1	+		+		12
X		+		-	
6	+	7	X	9	69
8		20		3	

Puzzle 22

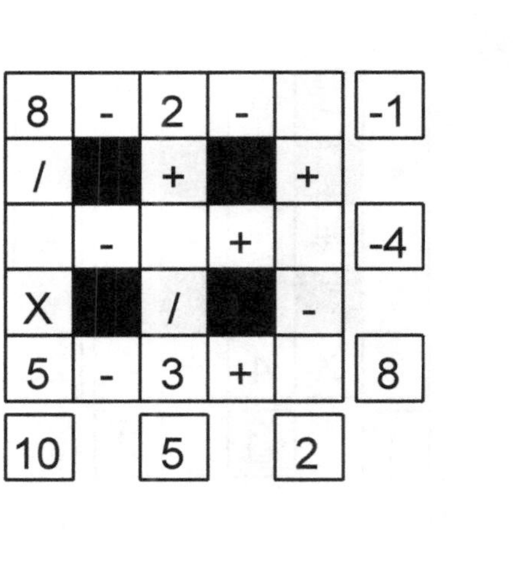

8	-	2	-		-1
/		+		+	
	-		+		-4
X		/		-	
5	-	3	+		8
10		5		2	

Puzzle 23

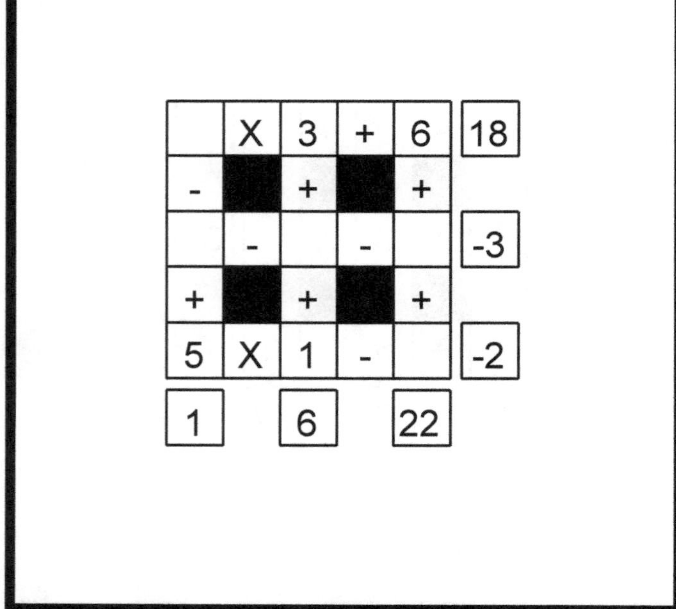

	X	3	+	6	18
-		+		+	
	-		-		-3
+		+		+	
5	X	1	-		-2
1		6		22	

Puzzle 24

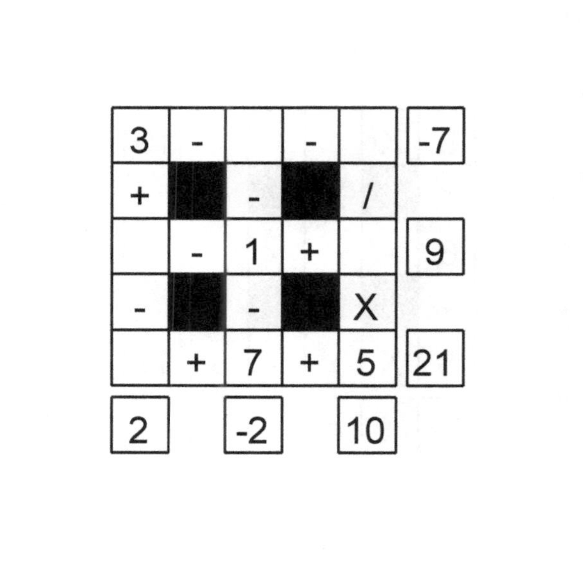

3	-		-		-7
+		-		/	
	-	1	+		9
-		-		X	
	+	7	+	5	21
2		-2		10	

Puzzle 25

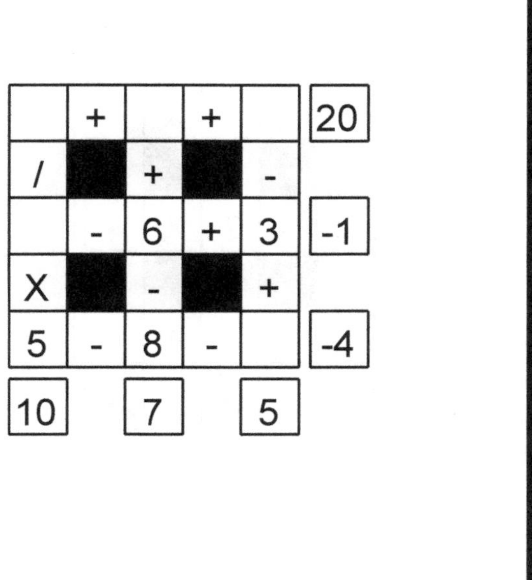

	+		+		20
/		+		-	
	-	6	+	3	-1
X		-		+	
5	-	8	-		-4
10		7		5	

Puzzle 26

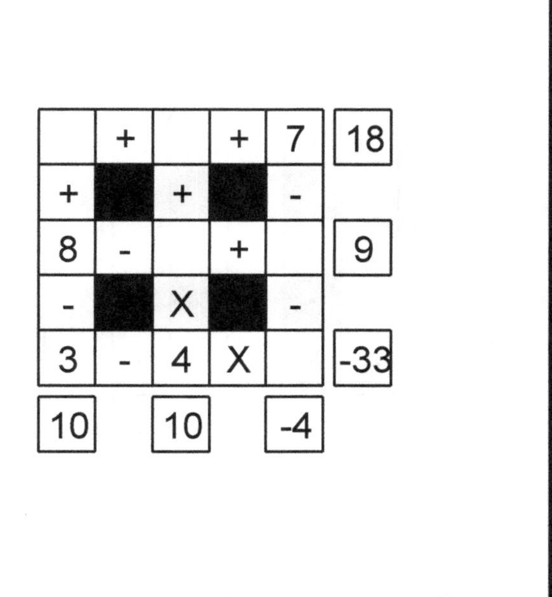

	+		+	7	18
+		+		-	
8	-		+		9
-		X		-	
3	-	4	X		-33
10		10		-4	

Puzzle 27

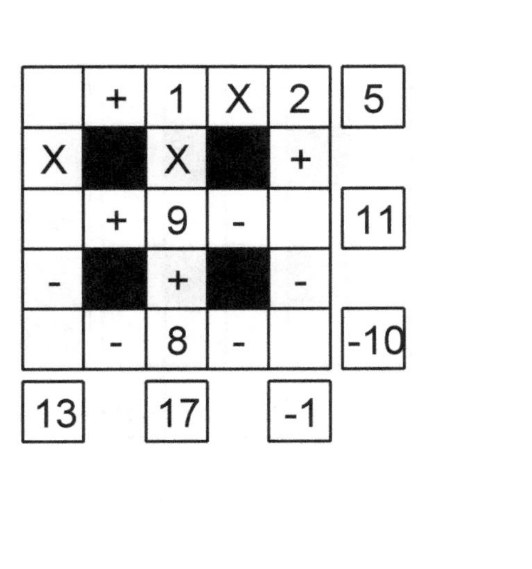

	+	1	X	2	5
X		X		+	
	+	9	-		11
-		+		-	
	-	8	-		-10
13		17		-1	

Puzzle 28

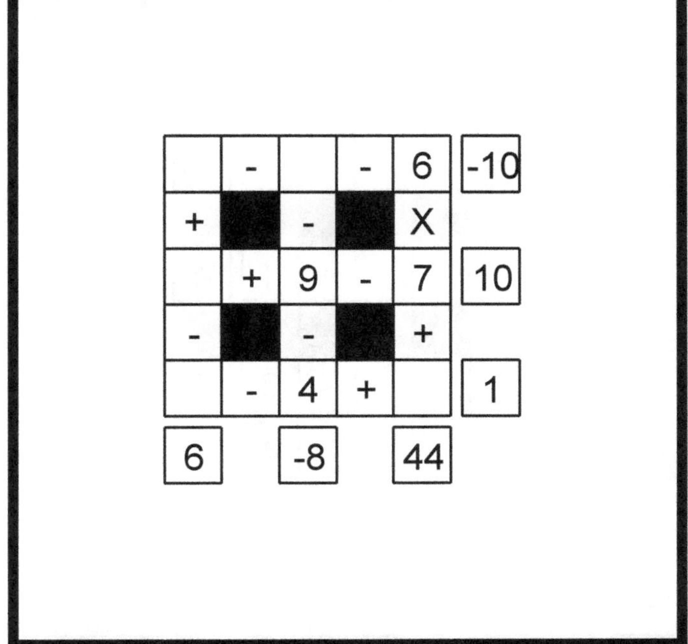

	-		-	6	-10
+		-		X	
	+	9	-	7	10
-		-		+	
	-	4	+		1
6		-8		44	

Puzzle 29

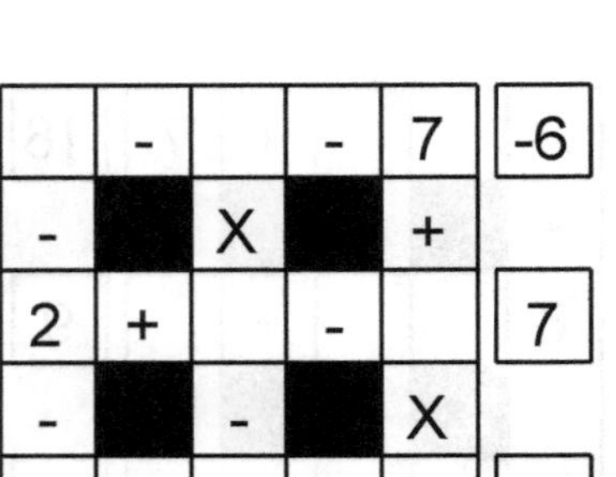

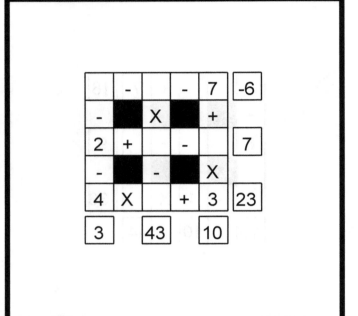

	-		-	7	-6
-		X		+	
2	+		-		7
-		-		X	
4	X		+	3	23
3		43		10	

Puzzle 30

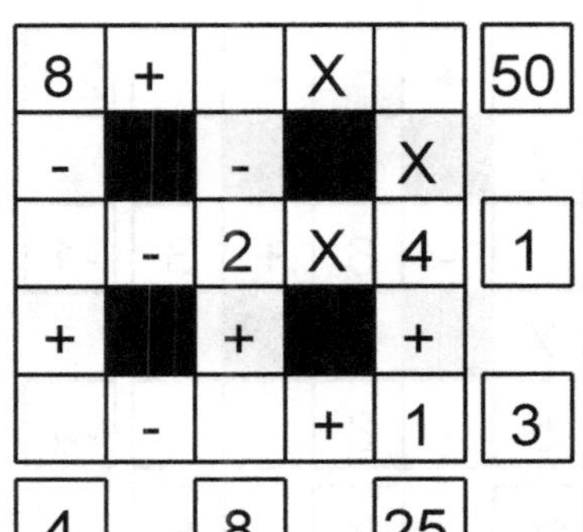

8	+		X		50
-		-		X	
	-	2	X	4	1
+		+		+	
	-		+	1	3
4		8		25	

Puzzle 31

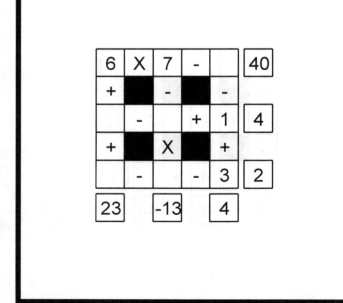

6	X	7	-		40
+		-		-	
	-		+	1	4
+		X		+	
	-		-	3	2
23		-13		4	

Puzzle 32

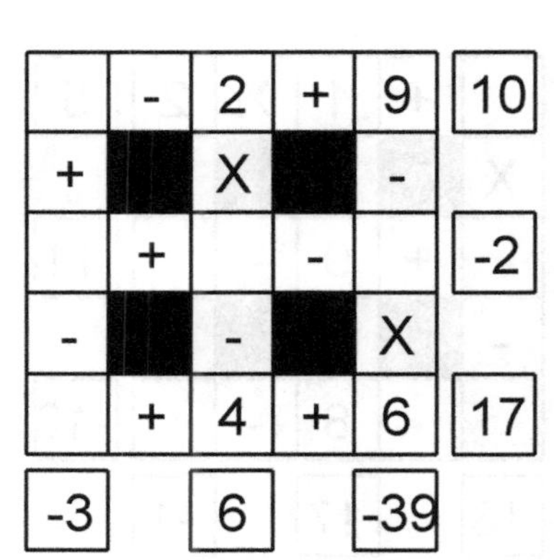

	-	2	+	9	10
+		X		-	
	+		-		-2
-		-		X	
	+	4	+	6	17
-3		6		-39	

Math Squares

Puzzle 33

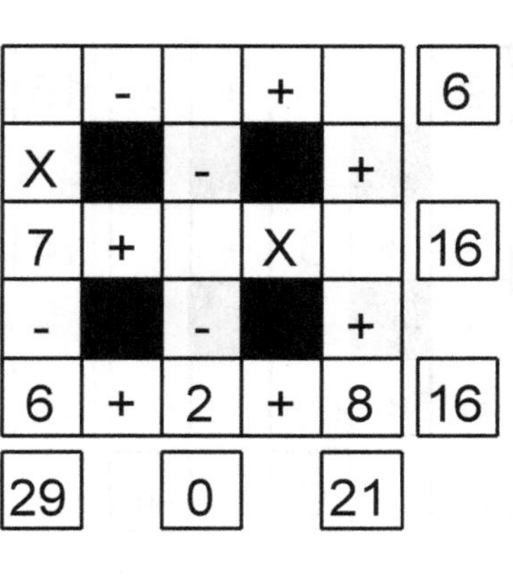

Puzzle 34

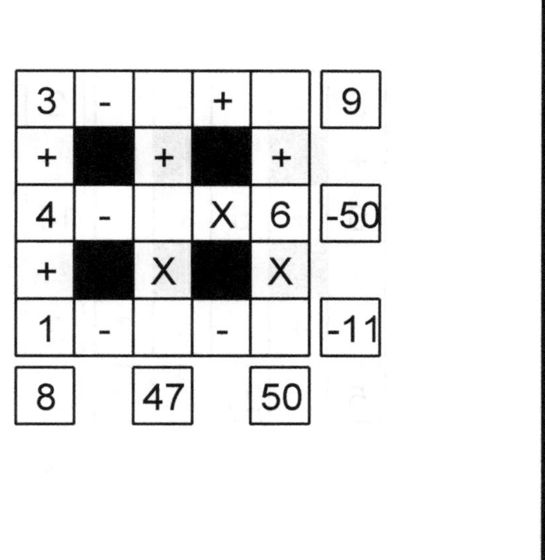

Puzzle 35

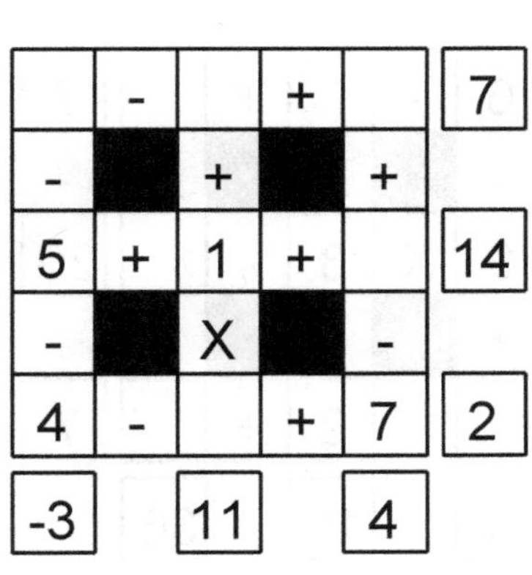

Puzzle 36

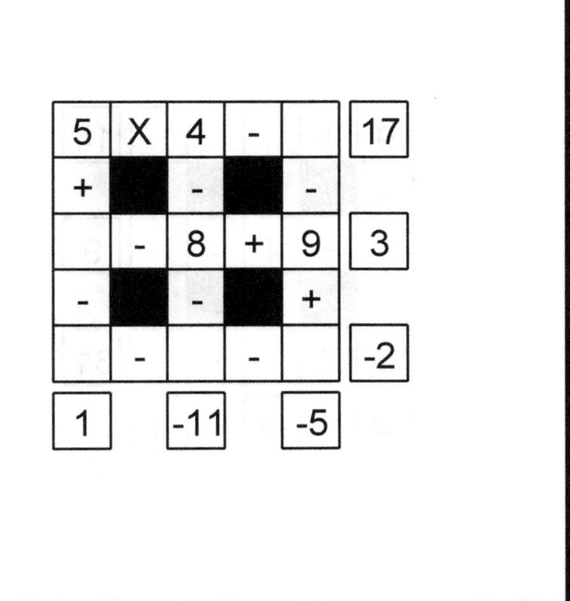

Puzzle 37

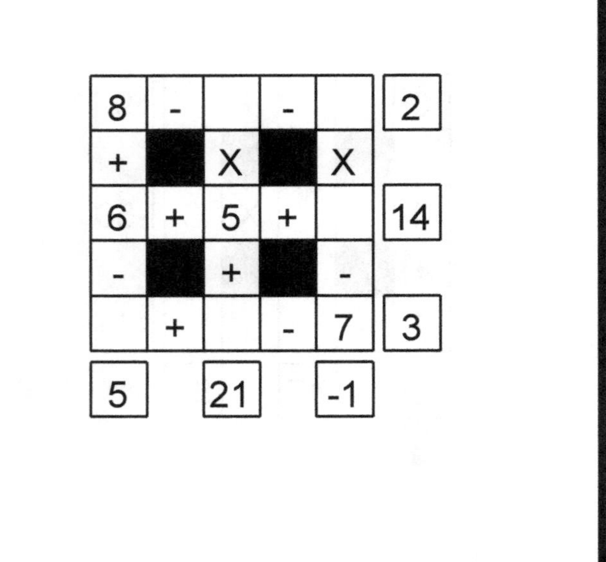

8	-		-		2
+	■	X	■	X	
6	+	5	+		14
-	■	+	■	-	
	+		-	7	3
5		21		-1	

Puzzle 38

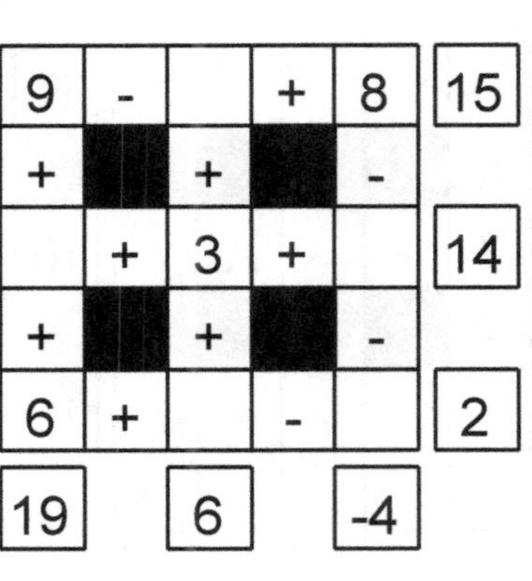

9	-		+	8	15
+	■	+	■	-	
	+	3	+		14
+	■	+	■	-	
6	+		-		2
19		6		-4	

Puzzle 39

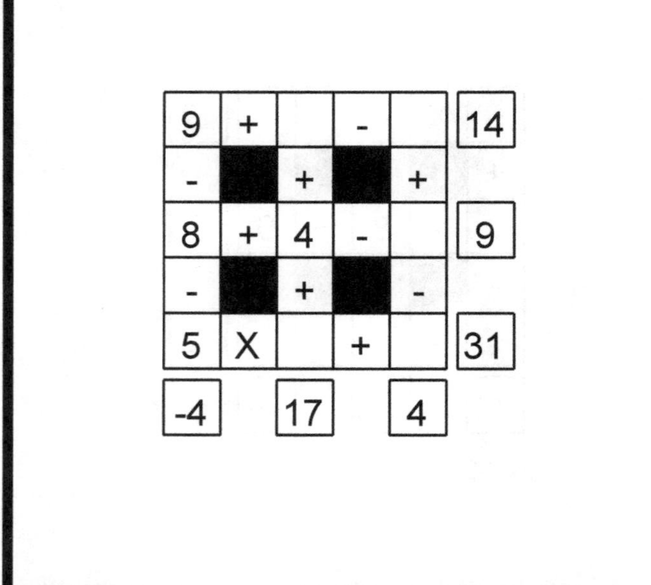

9	+		-		14
-	■	+	■	+	
8	+	4	-		9
-	■	+	■	-	
5	X		+		31
-4		17		4	

Puzzle 40

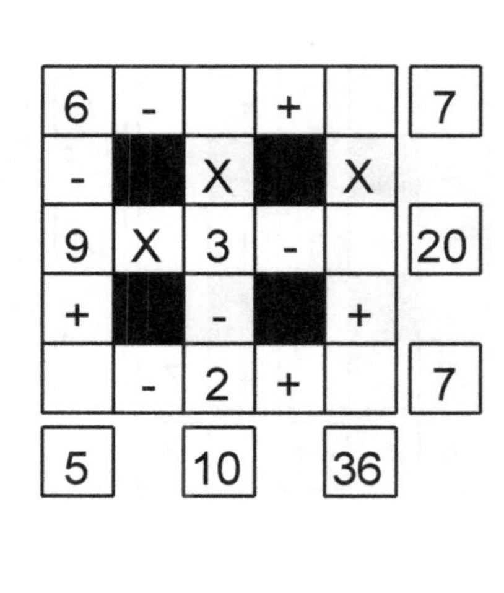

6	-		+		7
-	■	X	■	X	
9	X	3	-		20
+	■	-	■	+	
	-	2	+		7
5		10		36	

SUDOKU

How to: SUDOKU

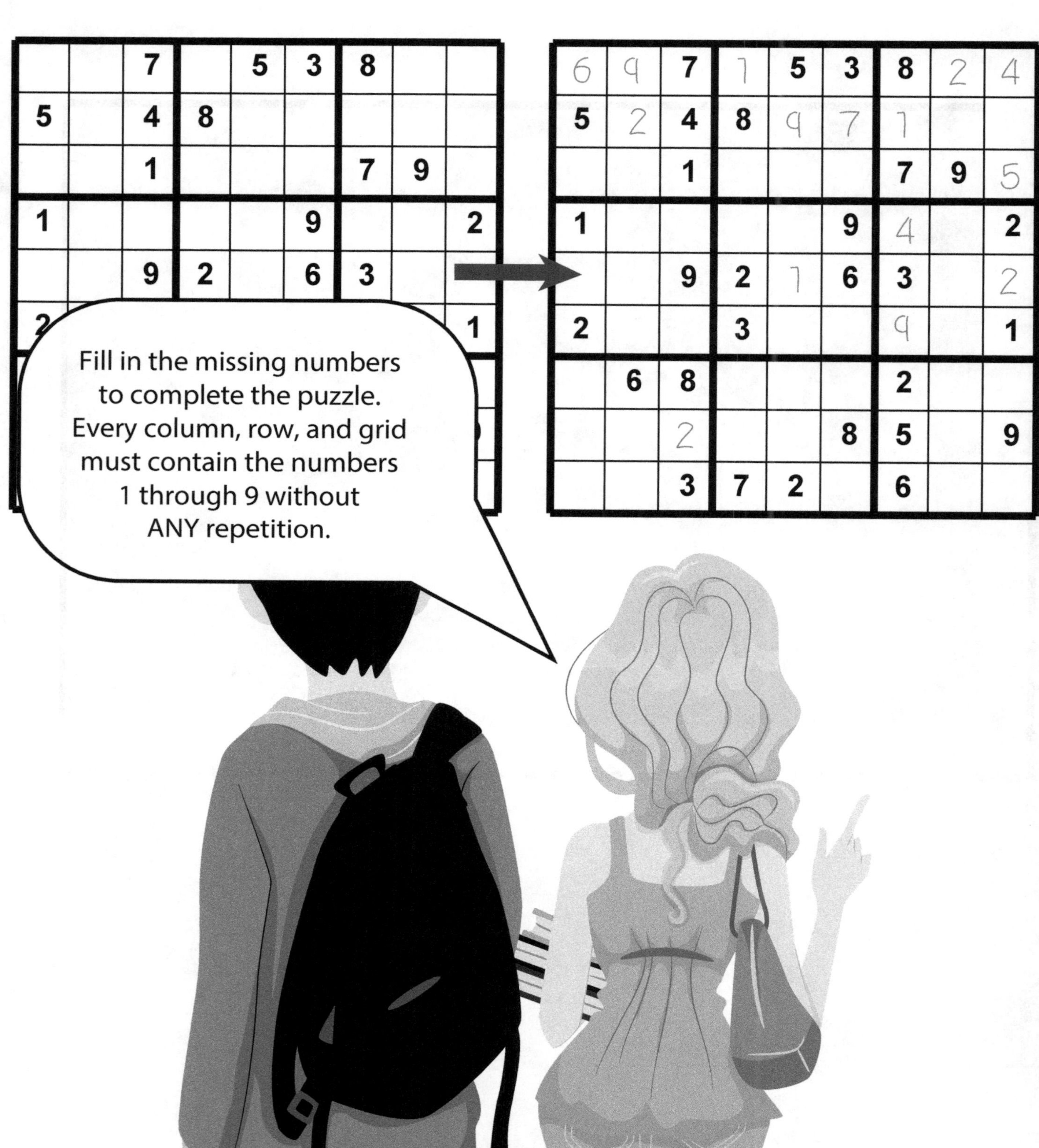

Fill in the missing numbers to complete the puzzle. Every column, row, and grid must contain the numbers 1 through 9 without ANY repetition.

Puzzle 1

						4	6	
4			3				8	
	5			9		3		7
	8			1	2	5	7	
2								8
	9	6	4	8			2	
9		5		4			3	
	4				8			6
	6	1						

Puzzle 2

	5	4		1		3	8	
	3	9						
1					3		6	
		6		8			1	
	2		7		5		4	
	8			4		6		
	1		8					2
						1	5	
	9	7		5		8	3	

Puzzle 3

3	5		8				9	
		6		3				7
	8		6		2			1
	4				8	3		
	9			1			6	
		2	5				1	
4			9		6		5	
5				2		9		
	3				5		7	2

Puzzle 4

	8		4			5	3	
7	4	6			8			
		3		2				
	9			6		1		
	3	1				6	5	
		7		5			8	
				4		8		
			1			7	9	5
	5	8			3		1	

Puzzle 5

			8				5	3
9		2		5			1	
				1	9	4	2	
				7	1			4
	1						9	
2			9	6				
	3	6	7	8				
	4			3		2		7
7	2				4			

Puzzle 6

		5			9		8	
		1	8		7		4	
7	8	4	1					
4			2					
3		7				8		5
					6			9
					8	3	9	4
	7		4		1	5		
	4		6			1		

Puzzle 7

4					1			
		5				7	3	
			4	2			9	
	4		2				5	7
	7	2	5		6	9	4	
5	8				4		2	
	5			1	9			
	6	4				2		
			8					9

Puzzle 8

	6	4			1			2
			9				3	5
8						1		
3	8	6			9			
		5	8	1	2	4		
			6			5	9	8
		2						9
6	9				8			
4			2			3	5	

Puzzle 9

5	7		2		8	6		
4			6					
	8	9			4			
			5			1	3	7
			3		1			
3	6	1			2			
			9			8	6	
					7			1
		8	1		5		9	4

Puzzle 10

4		7		3	5			
9			2	6	4		8	
	2							
	3				8		1	
5	9						2	7
	7		5				3	
							6	
	6		3	8	1			4
			4	9		2		3

Puzzle 11

	7			3		4		9
			1				7	3
6			9			1		8
	1				3		6	4
				2				
8	4		7				3	
2		4			9			6
7	6				5			
3		9		7			4	

Puzzle 12

1							7	
	5			9		3		2
	8		7		1		4	
4	6		3			8		
		8		2		5		
		1			7		9	3
	4		9		8		5	
8		5		6			3	
	9							4

Puzzle 13

2	9			5				
		4		6			1	2
					2	7	8	
	7			2				4
	8		1		3		9	
3				8			7	
	2	5	4					
7	3			1		4		
				3			2	8

Puzzle 14

7					9			
	5			2	7	8	9	
		1		4			7	5
	9					5		
5		7				2		3
		3					8	
6	8			1		9		
	7	9	3	5			1	
			6					8

Puzzle 15

	9		4	8		7	1	
		5			1			
		3				8	6	
	2			4	6			3
	6			1			9	
4			3	9			7	
	5	1				6		
			1			9		
	8	2		6	9		4	

Puzzle 16

	7		5		1	2		
	3	5	7				9	
2				6				
3				2		6		
	6		3		8		5	
		2		9				7
				7				9
	9				4	3	8	
		6	8		9		2	

Puzzle 17

				8	2			7
				7	6		5	
9	7		3			1		
		9				5	7	
6			7		1			2
	4	1				3		
		2			3		9	5
	1		6	9				
3			5	2				

Puzzle 18

		7		5	3	8		
5		4	8					
		1				7	9	
1					9			2
		9	2		6	3		
2			3					1
	6	8				2		
					8	5		9
		3	7	2		6		

Puzzle 19

	8		5					7
	3		9		7	6	4	
					6	1	3	
		4			9			2
1				6				4
3			2			5		
	9	3	7					
	1	5	4		2		8	
7					3		9	

Puzzle 20

			5			2		
	8	9	1					3
2	6					9	1	
9			8		5			
		5	2		4	6		
			6		3			1
	7	3					2	9
6					7	1	5	
		2			1			

Puzzle 21

5		6		9		1	2	
					4	7	9	6
			2					8
				8	1		7	2
8	7		5	6				
4					9			
3	2	7	8					
	1	8		4		2		5

Puzzle 22

9				7	3	2		
			8		9		7	
7	5		4				8	
8	4	7				9		
		5				4	2	1
	7				8		6	3
	8		7		5			
		2	6	9				7

Puzzle 23

	3	8			6			
		9	4				5	
1		4	8		9	7		2
			2					1
		5		7		2		
8					4			
9		2	1		7	5		8
	1				8	6		
			6			1	2	

Puzzle 24

2			3			1		7
					1	8		
		3			9	4	2	6
5	2			9				
4				7				8
				4			5	9
3	5	4	2			9		
		7	9					
6		2			7			3

Puzzle 25

6	1			3				8
	2				5	3		
	5		2				7	
				1		2	4	
	8		3		4		5	
	3	4		5				
	9				1		3	
		7	8				1	
3				6			8	2

Puzzle 26

		7		6				9
				3			6	4
6		1	4					
5	1		6					7
8	7						1	2
9					2		3	8
					7	8		3
7	8			5				
3				1		4		

Puzzle 27

	8		2	6				
						8		
7	9	2		1		4		
	2		5			3		4
3	5						1	8
8		6			3		9	
		9		2		7	4	5
		4						
				3	9		6	

Puzzle 28

9					7	6		3
				6	9	1		
	1				3		2	
4					6	8		
	8	9				5	3	
		3	1					9
	6		3				1	
		7	5	4				
3		4	6					8

Puzzle 29

3			8	1			2	
	2	1		7			8	
		8				3		1
	6		3				5	
			7	4	2			
	4				9		1	
4		2				8		
	7			3		1	4	
	8			5	7			3

Puzzle 30

	6				2			
	7	3	5			8		
	9	5		3	4			1
	3		4					
5	4						1	7
					6		9	
3			8	4		6	7	
		4			3	5	8	
			9				3	

Puzzle 31

	4			6				7
6	7				1	8		
	8	9				1	4	6
		6		3			1	
	2			9		3		
9	1	4				7	2	
		2	9				3	4
7				2			8	

Puzzle 32

1				5		2		
			3			5		4
3	7			2			1	6
			2			6	8	
			1		7			
	2	8			6			
6	9			3			2	1
8		3			2			
		2		7				5

Puzzle 33

	1		7		6			
4		3	1	8		9		
	6			3			5	
	3	1				4		
			2	4	9			
		4				5	9	
	5			1			8	
		8		9	3	6		7
			6		8		4	

Puzzle 34

				7	2		5	
7			9	4			8	2
1	4				5			9
5						6		
	6						7	
		3						1
6			2				1	4
2	3			9	1			8
	1		3	6				

Puzzle 35

	3				7	1		4
2				8				
	9							3
	2	7		6	1		9	
	1	8				6	4	
	4		2	9		7	3	
7							1	
				3				6
4		3	6				8	

Puzzle 36

			5		3		2	
				6	1			9
		1	2					7
			9	3		1	4	5
	5			8			3	
2	4	3		1	5			
7					8	2		
6			7	9				
	3		1		6			

Puzzle 37

	7	8	5		2			1
		3						4
	5					7	6	
	2		9		1			3
	3						9	
9			3		7		2	
	8	2					7	
6						3		
3			2		4	6	8	

Puzzle 38

	4	1	3	5				8
			2	7				
3		7			9	1		2
1	8		5					
					3		5	7
6		5	1			9		4
				4	5			
4				6	2	8	1	

Puzzle 39

6	5	7			1	9		
2								
	1	4	7		5		6	
		1		4			2	
		3				5		
	6			7		3		
	7		8		4	6	3	
								2
		9	2			4	5	1

Puzzle 40

		6					3	
		4	8					
	7		9	6	4			
3		7	4				5	1
		2	7		1	8		
8	4				2	7		3
			1	7	9		2	
					5	3		
	1					6		

Answer Keys

HIDDEN PICTURES

Puzzle 1

Puzzle 2

Puzzle 3

Puzzle 4

Puzzle 5

Puzzle 6

Puzzle 7

Puzzle 8

Puzzle 9

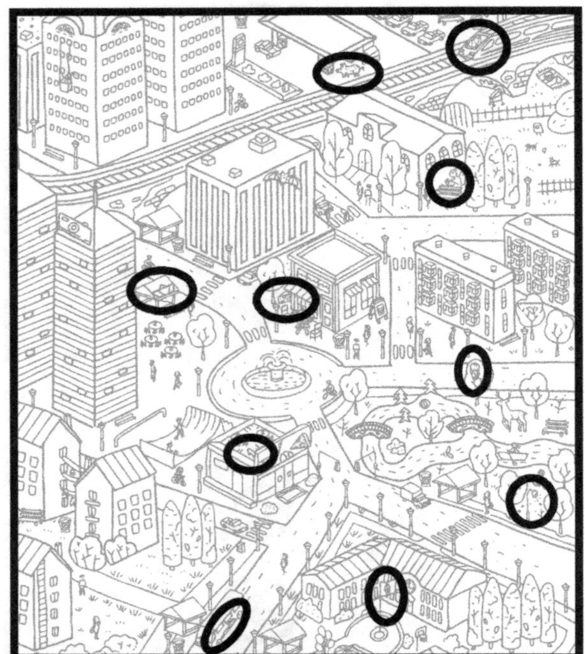

Puzzle 10

Puzzle 1

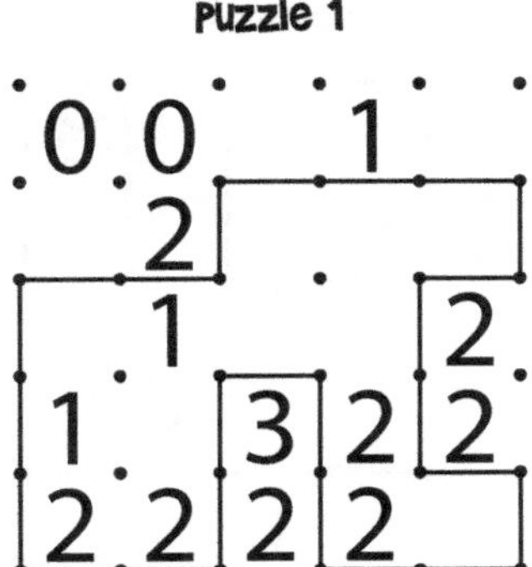

Puzzle 2

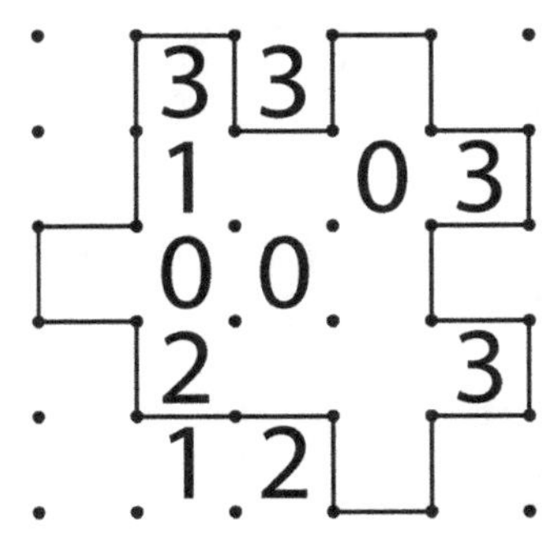

Puzzle 3

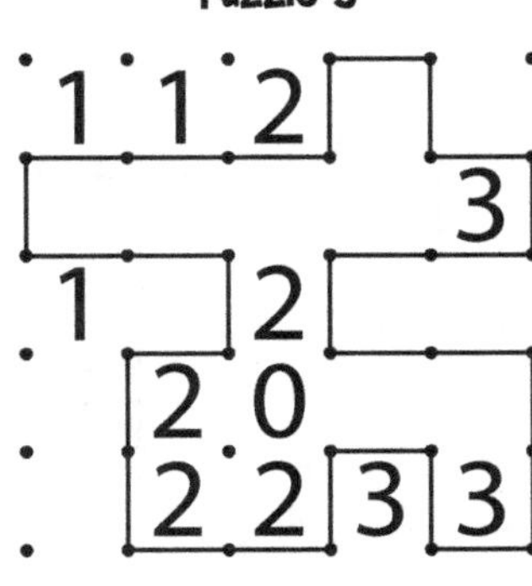

Puzzle 4

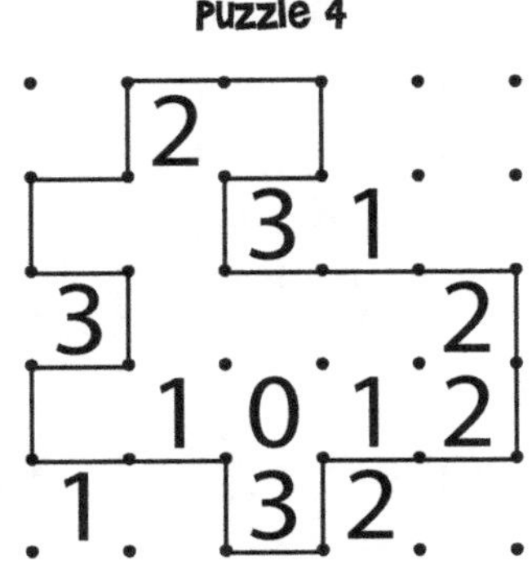

Puzzle 5

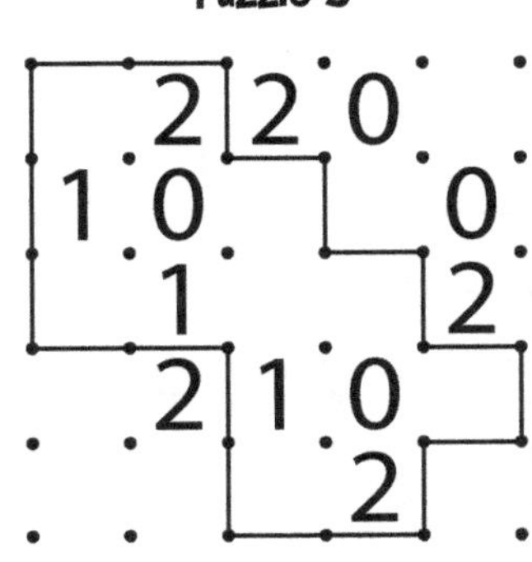

Puzzle 6

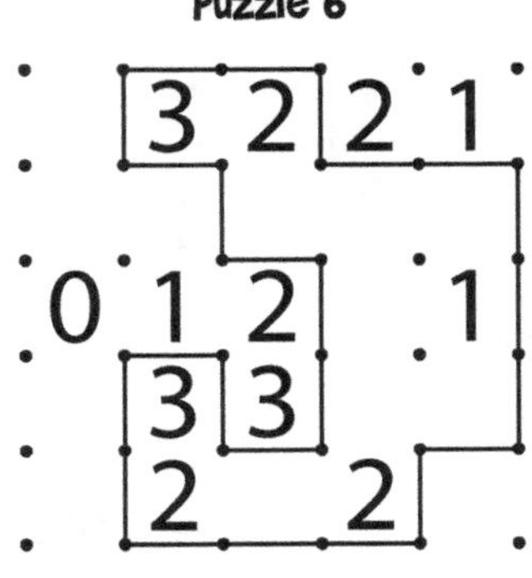

Puzzle 7

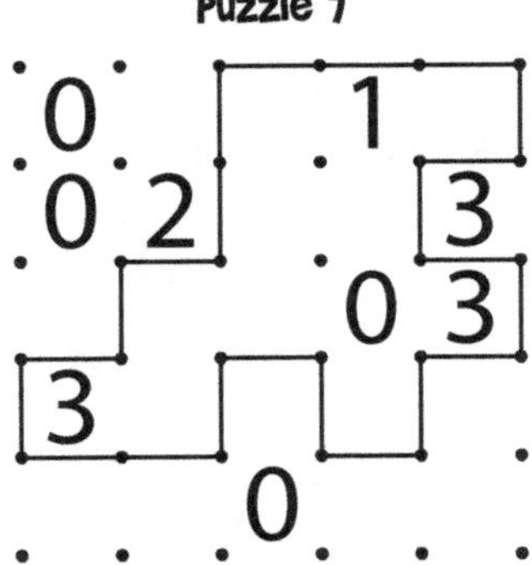

Puzzle 8

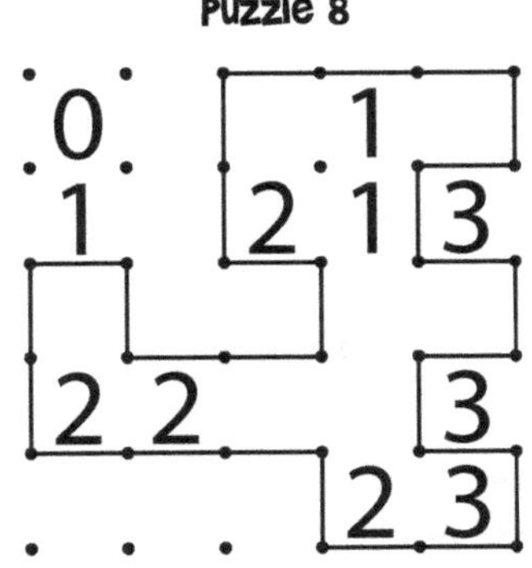

Puzzle 9

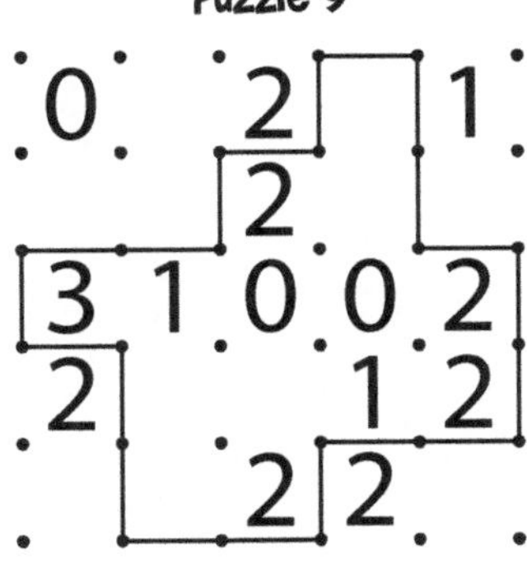

Puzzle 10

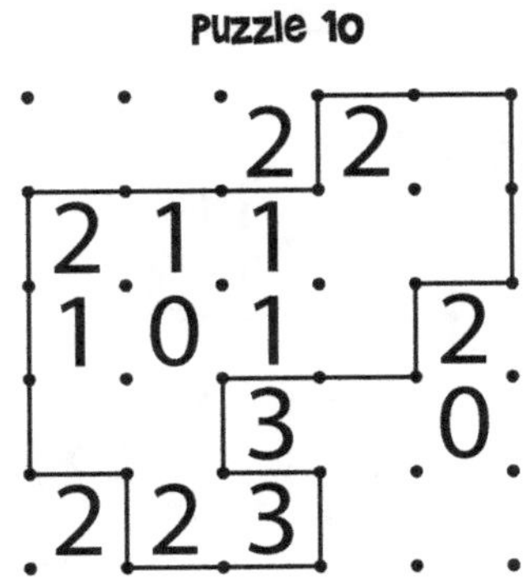

Puzzle 11

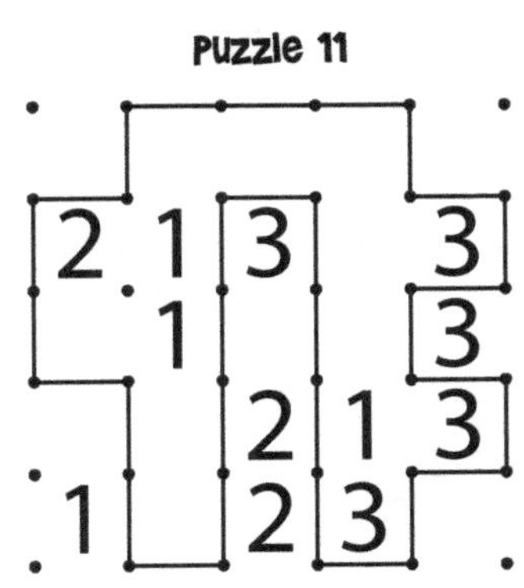

Puzzle 12

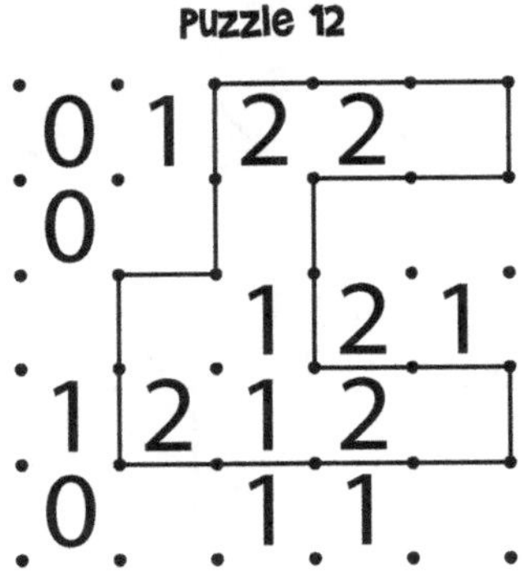

Puzzle 13

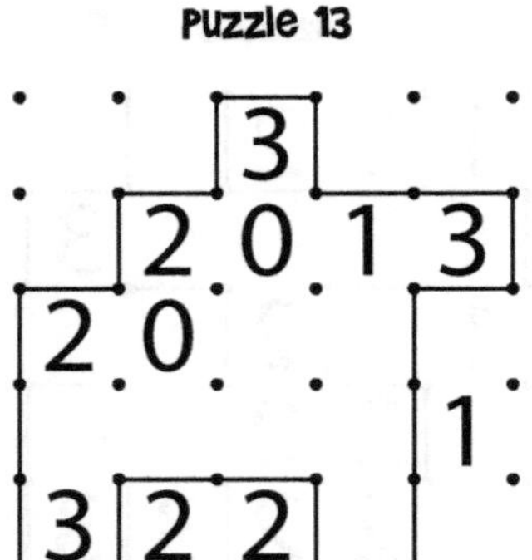

Puzzle 14

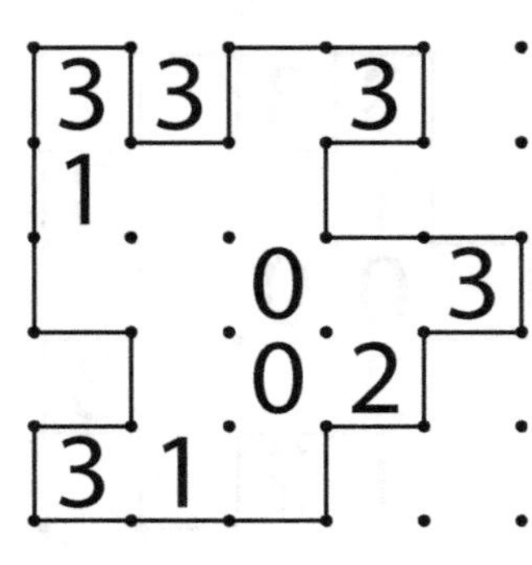

Puzzle 15

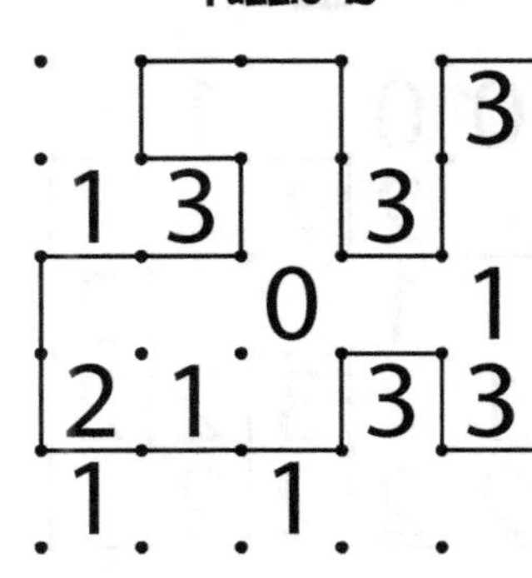

Puzzle 16

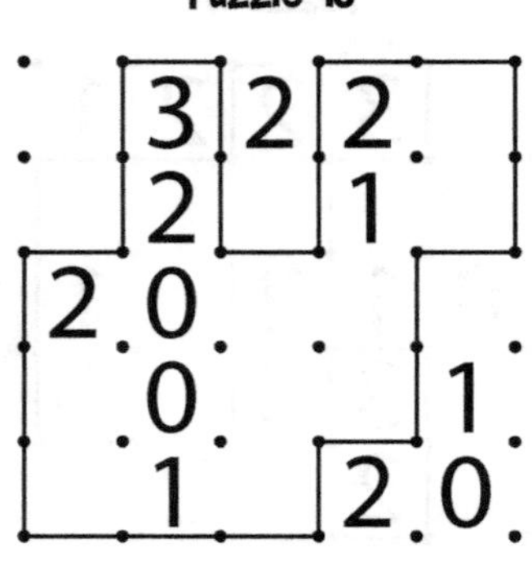

Puzzle 17

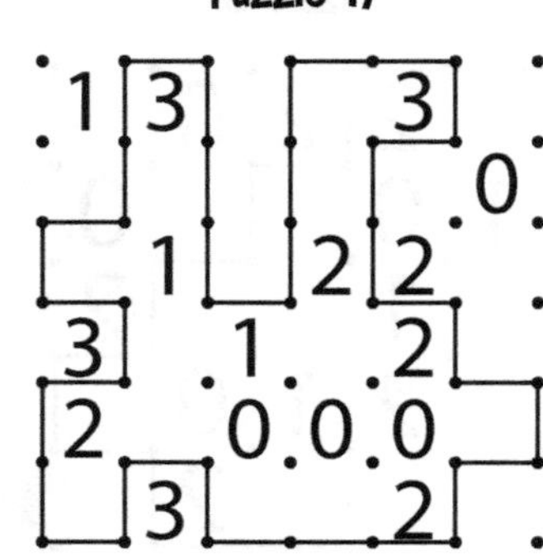

Puzzle 18

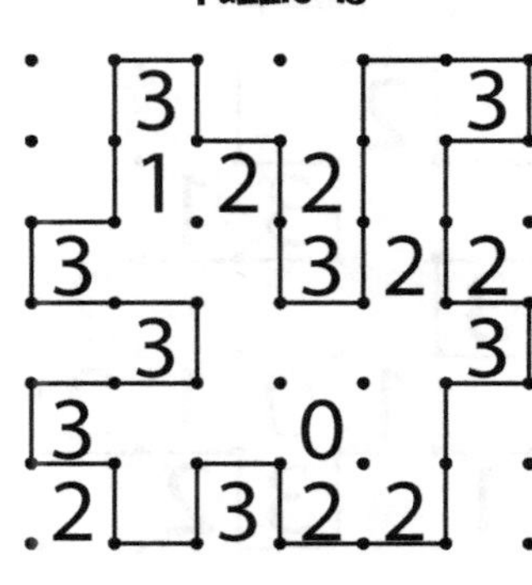

Puzzle 19

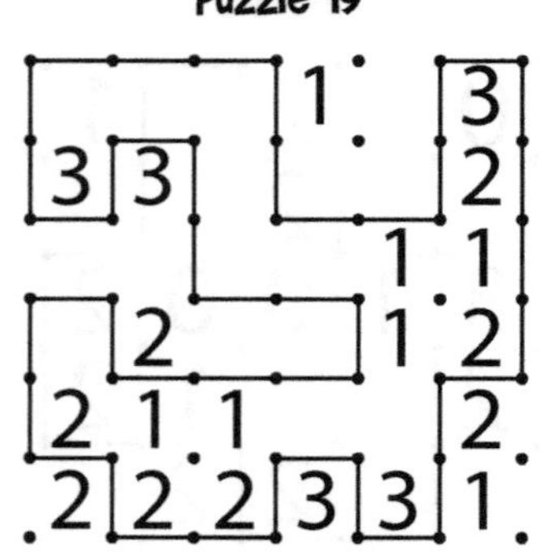

Puzzle 20

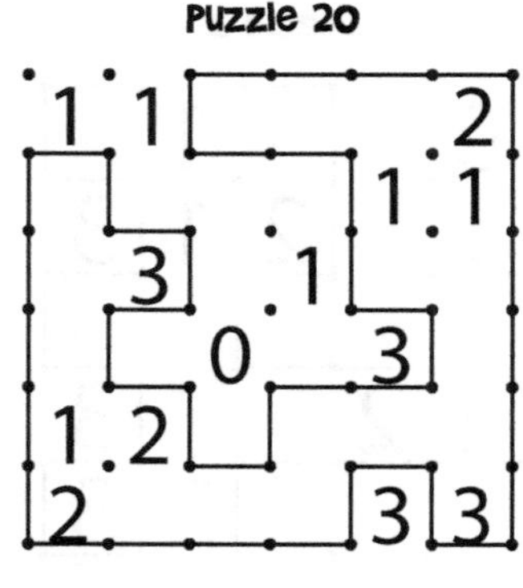

Puzzle 21

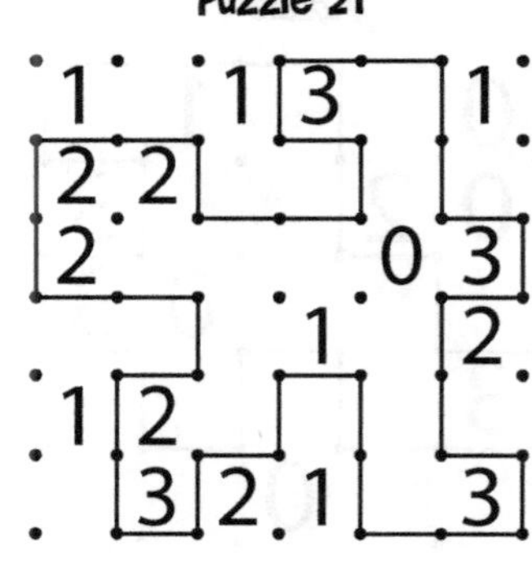

Puzzle 22

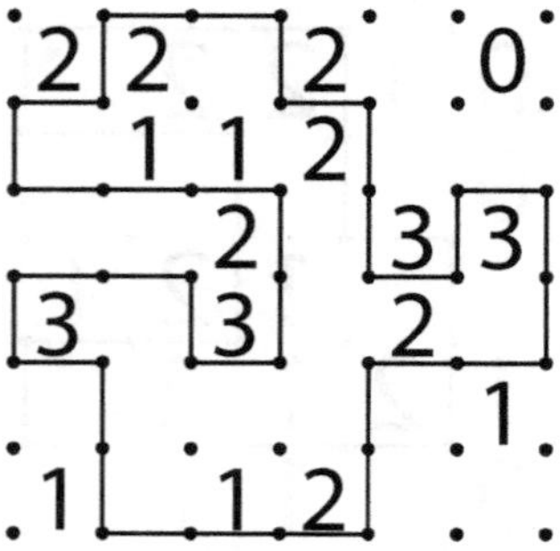

Puzzle 23

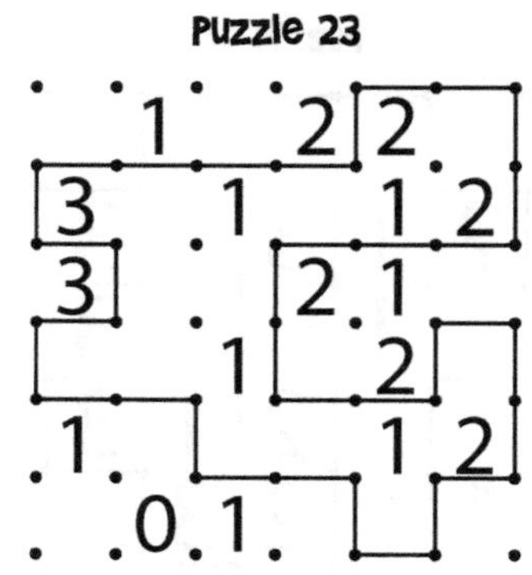

Puzzle 24

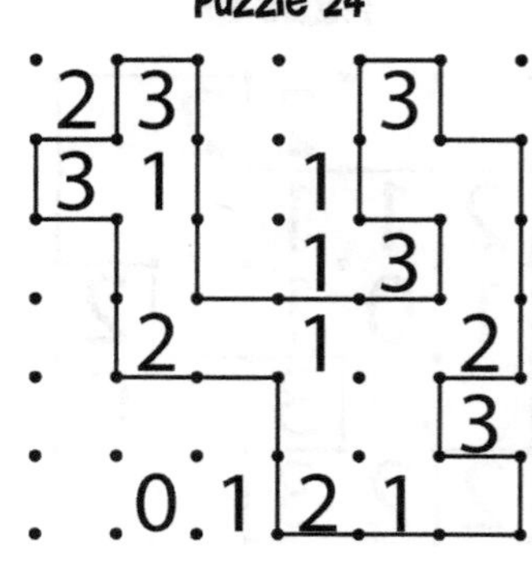

Slitherlink

Puzzle 25

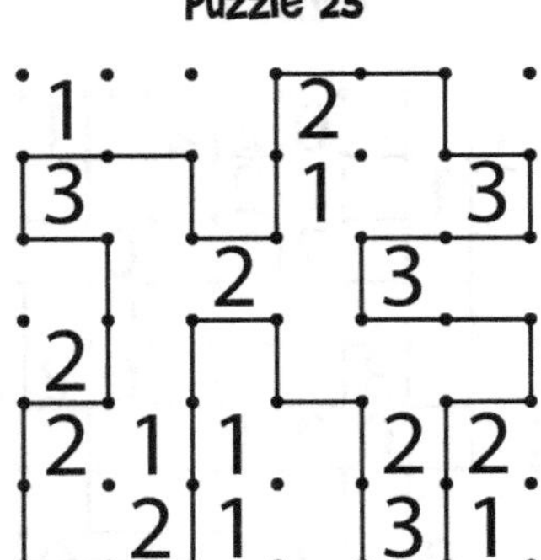

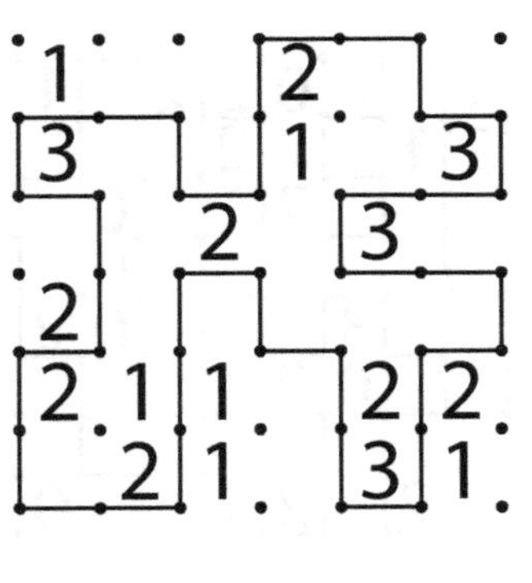

Puzzle 26

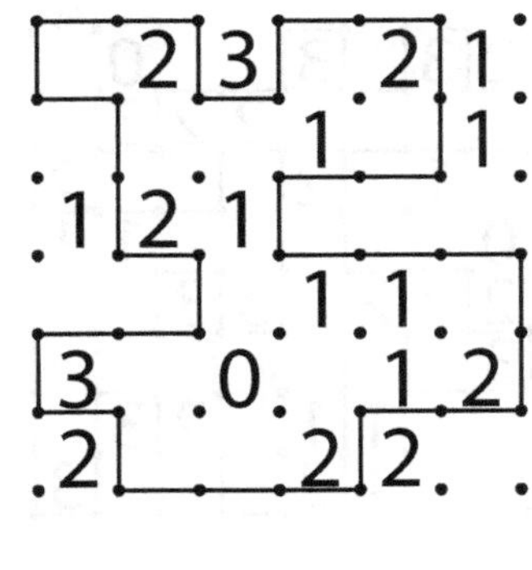

Puzzle 27

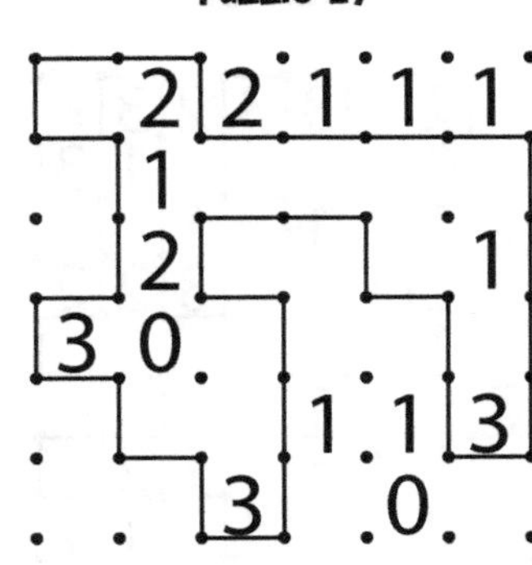

Puzzle 28

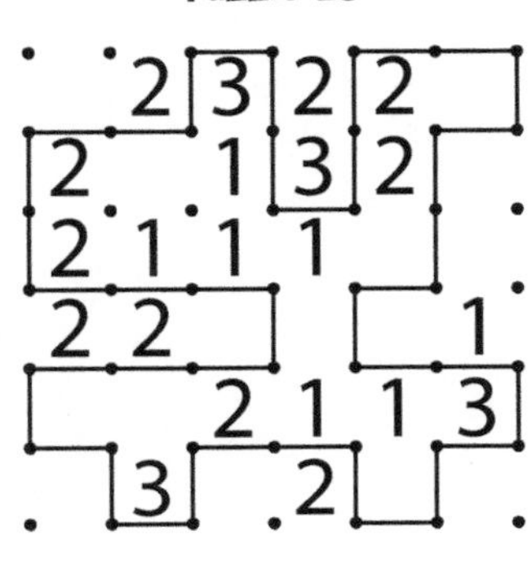

Puzzle 29

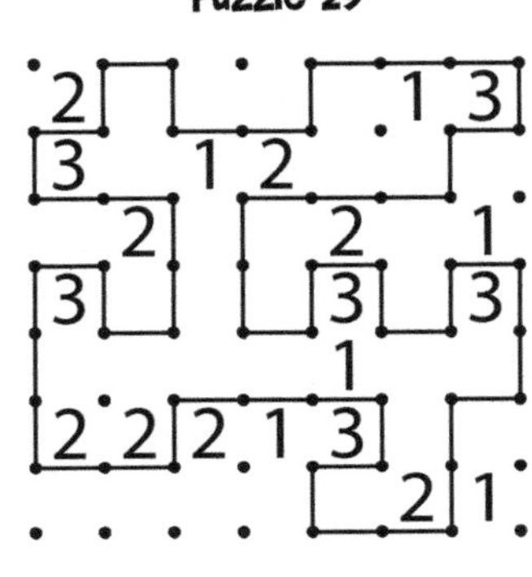

Puzzle 30

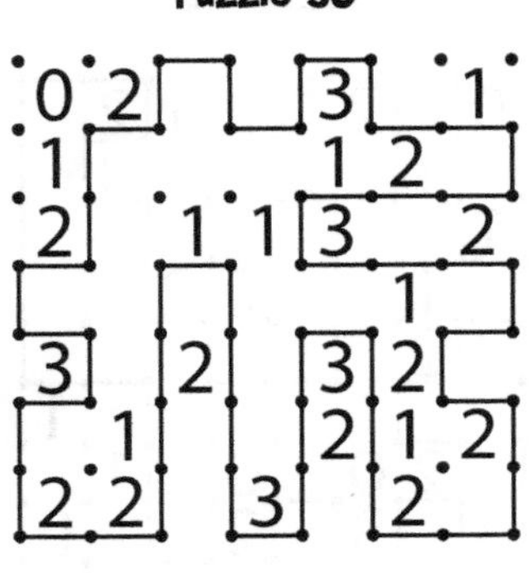

Puzzle 31

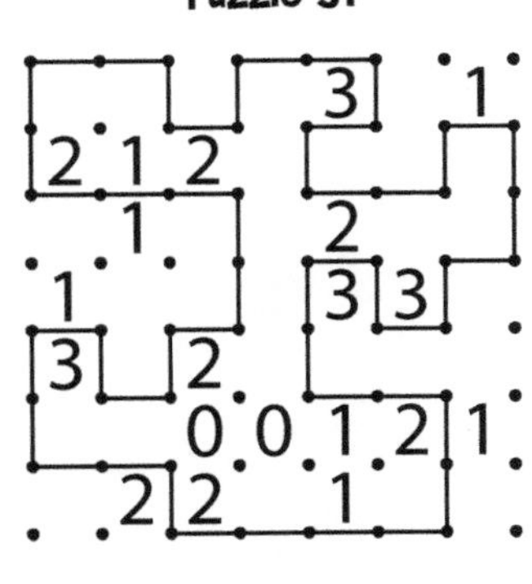

Puzzle 32

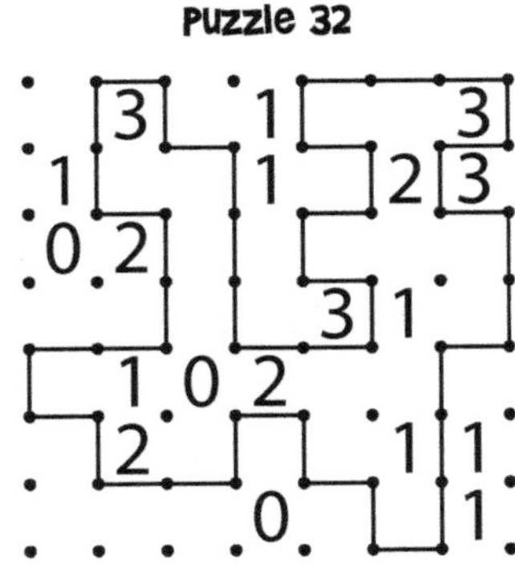

Puzzle 33

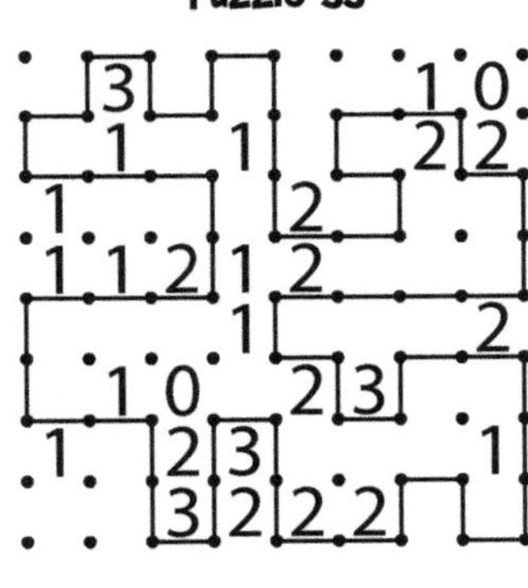

Puzzle 34

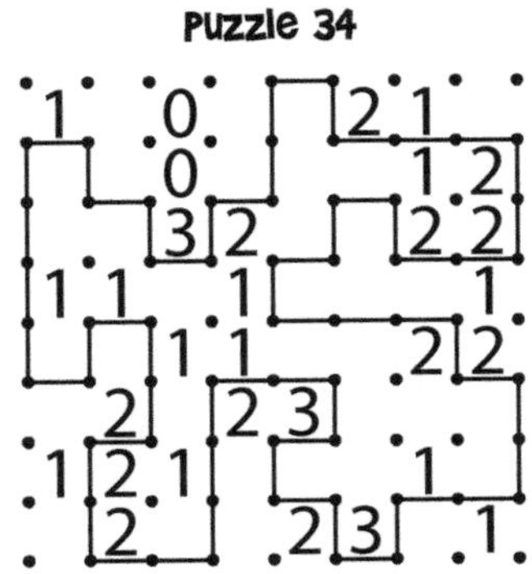

Puzzle 35

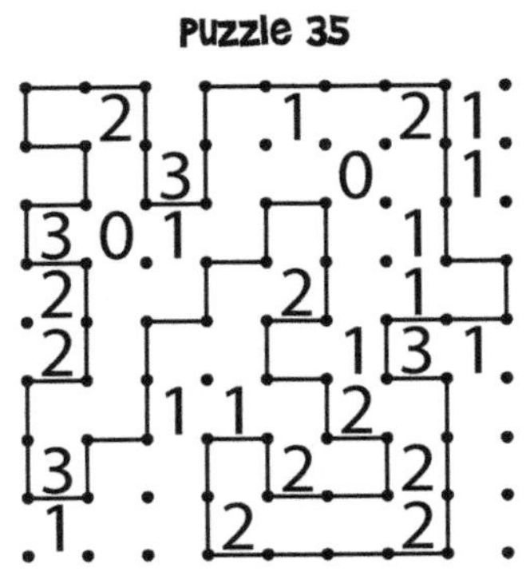

Puzzle 36

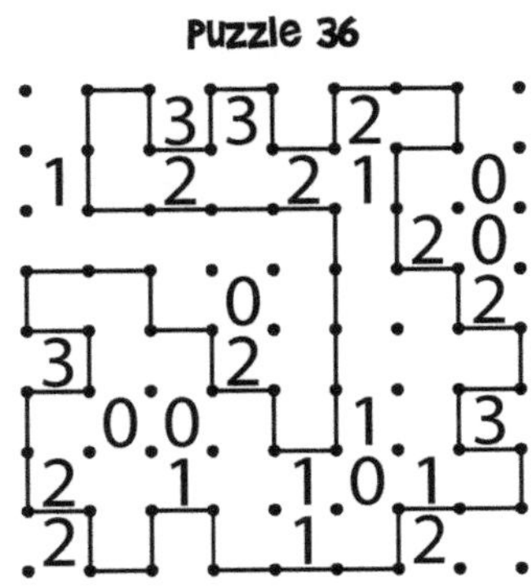

Puzzle 37

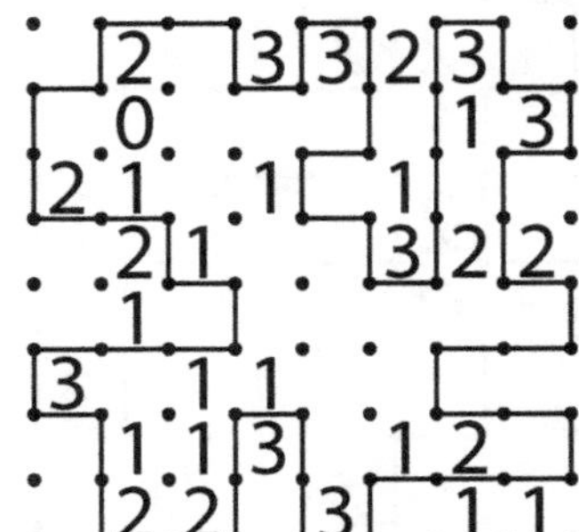

Puzzle 38

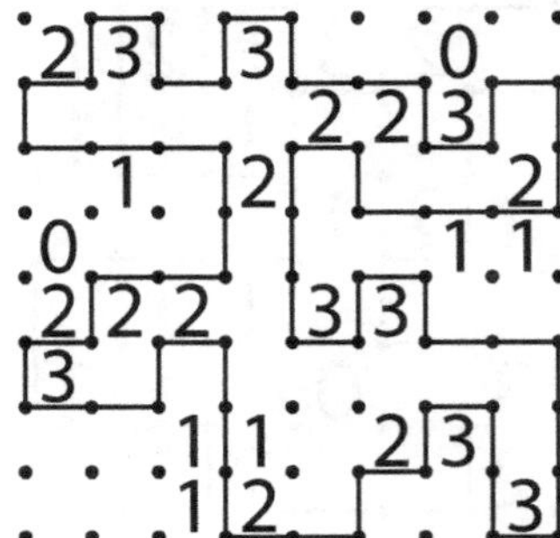

Puzzle 39

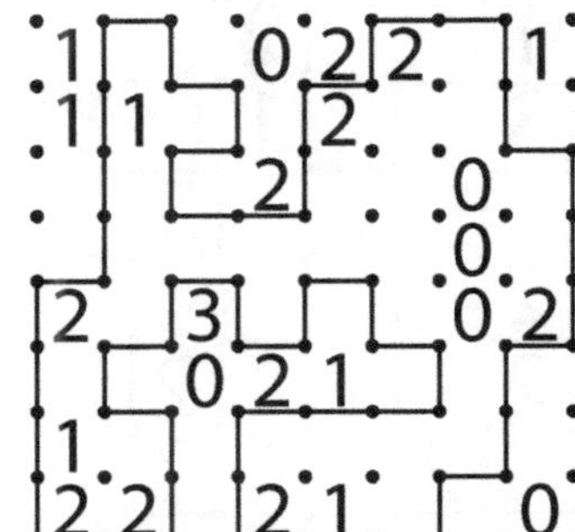

Puzzle 40

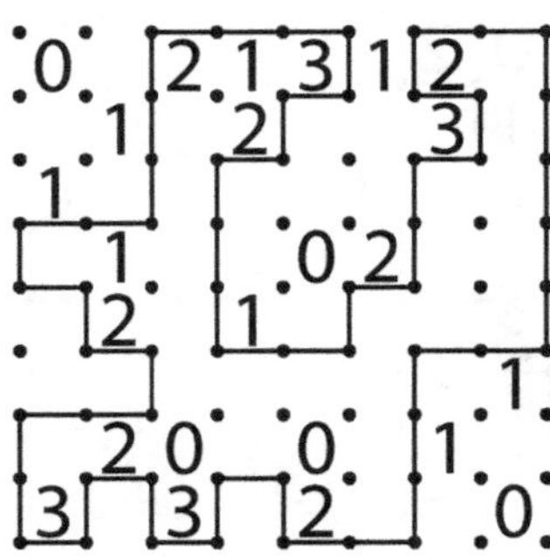

Puzzle 1

	Red	Yellow	Green	Blue
Brian	X	X	X	O
Greg	X	X	O	X
Ryan	O	X	X	X
Don	X	O	X	X

Puzzle 2

	Chocolate Chip	Sugar	Oatmeal	Peanut Butter
Michelle	X	O	X	X
Donna	O	X	X	X
Sabrina	X	X	O	X
Julie	X	X	X	O

Puzzle 3

	Black	White	Red	Grey
Van	X	X	X	O
Car	X	X	O	X
Pick-Up Truck	X	O	X	X
Motorcycle	O	X	X	X

Puzzle 4

	Fish	Bird	Dog	Cat
Fred	O	X	X	X
Sam	X	O	X	X
Bob	X	X	O	X
Carl	X	X	X	O

Puzzle 5

	Writing	Math	Reading	Spelling	Science
Martin	O	X	X	X	X
Edgar	X	X	O	X	X
Gertrude	X	X	X	X	O
Henry	X	X	X	O	X
Katherine	X	O	X	X	X

Puzzle 6

	Black	Grey	White	Blue	Green
Bears	X	O	X	X	X
Hornets	O	X	X	X	X
Eagles	X	X	X	X	O
Bulldogs	X	X	O	X	X
Tigers	X	X	X	O	X

Puzzle 7

	First	Second	Third	Fourth	Fifth
Clown	O	X	X	X	X
Trapeze	X	O	X	X	X
Tiger Tamer	X	X	X	X	O
Dancing Dogs	X	X	X	O	X
Elephants	X	X	O	X	X

Puzzle 8

	Red	Black	Green	Purple	1st	2nd	3rd	4th
Amy	O	X	X	X	X	O	X	X
Cathy	X	O	X	X	O	X	X	X
Frank	X	X	O	X	X	X	X	O
James	X	X	X	O	X	X	O	X

	Red	Black	Green	Purple
1st	X	O	X	X
2nd	O	X	X	X
3rd	X	X	X	O
4th	X	X	O	X

Amy was captain of the Red team, and placed 2nd.

Cathy was captain of the Black team, and placed 1st.

Frank was captain of the Green team, and placed 4th.

James was captain of the Purple team, and placed 3rd.

Puzzle 9

	January	February	March	April	Hamster	Fish	Turtle	Dog
Sally	O	X	X	X	X	X	X	O
Drew	X	X	X	O	O	X	X	X
Scott	X	X	O	X	X	O	X	X
Holly	X	O	X	X	X	X	O	X

	January	February	March	April
Hamster	X	X	X	O
Fish	X	X	O	X
Turtle	X	O	X	X
Dog	O	X	X	X

Sally was the January Student of the Month, and brought a dog to class.

Holly was the February Student of the Month, and brought a turtle to class.

Scott was the March Student of the Month, and brought a fish to class.

Drew was the April Student of the Month, and brought a hamster to class.

Puzzle 10

	Smith	Scott	Stewart	Shaw	Soccer	Football	Basketball	Baseball
John	X	X	X	O	O	X	X	X
Jeremy	X	X	O	X	X	X	X	O
Josh	O	X	X	X	X	X	O	X
Jacob	X	O	X	X	X	O	X	X

	Smith	Scott	Stewart	Shaw
Soccer	X	X	X	O
Football	X	O	X	X
Basketball	O	X	X	X
Baseball	X	X	O	X

John Shaw plays soccer.

Jeremy Stewart plays baseball.

Josh Smith plays basketball.

Jacob Scott plays football.

Puzzle 1

Puzzle 2

Puzzle 3

Puzzle 4

Puzzle 5

Puzzle 6

Puzzle 7

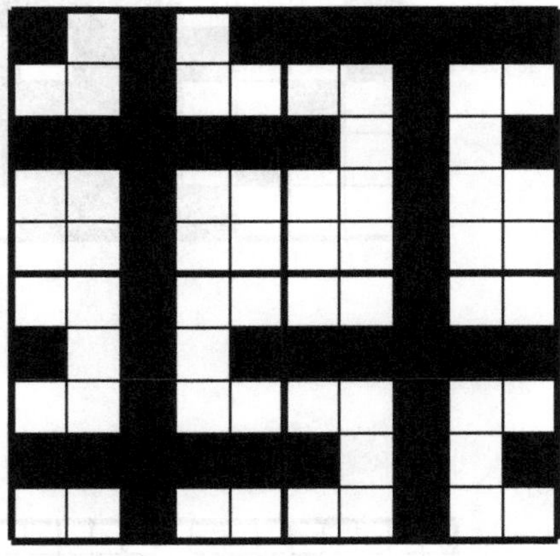

Puzzle 8

Puzzle 9

Puzzle 10

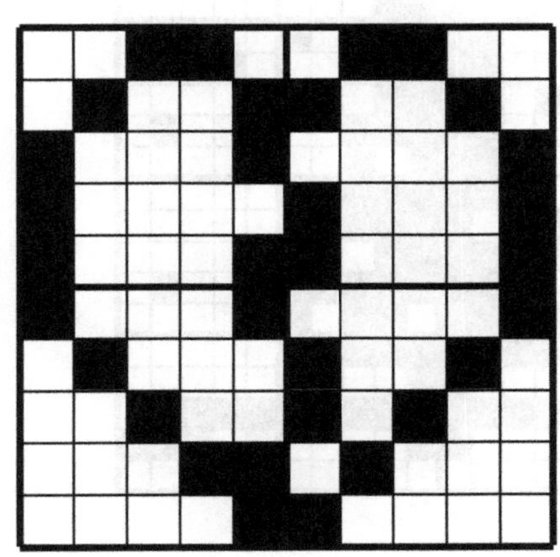

Puzzle 11

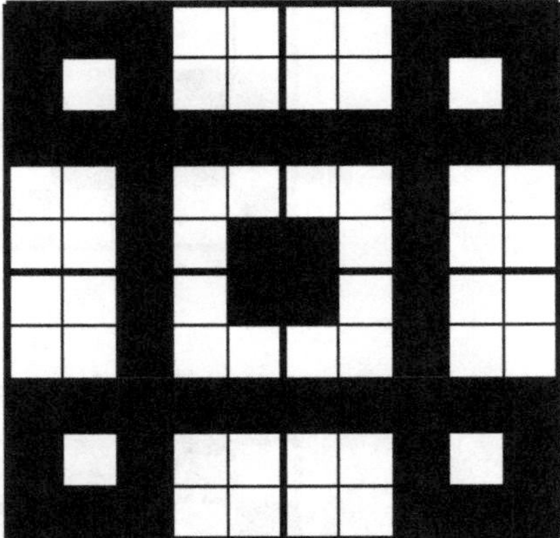

Puzzle 12

Puzzle 13

Puzzle 14

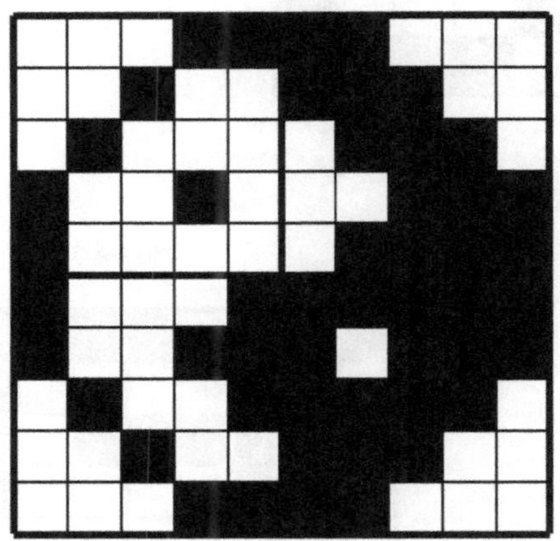

Puzzle 15

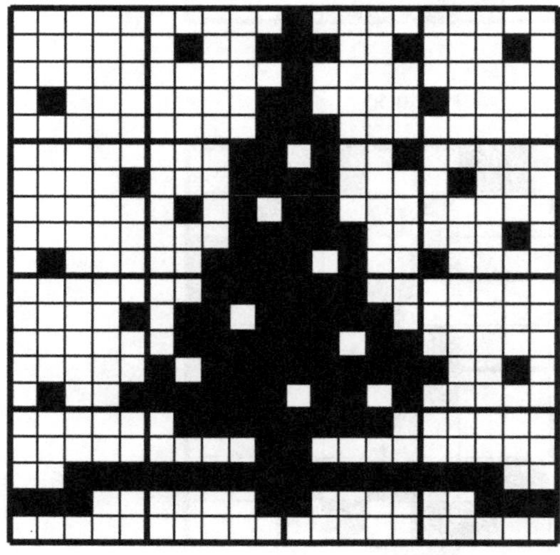

Puzzle 16

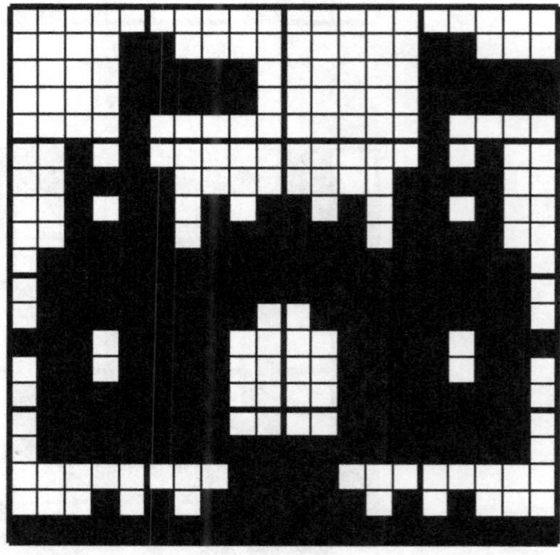

Puzzle 17

Puzzle 18

Puzzle 19

Puzzle 20

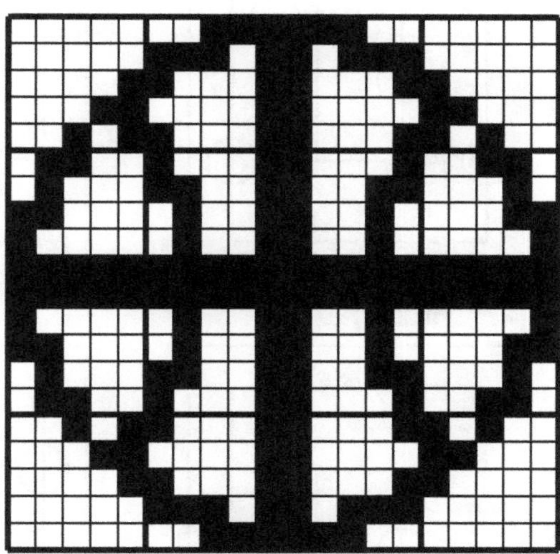

Puzzle 21

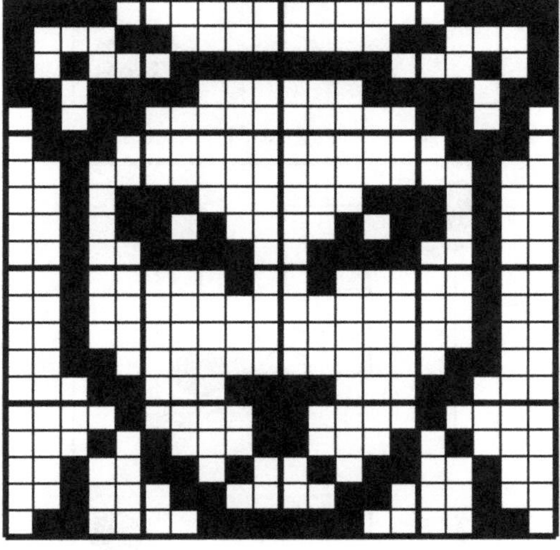

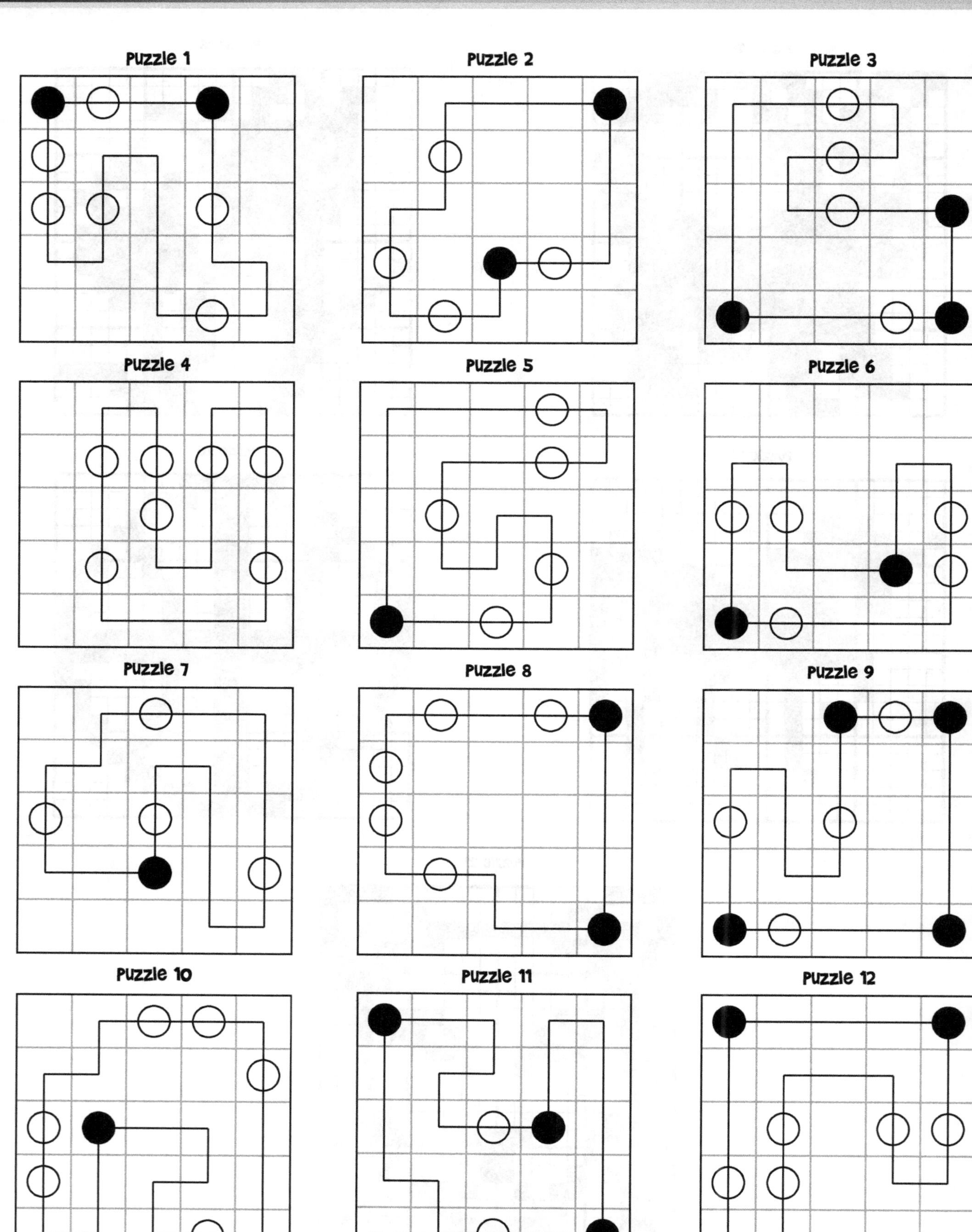
Puzzle 1
Puzzle 2
Puzzle 3
Puzzle 4
Puzzle 5
Puzzle 6
Puzzle 7
Puzzle 8
Puzzle 9
Puzzle 10
Puzzle 11
Puzzle 12

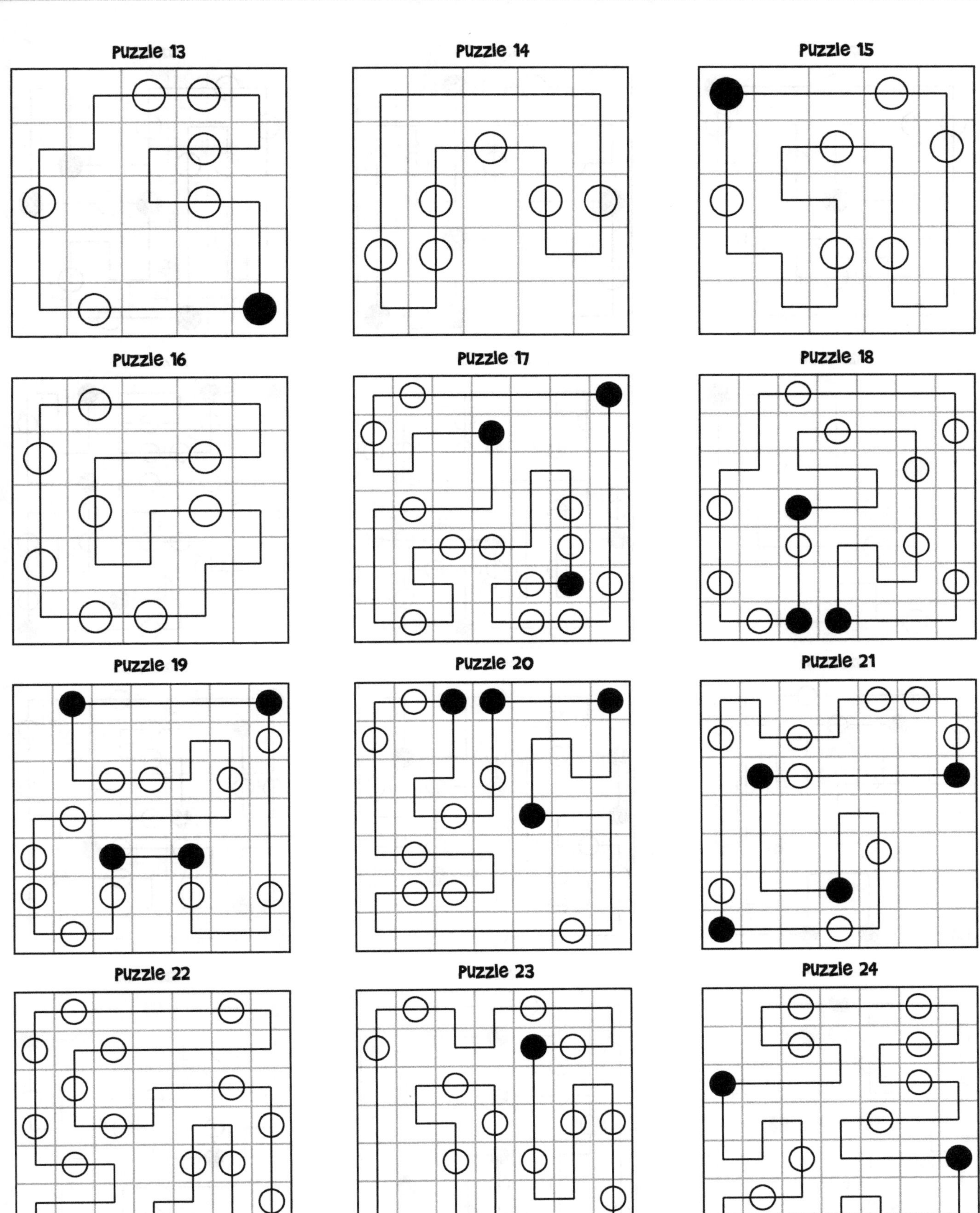
Puzzle 13
Puzzle 14
Puzzle 15
Puzzle 16
Puzzle 17
Puzzle 18
Puzzle 19
Puzzle 20
Puzzle 21
Puzzle 22
Puzzle 23
Puzzle 24

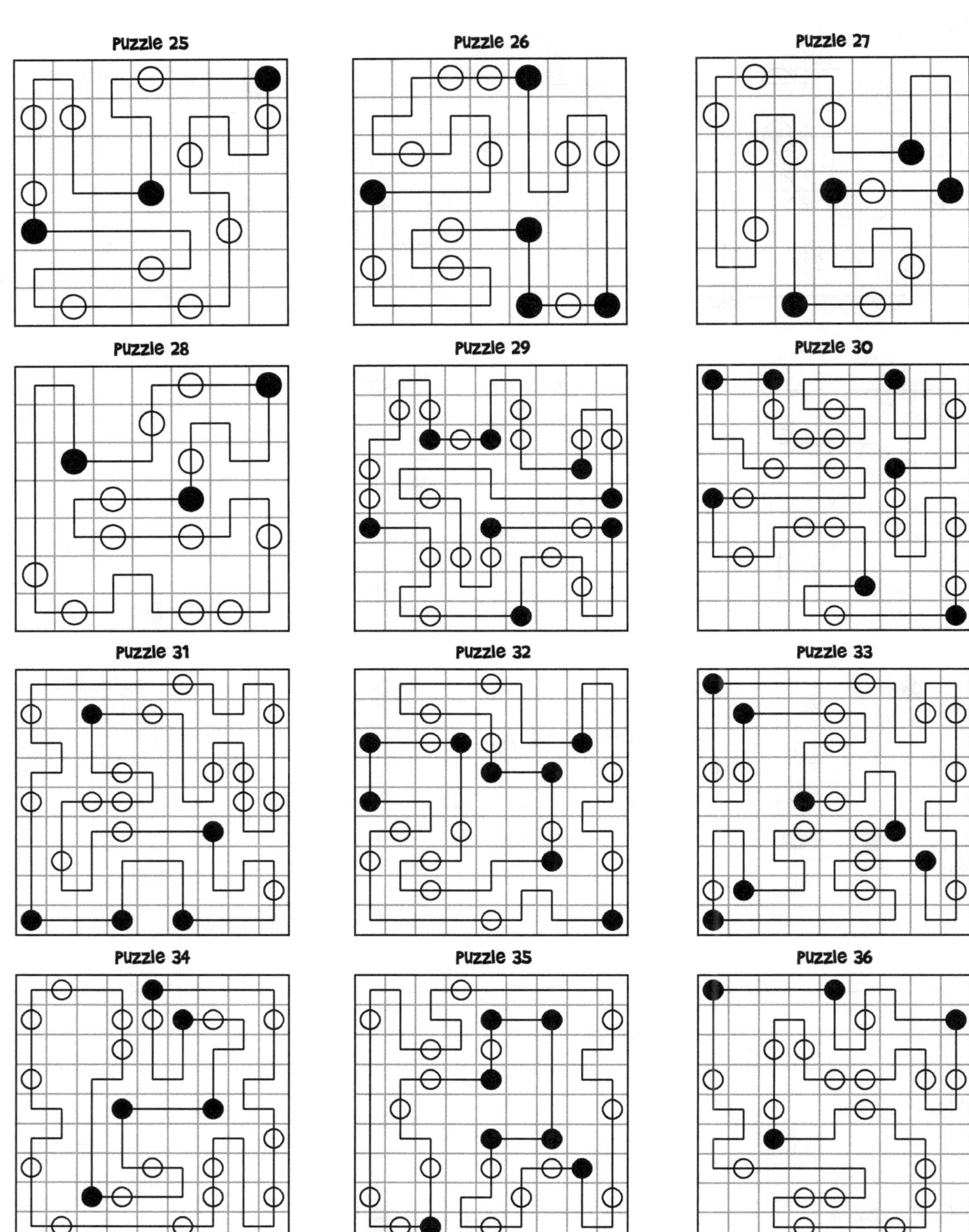
Puzzle 25
Puzzle 26
Puzzle 27
Puzzle 28
Puzzle 29
Puzzle 30
Puzzle 31
Puzzle 32
Puzzle 33
Puzzle 34
Puzzle 35
Puzzle 36

Puzzle 37

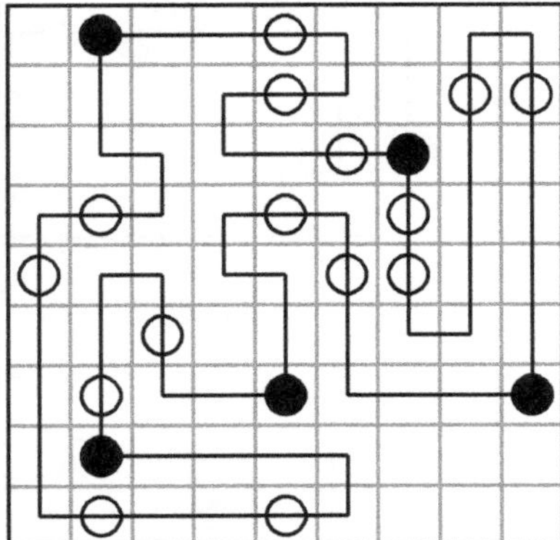

Puzzle 38

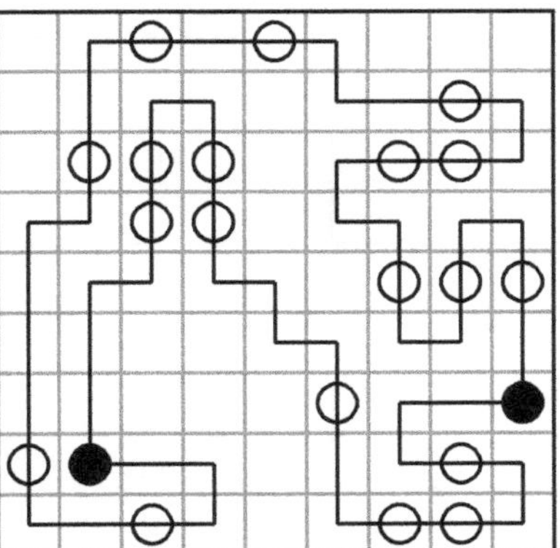

Puzzle 39

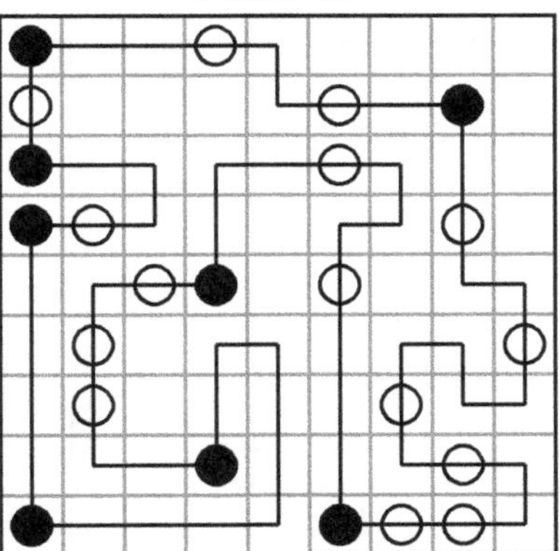

Puzzle 40

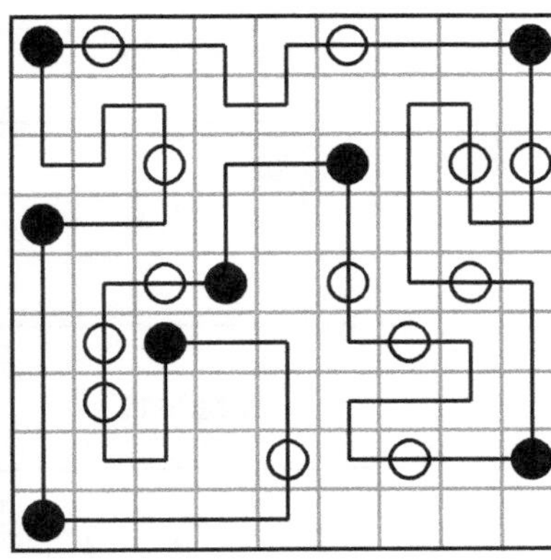

Matchsticks

Puzzle 1

1 + 2 = 3

Puzzle 2

4 + 5 = 9

Puzzle 3

2 - 2 = 0

Puzzle 4

6 + 3 = 9

Puzzle 5

0 + 3 = 3

Puzzle 6

8 + 1 = 9

Puzzle 7

1 + 1 = 2

Puzzle 8

1 - 1 = 0

Puzzle 9

9 + 0 = 9

Puzzle 10

2 - 2 = 0

Puzzle 11

4 - 1 = 3

Puzzle 12

2 + 1 = 3

Puzzle 13

7 - 4 = 3

Puzzle 14

4 + 1 = 5

Puzzle 15

6 + 3 = 9

Puzzle 16

5 + 4 = 9

Puzzle 17

3 + 3 = 6

Puzzle 18

9 - 3 = 6

Puzzle 19

7 - 2 = 5

Puzzle 20

6 + 0 = 6

Puzzle 21

9 + 4 = 13

Puzzle 22

8 + 8 = 16

Puzzle 23

9 + 6 = 15

Puzzle 24

12 - 2 = 10

Puzzle 25

5 + 4 = 9

Puzzle 26

10 - 4 = 6

Puzzle 27

5 + 0 = 5

Puzzle 28

9 + 6 = 15

Matchsticks

Puzzle 29

11 + 2 = 13

Puzzle 30

10 - 5 = 5

Puzzle 31

12 - 12 = 0

Puzzle 32

2 + 16 = 18

Puzzle 33

16 + 3 = 19

Puzzle 34

5 + 5 = 10

Puzzle 35

3 + 5 = 8

Puzzle 36

0 - 0 = 0

Puzzle 37

5 + 0 = 5

Puzzle 38

6 + 4 = 10

Puzzle 39

13 + 10 = 23

Puzzle 40

15 + 15 = 30

Puzzle 41

11 + 11 = 22

Puzzle 42

2 + 16 = 18

Puzzle 43

16 + 3 = 19

Puzzle 44

6 + 5 = 11

Puzzle 45

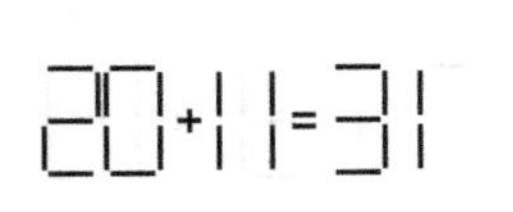

Puzzle 46

20 - 4 = 16

Puzzle 47

65 + 20 = 85

Puzzle 48

52 + 8 = 60

Puzzle 49

15 + 3 = 18

Puzzle 50

9 + 12 = 21

Puzzle 51

15 + 12 = 27

Puzzle 52

32 + 4 = 36

Puzzle 53

23 + 5 = 28

Puzzle 54

4 + 9 = 13

Puzzle 55

21 + 21 = 42

Puzzle 56

33 - 33 = 0

Matchsticks

Puzzle 57

8+20=28

Puzzle 58

47-3=44

Puzzle 59

10+9=19

Puzzle 60

36+17=53

Puzzle 61

4+6=10

Puzzle 62

5+12=17

Puzzle 63

10+1=11

Puzzle 64

12+12=24

Puzzle 65

20+8=28

Puzzle 66

43+2=45

Puzzle 67

31+1=32

Puzzle 68

12+9=21

Puzzle 69

10+9=19

Puzzle 70

1+6=7

Puzzle 71

10-7=3

Puzzle 72

7+1=8

Puzzle 73

8+9=17

Puzzle 74

2+0=2

Puzzle 75

9+9=18

Puzzle 76

7+3=10

Puzzle 77

4+1=5

Puzzle 78

9-2=7

Puzzle 79

18-1=17

Puzzle 80

67+16=83

Puzzle 81

0+6=6

Puzzle 82

8-6=2

Puzzle 83

10-6=4

Puzzle 84

29-6=23

Puzzle 85

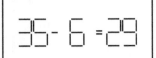

35 - 6 = 29

Puzzle 86

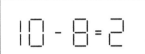

10 - 8 = 2

Puzzle 87

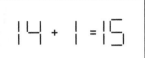

14 + 1 = 15

Puzzle 88

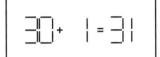

30 + 1 = 31

Puzzle 89

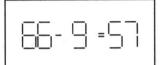

66 - 9 = 57

Puzzle 90

23 - 15 = 8

Puzzle 91

3 × 3 = 9

Puzzle 92

6 × 7 = 42

Puzzle 93

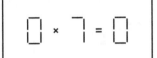

0 × 7 = 0

Puzzle 94

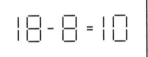

18 - 8 = 10

Puzzle 95

19 - 5 = 14

Puzzle 96

12 × 3 = 36

Puzzle 97

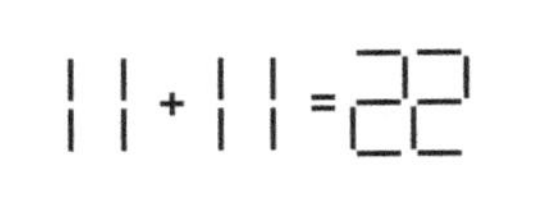

Puzzle 98

47 - 16 = 31

Puzzle 99

8 × 0 = 0

Puzzle 100

5 × 5 = 25

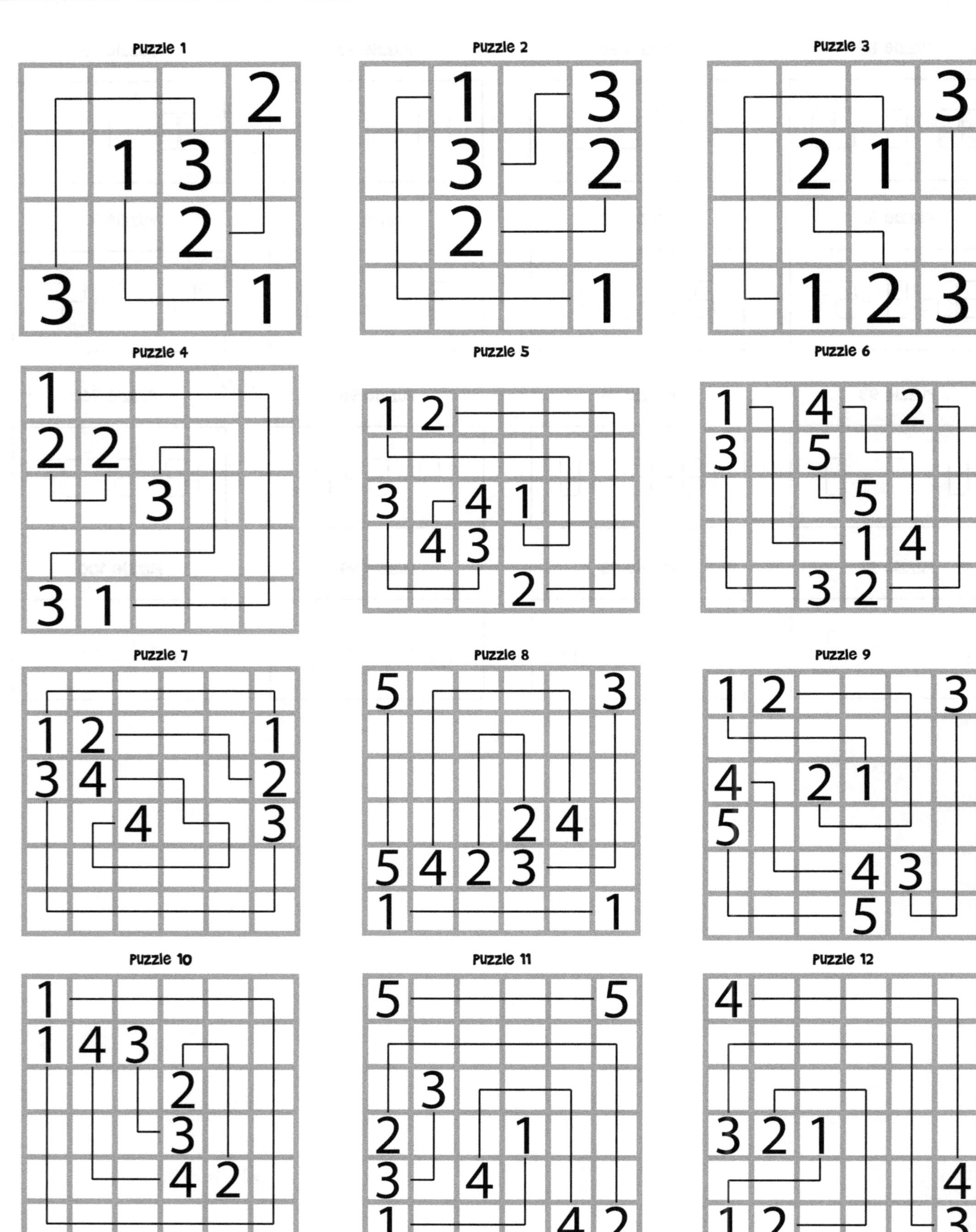
Puzzle 1
Puzzle 2
Puzzle 3
Puzzle 4
Puzzle 5
Puzzle 6
Puzzle 7
Puzzle 8
Puzzle 9
Puzzle 10
Puzzle 11
Puzzle 12

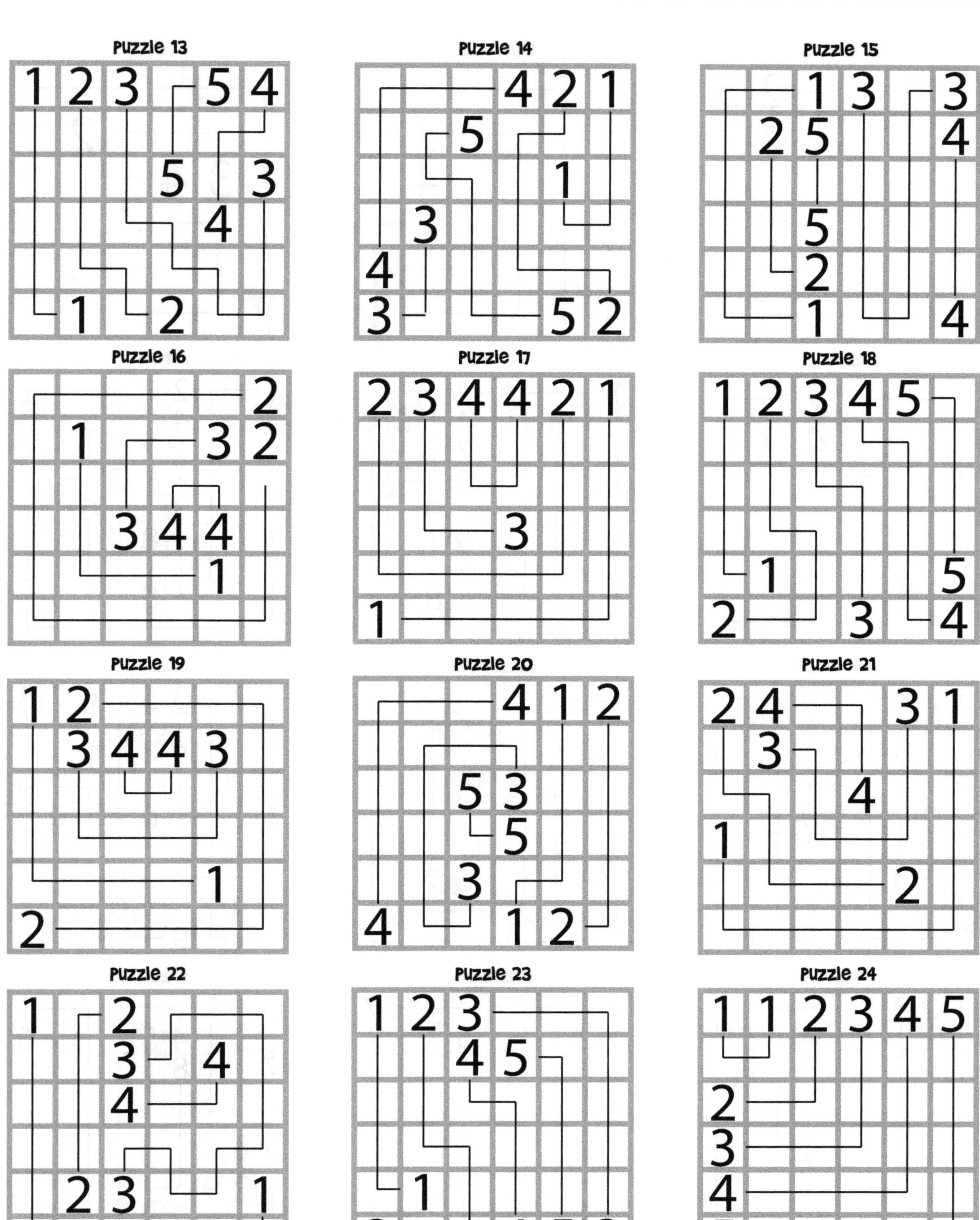
Puzzle 13
Puzzle 14
Puzzle 15
Puzzle 16
Puzzle 17
Puzzle 18
Puzzle 19
Puzzle 20
Puzzle 21
Puzzle 22
Puzzle 23
Puzzle 24

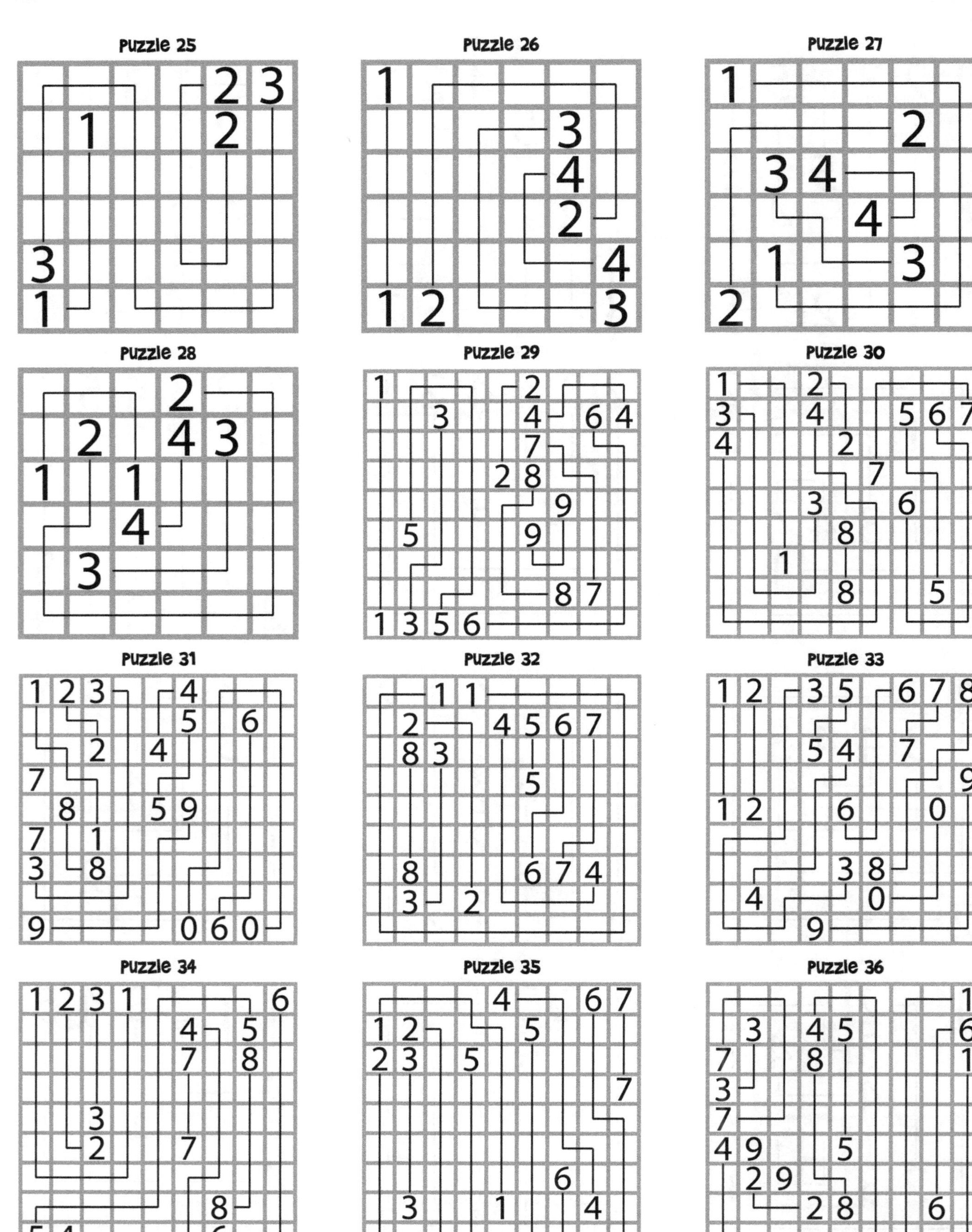
Puzzle 25
Puzzle 26
Puzzle 27
Puzzle 28
Puzzle 29
Puzzle 30
Puzzle 31
Puzzle 32
Puzzle 33
Puzzle 34
Puzzle 35
Puzzle 36

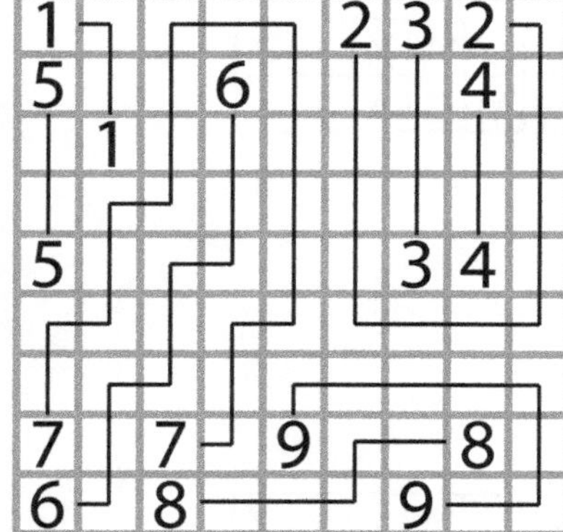

Puzzle 38

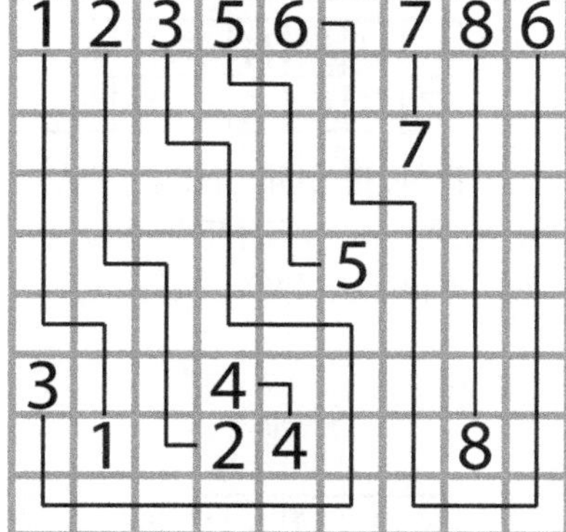

Puzzle 39

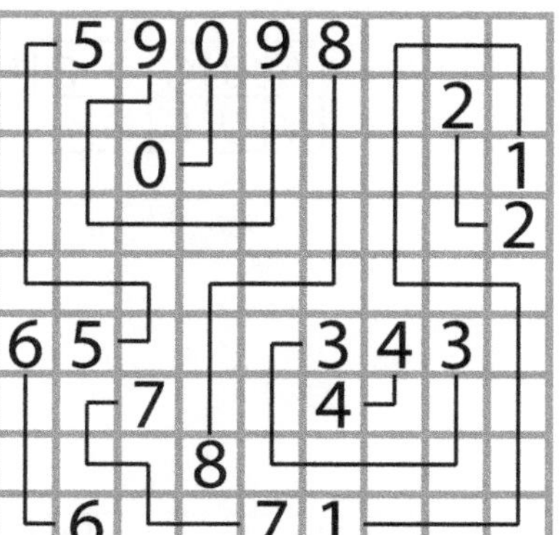

Puzzle 40

	1	2		4			5	
	3						6	5
						4		7
8								
				3			0	
9	0							
			2	1				
		8				6		
9								7

Puzzle 1

A	B	C	D	E	F	G	H	I	J	K	L	M	N	O	P	Q	R	S	T	U	V	W	X	Y	Z
Y	U	R	G	P	J	W	E	H	F	Z	S	O	K	Q	V	N	L	D	X	B	M	C	A	I	T

"LIVE IN THE SUNSHINE, SWIM
THE SEA, DRINK THE WILD AIR."
RALPH WALDO EMERSON

Puzzle 2

A	B	C	D	E	F	G	H	I	J	K	L	M	N	O	P	Q	R	S	T	U	V	W	X	Y	Z
J	F	H	V	L	T	B	A	Y	Z	C	M	W	E	I	N	R	S	X	Q	O	G	D	U	K	P

"ALL GREAT ACHIEVEMENTS REQUIRE
TIME."
MAYA ANGELOU

Puzzle 3

A	B	C	D	E	F	G	H	I	J	K	L	M	N	O	P	Q	R	S	T	U	V	W	X	Y	Z
L	C	D	A	W	V	I	R	U	X	Q	T	Z	B	N	J	G	E	K	O	Y	H	M	P	F	S

"LIFE ISN'T ABOUT FINDING
YOURSELF. LIFE IS ABOUT CREATING
YOURSELF."
GEORGE BERNARD SHAW

Puzzle 4

A	B	C	D	E	F	G	H	I	J	K	L	M	N	O	P	Q	R	S	T	U	V	W	X	Y	Z
S	T	F	O	C	J	B	Y	W	L	R	I	X	K	H	Z	E	P	G	N	Q	D	M	V	A	U

"MISTAKES ARE ALWAYS FORGIVABLE,
IF ONE HAS THE COURAGE TO
ADMIT THEM."
BRUCE LEE

Puzzle 5

A	B	C	D	E	F	G	H	I	J	K	L	M	N	O	P	Q	R	S	T	U	V	W	X	Y	Z
A	T	Q	I	H	G	F	Z	U	C	P	J	X	S	R	K	E	O	B	M	N	V	Y	D	W	L

"NOT ALL THOSE WHO WANDER
ARE LOST."
J. R. R. TOLKIEN

Puzzle 6

A	B	C	D	E	F	G	H	I	J	K	L	M	N	O	P	Q	R	S	T	U	V	W	X	Y	Z
J	V	K	L	G	Y	H	P	Z	T	S	D	E	O	I	C	X	N	B	F	Q	R	M	U	W	A

"THE TRUE SIGN OF INTELLIGENCE
IS NOT KNOWLEDGE BUT IMAGINATION."
ALBERT EINSTEIN

Puzzle 7

A	B	C	D	E	F	G	H	I	J	K	L	M	N	O	P	Q	R	S	T	U	V	W	X	Y	Z
F	G	R	W	S	X	Y	A	D	C	N	J	Q	O	T	K	I	B	H	E	M	L	Z	P	V	U

"GOOD HABITS FORMED AT YOUTH
MAKE ALL THE DIFFERENCE."
ARISTOTLE

Puzzle 8

A	B	C	D	E	F	G	H	I	J	K	L	M	N	O	P	Q	R	S	T	U	V	W	X	Y	Z
R	F	S	N	C	Z	X	J	D	A	G	O	T	U	M	Q	W	V	K	P	L	I	Y	H	E	B

"THOSE WHO DARE TO FAIL MISERABLY
CAN ACHIEVE GREATLY."
JOHN F. KENNEDY

Puzzle 9

A	B	C	D	E	F	G	H	I	J	K	L	M	N	O	P	Q	R	S	T	U	V	W	X	Y	Z
F	Z	O	V	W	A	E	M	D	T	U	X	B	J	R	L	N	K	Q	P	G	Y	H	S	C	I

"EDUCATION IS THE MOST POWERFUL
WEAPON WHICH YOU CAN USE TO
CHANGE THE WORLD."
NELSON MANDELA

Puzzle 10

A	B	C	D	E	F	G	H	I	J	K	L	M	N	O	P	Q	R	S	T	U	V	W	X	Y	Z
L	T	B	C	A	E	Z	W	H	O	K	F	P	Y	N	I	R	D	V	G	U	J	M	S	X	Q

"WHAT GOES UP MUST COME DOWN."
ISAAC NEWTON

Puzzle 11

A	B	C	D	E	F	G	H	I	J	K	L	M	N	O	P	Q	R	S	T	U	V	W	X	Y	Z
B	O	M	X	I	E	W	U	P	T	N	Z	J	L	V	A	C	S	H	G	K	D	R	F	Y	Q

"YOU CANNOT OPEN A BOOK WITHOUT
LEARNING SOMETHING."
CONFUCIUS

Puzzle 12

A	B	C	D	E	F	G	H	I	J	K	L	M	N	O	P	Q	R	S	T	U	V	W	X	Y	Z
R	K	P	D	S	U	T	C	X	Q	Y	V	L	A	G	B	O	W	M	E	H	Z	J	I	N	F

"DO I NOT DESTROY MY ENEMIES
WHEN I MAKE THEM MY FRIENDS?"
ABRAHAM LINCOLN

Puzzle 13

A	B	C	D	E	F	G	H	I	J	K	L	M	N	O	P	Q	R	S	T	U	V	W	X	Y	Z
O	V	P	L	S	N	B	W	Y	Q	F	Z	C	M	X	H	G	A	D	E	K	U	J	T	I	R

"EDUCATION IS THE KEY TO UNLOCKING
THE WORLD, A PASSPORT TO FREEDOM."
OPRAH WINFREY

Puzzle 14

A	B	C	D	E	F	G	H	I	J	K	L	M	N	O	P	Q	R	S	T	U	V	W	X	Y	Z
B	R	H	W	Z	P	J	T	Q	M	O	K	E	G	D	Y	U	S	V	C	L	F	X	A	I	N

"A CLOUDY DAY IS NO MATCH FOR
A SUNNY DISPOSITION."
WILLIAM ARTHUR WARD

Puzzle 15

A	B	C	D	E	F	G	H	I	J	K	L	M	N	O	P	Q	R	S	T	U	V	W	X	Y	Z
X	Q	U	I	J	L	T	C	O	F	B	R	N	W	Y	G	K	A	P	V	Z	S	M	E	D	H

"THE TIME YOU ENJOY WASTING
IS NOT WASTED TIME."
BERTRAND RUSSELL

Puzzle 16

A	B	C	D	E	F	G	H	I	J	K	L	M	N	O	P	Q	R	S	T	U	V	W	X	Y	Z
M	G	D	Z	I	A	T	K	Y	X	Q	S	P	U	V	E	H	C	B	N	L	R	J	W	F	O

"WE NEED MORE KINDNESS, MORE
COMPASSION, MORE JOY, MORE
LAUGHTER."
ELLEN DEGENERES

Puzzle 17

A	B	C	D	E	F	G	H	I	J	K	L	M	N	O	P	Q	R	S	T	U	V	W	X	Y	Z
D	R	N	B	J	T	W	G	I	C	F	A	X	V	L	Q	Z	S	O	P	Y	H	E	K	U	M

"FROM A SMALL SEED A MIGHTY
TRUNK MAY GROW."
AESCHYLUS

Puzzle 18

A	B	C	D	E	F	G	H	I	J	K	L	M	N	O	P	Q	R	S	T	U	V	W	X	Y	Z
X	F	Z	P	W	S	M	E	K	I	N	G	Q	H	Y	A	R	U	J	D	C	B	V	T	L	O

"IF WE DID ALL THE THINGS WE
ARE CAPABLE OF, WE WOULD LITERALLY
ASTOUND OURSELVES."
THOMAS A. EDISON

Puzzle 19

A	B	C	D	E	F	G	H	I	J	K	L	M	N	O	P	Q	R	S	T	U	V	W	X	Y	Z
F	R	Q	G	H	J	O	X	L	P	D	E	S	W	C	T	U	N	I	K	B	A	M	Z	V	Y

"FAILURE IS SIMPLY THE OPPORTUNITY
TO BEGIN AGAIN, THIS TIME
MORE INTELLIGENTLY."
HENRY FORD

Puzzle 20

A	B	C	D	E	F	G	H	I	J	K	L	M	N	O	P	Q	R	S	T	U	V	W	X	Y	Z
B	I	O	E	D	L	T	U	K	X	Y	M	P	A	H	F	N	V	G	J	W	C	S	Z	Q	R

"KEEP YOUR FACE TO THE SUNSHINE
AND YOU CANNOT SEE A SHADOW."
HELEN KELLER

Math Squares

Puzzle 1

2	+	3	+	5	10
-		+		-	
7	X	1	-	9	-2
+		+		-	
8	-	6	+	4	6
3		10		-8	

Puzzle 2

9	-	5	-	7	-3
+		X		+	
4	+	2	+	1	7
+		+		X	
8	-	3	+	6	11
21		13		13	

Puzzle 3

2	-	7	-	3	-8
+		+		+	
6	+	8	X	5	46
+		+		X	
4	+	9	+	1	14
12		24		8	

Puzzle 4

8	X	9	+	3	75
-		-		+	
5	X	1	+	4	9
+		+		+	
2	-	6	-	7	-11
5		14		14	

Puzzle 5

2	-	8	-	4	-10
+		+		-	
5	X	9	-	1	44
-		/		+	
7	+	3	X	6	25
0		11		9	

Puzzle 6

2	-	6	-	9	-13
X		-		+	
4	-	7	+	1	-2
-		+		-	
5	+	8	+	3	16
3		7		7	

Puzzle 7

5	X	9	+	8	53
-		/		-	
4	X	3	-	6	6
+		X		/	
1	+	7	X	2	15
2		21		5	

Puzzle 8

7	-	9	X	5	-38
+		/		+	
2	X	3	-	8	-2
X		-		-	
1	+	4	+	6	11
9		-1		7	

Puzzle 9

8	X	6	+	9	57
+		X		+	
7	+	1	-	5	3
-		+		X	
4	-	2	+	3	5
11		8		24	

Puzzle 10

9	-	2	+	1	8
/		X		+	
3	-	7	-	5	-9
X		+		-	
4	-	8	+	6	2
12		22		0	

Puzzle 11

2	+	3	X	6	20
+		+		+	
7	-	8	-	1	-2
-		-		+	
9	X	5	-	4	41
0		6		11	

Puzzle 12

8	+	9	+	6	23
X		-		-	
7	X	5	-	1	34
-		+		-	
2	+	4	+	3	9
54		8		2	

Math Squares

Puzzle 13

4	+	3	+	2	9
-		-		-	
8	X	5	+	9	49
-		+		-	
7	+	6	X	1	13
-11		4		-8	

Puzzle 14

4	+	8	-	5	7
+		+		X	
3	-	1	-	9	-7
-		-		+	
2	+	7	+	6	15
5		2		51	

Puzzle 15

3	-	9	-	1	-7
-		+		-	
7	-	6	-	2	-1
-		-		-	
8	X	5	-	4	36
-12		10		-5	

Puzzle 16

4	X	5	-	1	19
/		-		X	
2	+	7	-	3	6
-		X		+	
9	+	6	-	8	7
-7		-37		11	

Puzzle 17

7	-	9	-	8	-10
+		/		X	
2	+	3	-	1	4
-		-		-	
5	X	4	+	6	26
4		-1		2	

Puzzle 18

7	+	1	+	3	11
+		+		-	
9	-	2	+	5	12
-		+		+	
6	-	8	-	4	-6
10		11		2	

Puzzle 19

9	X	2	+	1	19
X		X		+	
6	-	8	-	7	-9
+		/		-	
5	X	4	-	3	17
59		4		5	

Puzzle 20

2	-	8	-	4	-10
X		+		+	
9	+	3	X	7	30
-		-		+	
1	+	5	-	6	0
17		6		17	

Puzzle 21

2	-	5	+	4	1
+		+		X	
1	+	8	+	3	12
X		+		-	
6	+	7	X	9	69
8		20		3	

Puzzle 22

8	-	2	-	7	-1
/		+		+	
4	-	9	+	1	-4
X		/		-	
5	-	3	+	6	8
10		5		2	

Puzzle 23

4	X	3	+	6	18
-		+		+	
8	-	2	-	9	-3
+		+		+	
5	X	1	-	7	-2
1		6		22	

Puzzle 24

3	-	6	-	4	-7
+		-		/	
8	-	1	+	2	9
-		-		X	
9	+	7	+	5	21
2		-2		10	

Math Squares

Puzzle 25

4	+	9	+	7	20
/		+		-	
2	-	6	+	3	-1
X		-		+	
5	-	8	-	1	-4
10		7		5	

Puzzle 26

5	+	6	+	7	18
+		+		-	
8	-	1	+	2	9
-		X		-	
3	-	4	X	9	-33
10		10		-4	

Puzzle 27

3	+	1	X	2	5
X		X		+	
6	+	9	-	4	11
-		+		-	
5	-	8	-	7	-10
13		17		-1	

Puzzle 28

1	-	5	-	6	-10
+		-		X	
8	+	9	-	7	10
-		-		+	
3	-	4	+	2	1
6		-8		44	

Puzzle 29

9	-	8	-	7	-6
-		X		+	
2	+	6	-	1	7
-		-		X	
4	X	5	+	3	23
3		43		10	

Puzzle 30

8	+	7	X	6	50
-		-		X	
9	-	2	X	4	1
+		+		+	
5	-	3	+	1	3
4		8		25	

Puzzle 31

6	X	7	-	2	40
+		-		-	
8	-	5	+	1	4
+		X		+	
9	-	4	-	3	2
23		-13		4	

Puzzle 32

3	-	2	+	9	10
+		X		-	
1	+	5	-	8	-2
-		-		X	
7	+	4	+	6	17
-3		6		-39	

Puzzle 33

5	-	3	+	4	6
X		-		+	
7	+	1	X	9	16
-		-		+	
6	+	2	+	8	16
29		0		21	

Puzzle 34

3	-	2	+	8	9
+		+		+	
4	-	9	X	6	-50
+		X		X	
1	-	5	-	7	-11
8		47		50	

Puzzle 35

6	-	2	+	3	7
-		+		+	
5	+	1	+	8	14
-		X		-	
4	-	9	+	7	2
-3		11		4	

Puzzle 36

5	X	4	-	3	17
+		-		-	
2	-	8	+	9	3
-		-		+	
6	-	7	-	1	-2
1		-11		-5	

Puzzle 37

8	-	4	-	2	2
+		X		X	
6	+	5	+	3	14
-		+		-	
9	+	1	-	7	3
5		21		-1	

Puzzle 38

9	-	2	+	8	15
+		+		-	
4	+	3	+	7	14
+		+		-	
6	+	1	-	5	2
19		6		-4	

Puzzle 39

9	+	7	-	2	14
-		+		+	
8	+	4	-	3	9
-		+		-	
5	X	6	+	1	31
-4		17		4	

Puzzle 40

6	-	4	+	5	7
-		X		X	
9	X	3	-	7	20
+		-		+	
8	-	2	+	1	7
5		10		36	

Puzzle 1

1	3	9	8	7	5	4	6	2
4	7	2	3	6	1	9	8	5
6	5	8	2	9	4	3	1	7
3	8	4	6	1	2	5	7	9
2	1	7	5	3	9	6	4	8
5	9	6	4	8	7	1	2	3
9	2	5	7	4	6	8	3	1
7	4	3	1	5	8	2	9	6
8	6	1	9	2	3	7	5	4

Puzzle 2

2	5	4	6	1	7	3	8	9
6	3	9	4	2	8	5	7	1
1	7	8	5	9	3	2	6	4
9	4	6	3	8	2	7	1	5
3	2	1	7	6	5	9	4	8
7	8	5	1	4	9	6	2	3
5	1	3	8	7	6	4	9	2
8	6	2	9	3	4	1	5	7
4	9	7	2	5	1	8	3	6

Puzzle 3

3	5	4	8	7	1	2	9	6
2	1	6	4	3	9	5	8	7
7	8	9	6	5	2	4	3	1
1	4	5	7	6	8	3	2	9
8	9	3	2	1	4	7	6	5
6	7	2	5	9	3	8	1	4
4	2	7	9	8	6	1	5	3
5	6	1	3	2	7	9	4	8
9	3	8	1	4	5	6	7	2

Puzzle 4

9	8	2	4	1	7	5	3	6
7	4	6	5	3	8	9	2	1
5	1	3	6	2	9	4	7	8
8	9	5	3	6	2	1	4	7
2	3	1	8	7	4	6	5	9
4	6	7	9	5	1	3	8	2
1	7	9	2	4	5	8	6	3
3	2	4	1	8	6	7	9	5
6	5	8	7	9	3	2	1	4

Puzzle 5

4	6	1	8	2	7	9	5	3
9	8	2	4	5	3	7	1	6
3	7	5	6	1	9	4	2	8
8	9	3	2	7	1	5	6	4
6	1	7	3	4	5	8	9	2
2	5	4	9	6	8	3	7	1
5	3	6	7	8	2	1	4	9
1	4	9	5	3	6	2	8	7
7	2	8	1	9	4	6	3	5

Puzzle 6

6	2	5	3	4	9	7	8	1
9	3	1	8	5	7	2	4	6
7	8	4	1	6	2	9	5	3
4	9	8	2	3	5	6	1	7
3	6	7	9	1	4	8	2	5
1	5	2	7	8	6	4	3	9
2	1	6	5	7	8	3	9	4
8	7	3	4	9	1	5	6	2
5	4	9	6	2	3	1	7	8

Puzzle 7

4	9	7	3	5	1	6	8	2
1	2	5	9	6	8	7	3	4
8	3	6	4	2	7	1	9	5
6	4	1	2	9	3	8	5	7
3	7	2	5	8	6	9	4	1
5	8	9	1	7	4	3	2	6
2	5	8	6	1	9	4	7	3
9	6	4	7	3	5	2	1	8
7	1	3	8	4	2	5	6	9

Puzzle 8

5	6	4	3	8	1	9	7	2
1	2	7	9	6	4	8	3	5
8	3	9	7	2	5	1	4	6
3	8	6	4	5	9	7	2	1
9	7	5	8	1	2	4	6	3
2	4	1	6	3	7	5	9	8
7	5	2	1	4	3	6	8	9
6	9	3	5	7	8	2	1	4
4	1	8	2	9	6	3	5	7

Puzzle 9

5	7	3	2	1	8	6	4	9
4	1	2	6	3	9	5	7	8
6	8	9	7	5	4	2	1	3
8	2	4	5	9	6	1	3	7
7	9	5	3	8	1	4	2	6
3	6	1	4	7	2	9	8	5
1	5	7	9	4	3	8	6	2
9	4	6	8	2	7	3	5	1
2	3	8	1	6	5	7	9	4

Puzzle 10

4	1	7	8	3	5	6	9	2
9	5	3	2	6	4	7	8	1
6	2	8	9	1	7	3	4	5
2	3	4	6	7	8	5	1	9
5	9	6	1	4	3	8	2	7
8	7	1	5	2	9	4	3	6
3	4	9	7	5	2	1	6	8
7	6	2	3	8	1	9	5	4
1	8	5	4	9	6	2	7	3

Puzzle 11

1	7	5	6	3	8	4	2	9
4	9	8	1	5	2	6	7	3
6	2	3	9	4	7	1	5	8
5	1	7	8	9	3	2	6	4
9	3	6	5	2	4	8	1	7
8	4	2	7	6	1	9	3	5
2	5	4	3	1	9	7	8	6
7	6	1	4	8	5	3	9	2
3	8	9	2	7	6	5	4	1

Puzzle 12

1	3	6	5	4	2	9	7	8
7	5	4	8	9	6	3	1	2
9	8	2	7	3	1	6	4	5
4	6	9	3	1	5	8	2	7
3	7	8	4	2	9	5	6	1
5	2	1	6	8	7	4	9	3
2	4	3	9	7	8	1	5	6
8	1	5	2	6	4	7	3	9
6	9	7	1	5	3	2	8	4

SUDOKU

Puzzle 13

2	9	7	8	5	1	6	4	3
8	5	4	3	6	7	9	1	2
6	1	3	9	4	2	7	8	5
5	7	1	6	2	9	8	3	4
4	8	2	1	7	3	5	9	6
3	6	9	5	8	4	2	7	1
1	2	5	4	9	8	3	6	7
7	3	8	2	1	6	4	5	9
9	4	6	7	3	5	1	2	8

Puzzle 14

7	4	8	5	6	9	3	2	1
3	5	6	1	2	7	8	9	4
9	2	1	8	4	3	6	7	5
8	9	2	4	3	1	5	6	7
5	1	7	9	8	6	2	4	3
4	6	3	2	7	5	1	8	9
6	8	5	7	1	4	9	3	2
2	7	9	3	5	8	4	1	6
1	3	4	6	9	2	7	5	8

Puzzle 15

2	9	6	4	8	3	7	1	5
8	7	5	6	2	1	4	3	9
1	4	3	9	5	7	8	6	2
5	2	9	7	4	6	1	8	3
3	6	7	2	1	8	5	9	4
4	1	8	3	9	5	2	7	6
9	5	1	8	3	4	6	2	7
6	3	4	1	7	2	9	5	8
7	8	2	5	6	9	3	4	1

Puzzle 16

9	7	8	5	4	1	2	6	3
6	3	5	7	8	2	1	9	4
2	1	4	9	6	3	8	7	5
3	5	9	4	2	7	6	1	8
4	6	7	3	1	8	9	5	2
1	8	2	6	9	5	4	3	7
8	2	3	1	7	6	5	4	9
7	9	1	2	5	4	3	8	6
5	4	6	8	3	9	7	2	1

Puzzle 17

1	5	6	9	8	2	4	3	7
4	2	3	1	7	6	8	5	9
9	7	8	3	4	5	1	2	6
2	3	9	8	6	4	5	7	1
6	8	5	7	3	1	9	4	2
7	4	1	2	5	9	3	6	8
8	6	2	4	1	3	7	9	5
5	1	4	6	9	7	2	8	3
3	9	7	5	2	8	6	1	4

Puzzle 18

6	9	7	1	5	3	8	2	4
5	2	4	8	9	7	1	3	6
3	8	1	4	6	2	7	9	5
1	3	6	5	7	9	4	8	2
8	4	9	2	1	6	3	5	7
2	7	5	3	8	4	9	6	1
7	6	8	9	4	5	2	1	3
4	1	2	6	3	8	5	7	9
9	5	3	7	2	1	6	4	8

Puzzle 19

4	8	6	5	3	1	9	2	7
5	3	1	9	2	7	6	4	8
9	7	2	8	4	6	1	3	5
8	5	4	1	7	9	3	6	2
1	2	9	3	6	5	8	7	4
3	6	7	2	8	4	5	1	9
2	9	3	7	1	8	4	5	6
6	1	5	4	9	2	7	8	3
7	4	8	6	5	3	2	9	1

Puzzle 20

7	3	1	5	4	9	2	8	6
5	8	9	1	6	2	4	7	3
2	6	4	7	3	8	9	1	5
9	4	6	8	1	5	7	3	2
3	1	5	2	7	4	6	9	8
8	2	7	6	9	3	5	4	1
1	7	3	4	5	6	8	2	9
6	9	8	3	2	7	1	5	4
4	5	2	9	8	1	3	6	7

Puzzle 21

5	4	6	7	9	8	1	2	3
2	8	3	1	5	4	7	9	6
7	9	1	2	3	6	4	5	8
6	3	4	9	8	1	5	7	2
1	5	2	4	7	3	6	8	9
8	7	9	5	6	2	3	4	1
4	6	5	3	2	9	8	1	7
3	2	7	8	1	5	9	6	4
9	1	8	6	4	7	2	3	5

Puzzle 22

9	6	8	5	7	3	2	1	4
3	2	4	8	1	9	6	7	5
7	5	1	4	2	6	3	8	9
8	4	7	1	5	2	9	3	6
2	1	3	9	6	4	7	5	8
6	9	5	3	8	7	4	2	1
1	7	9	2	4	8	5	6	3
4	8	6	7	3	5	1	9	2
5	3	2	6	9	1	8	4	7

Puzzle 23

2	3	8	7	5	6	4	1	9
6	7	9	4	1	2	8	5	3
1	5	4	8	3	9	7	6	2
7	9	6	2	8	5	3	4	1
3	4	5	9	7	1	2	8	6
8	2	1	3	6	4	9	7	5
9	6	2	1	4	7	5	3	8
4	1	3	5	2	8	6	9	7
5	8	7	6	9	3	1	2	4

Puzzle 24

2	8	5	3	6	4	1	9	7
9	4	6	7	2	1	8	3	5
1	7	3	8	5	9	4	2	6
5	2	8	1	9	3	7	6	4
4	6	9	5	7	2	3	1	8
7	3	1	6	4	8	2	5	9
3	5	4	2	8	6	9	7	1
8	1	7	9	3	5	6	4	2
6	9	2	4	1	7	5	8	3

Puzzle 25

6	1	9	4	3	7	5	2	8
7	2	8	1	9	5	3	6	4
4	5	3	2	8	6	1	7	9
5	7	6	9	1	8	2	4	3
9	8	2	3	7	4	6	5	1
1	3	4	6	5	2	8	9	7
8	9	5	7	2	1	4	3	6
2	6	7	8	4	3	9	1	5
3	4	1	5	6	9	7	8	2

Puzzle 26

4	5	7	8	6	1	3	2	9
2	9	8	7	3	5	1	6	4
6	3	1	4	2	9	7	8	5
5	1	2	6	8	3	9	4	7
8	7	3	5	9	4	6	1	2
9	4	6	1	7	2	5	3	8
1	6	9	2	4	7	8	5	3
7	8	4	3	5	6	2	9	1
3	2	5	9	1	8	4	7	6

Puzzle 27

4	8	3	2	6	7	1	5	9
6	1	5	3	9	4	8	2	7
7	9	2	8	1	5	4	3	6
9	2	1	5	8	6	3	7	4
3	5	7	9	4	2	6	1	8
8	4	6	1	7	3	5	9	2
1	3	9	6	2	8	7	4	5
2	6	4	7	5	1	9	8	3
5	7	8	4	3	9	2	6	1

Puzzle 28

9	4	5	2	1	7	6	8	3
7	3	2	8	6	9	1	4	5
8	1	6	4	5	3	9	2	7
4	5	1	9	3	6	8	7	2
6	8	9	7	2	4	5	3	1
2	7	3	1	8	5	4	6	9
5	6	8	3	9	2	7	1	4
1	2	7	5	4	8	3	9	6
3	9	4	6	7	1	2	5	8

Puzzle 29

3	9	4	8	1	5	6	2	7
6	2	1	9	7	3	5	8	4
7	5	8	6	2	4	3	9	1
9	6	7	3	8	1	4	5	2
8	1	5	7	4	2	9	3	6
2	4	3	5	6	9	7	1	8
4	3	2	1	9	6	8	7	5
5	7	6	2	3	8	1	4	9
1	8	9	4	5	7	2	6	3

Puzzle 30

4	6	1	7	8	2	9	5	3
2	7	3	5	1	9	8	4	6
8	9	5	6	3	4	7	2	1
9	3	7	4	5	1	2	6	8
5	4	6	2	9	8	3	1	7
1	8	2	3	7	6	4	9	5
3	1	9	8	4	5	6	7	2
7	2	4	1	6	3	5	8	9
6	5	8	9	2	7	1	3	4

Puzzle 31

3	4	1	8	6	9	2	5	7
6	7	5	2	4	1	8	9	3
2	8	9	5	7	3	1	4	6
4	9	6	7	3	8	5	1	2
1	3	8	6	5	2	4	7	9
5	2	7	1	9	4	3	6	8
9	1	4	3	8	6	7	2	5
8	5	2	9	1	7	6	3	4
7	6	3	4	2	5	9	8	1

Puzzle 32

1	6	4	7	5	9	2	3	8
2	8	9	3	6	1	5	7	4
3	7	5	8	2	4	9	1	6
5	4	1	2	9	3	6	8	7
9	3	6	1	8	7	4	5	2
7	2	8	5	4	6	1	9	3
6	9	7	4	3	5	8	2	1
8	5	3	6	1	2	7	4	9
4	1	2	9	7	8	3	6	5

Puzzle 33

5	1	9	7	2	6	8	3	4
4	2	3	1	8	5	9	7	6
8	6	7	9	3	4	2	5	1
9	3	1	8	5	7	4	6	2
6	8	5	2	4	9	7	1	3
2	7	4	3	6	1	5	9	8
7	5	6	4	1	2	3	8	9
1	4	8	5	9	3	6	2	7
3	9	2	6	7	8	1	4	5

Puzzle 34

3	8	9	1	7	2	4	5	6
7	5	6	9	4	3	1	8	2
1	4	2	6	8	5	7	3	9
5	2	8	4	1	7	6	9	3
4	6	1	8	3	9	2	7	5
9	7	3	5	2	6	8	4	1
6	9	7	2	5	8	3	1	4
2	3	4	7	9	1	5	6	8
8	1	5	3	6	4	9	2	7

Puzzle 35

8	3	6	9	5	7	1	2	4
2	7	1	3	8	4	9	6	5
5	9	4	1	2	6	8	7	3
3	2	7	4	6	1	5	9	8
9	1	8	5	7	3	6	4	2
6	4	5	2	9	8	7	3	1
7	6	2	8	4	5	3	1	9
1	8	9	7	3	2	4	5	6
4	5	3	6	1	9	2	8	7

Puzzle 36

4	9	6	5	7	3	8	2	1
3	7	2	8	6	1	4	5	9
5	8	1	2	4	9	3	6	7
8	6	7	9	3	2	1	4	5
1	5	9	4	8	7	6	3	2
2	4	3	6	1	5	9	7	8
7	1	4	3	5	8	2	9	6
6	2	8	7	9	4	5	1	3
9	3	5	1	2	6	7	8	4

Puzzle 37

4	7	8	5	6	2	9	3	1
1	6	3	7	9	8	2	5	4
2	5	9	4	1	3	7	6	8
7	2	6	9	8	1	5	4	3
8	3	4	6	2	5	1	9	7
9	1	5	3	4	7	8	2	6
5	8	2	1	3	6	4	7	9
6	4	7	8	5	9	3	1	2
3	9	1	2	7	4	6	8	5

Puzzle 38

2	4	1	3	5	6	7	9	8
8	9	6	2	7	1	5	4	3
3	5	7	4	8	9	1	6	2
1	8	4	5	2	7	6	3	9
5	7	3	6	9	4	2	8	1
9	6	2	8	1	3	4	5	7
6	2	5	1	3	8	9	7	4
7	1	8	9	4	5	3	2	6
4	3	9	7	6	2	8	1	5

Puzzle 39

6	5	7	3	2	1	9	4	8
2	3	8	4	9	6	1	7	5
9	1	4	7	8	5	2	6	3
7	9	1	5	4	3	8	2	6
4	2	3	6	1	8	5	9	7
8	6	5	9	7	2	3	1	4
1	7	2	8	5	4	6	3	9
5	4	6	1	3	9	7	8	2
3	8	9	2	6	7	4	5	1

Puzzle 40

9	8	6	2	5	7	1	3	4
2	5	4	8	1	3	9	7	6
1	7	3	9	6	4	5	8	2
3	9	7	4	8	6	2	5	1
5	6	2	7	3	1	8	4	9
8	4	1	5	9	2	7	6	3
6	3	8	1	7	9	4	2	5
7	2	9	6	4	5	3	1	8
4	1	5	3	2	8	6	9	7

Dragon
Fruit

Ready for new Challenges?

Test your Critical Thinking!

If you're looking for a fun sudoku book for beginners, here's the perfect first sudoku puzzle book for you! *Sudoku for Kids* starts out with super easy 4x4 puzzles, and then conquers the popular 9x9 sudoku puzzle.

Learn to expand your critical thinking and logic skills with the addicting fun of sudoku!

Practice Positive Thinking!

Make a habit out of positive thinking with the *Positive Thinking Journal!* This gratitude diary for children gives your kids hundreds of gratitude journal prompts, self-care planner activities, and positive thinking exercises that help boost their self-esteem.

Help your kids focus on the happy things in life. Tiny acts of gratitude can change the way your kids think and feel day-to-day. Explore mindfulness for kids with affirmations coloring pages, too!

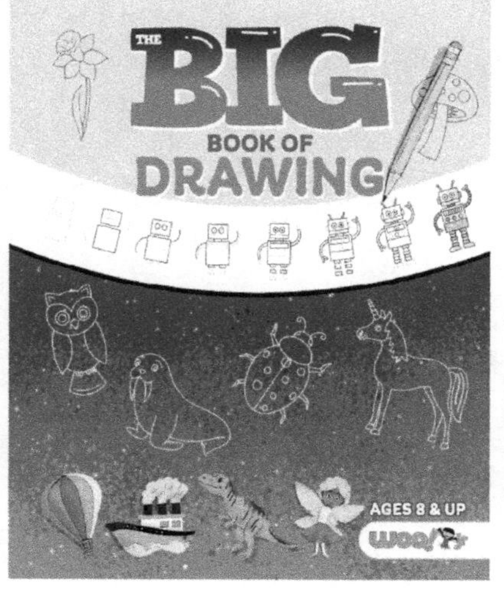

Explore your Creative Side!

This step-by-step drawing guide is essential for all kids! With over 500 things to draw, your child will be entertained for hours while learning a new skill. *The Big Book of Drawing for Kids* makes learning how to draw easy!

Inside this giant activity book for kids, learn to draw: objects in nature, in space, musical instruments, tons of animals both real and mythological, holiday images, sporty items, robots, treats, and more!

Buy on Amazon or Mango.bz/books

CPSIA information can be obtained
at www.ICGtesting.com
Printed in the USA
BVHW010006060822
643962BV00007B/277